D1561797

STAGING THE ABSOLUTE

**THOMAS
SEIFRID**

STAGING THE
ABSOLUTE
Ritual in Russia's Modern Era

UNIVERSITY OF TORONTO PRESS
Toronto Buffalo London

ISBN 978-1-4875-5180-3 (cloth)
ISBN 978-1-4875-5182-7 (EPUB)
ISBN 978-1-4875-5181-0 (PDF)

Library and Archives Canada Cataloguing in Publication

Title: Staging the absolute : ritual in Russia's modern era / Thomas Seifrid.
Names: Seifrid, Thomas, author.
Description: Includes bibliographical references and index.
Identifiers: Canadiana (print) 20230484034 | Canadiana (ebook)
20230484077 | ISBN 9781487551803 (cloth) | ISBN 9781487551827 (EPUB) |
ISBN 9781487551810 (PDF)
Subjects: LCSH: Russian literature – 20th century – History and
criticism. | LCSH: Soviet Union – Symbolic representation. |
LCSH: Theater and society – Soviet Union. | LCSH: Festivals – Soviet
Union. | LCSH: City planning – Soviet Union.
Classification: LCC PG3022.S45 2024 | DDC 891.709/004 – dc23

Cover design: Liz Harasymczuk
Cover image: *May Day*, The New York Public Library
Digital Collections (1919)

We wish to acknowledge the land on which the University of Toronto
Press operates. This land is the traditional territory of the Wendat, the
Anishnaabeg, the Haudenosaunee, the Métis, and the Mississaugas of the
Credit First Nation.

University of Toronto Press acknowledges the financial support of the
Government of Canada, the Canada Council for the Arts, and the Ontario
Arts Council, an agency of the Government of Ontario, for its publishing
activities.

 Canada Council
for the Arts
Conseil des Arts
du Canada

 ONTARIO ARTS COUNCIL
CONSEIL DES ARTS DE L'ONTARIO
an Ontario government agency
un organisme du gouvernement de l'Ontario

Funded by the   Financé par le
Government gouvernement
of Canada   du Canada

For Lisa

Contents

Illustrations

Acknowledgments

Over the years while I was writing this book I accumulated more debts of gratitude than can adequately be listed here. Among those that particularly stand out is the one to my colleagues in the Department of Slavic Languages and Literatures at the University of Southern California, for constant lively exchange of ideas and collegial relations. The Department of Slavic Languages and Literatures at UC Berkeley hosted a talk that represented a very early version of the ideas developed here. I likewise thank Irina Shevelenko at the University of Wisconsin (Madison) for inviting me to participate in a conference titled "Reframing Russian Modernism," where I presented another early overview of my ideas about ritual in modern Russian culture. Equally, I thank the University of Wisconsin Press for granting permission to republish the elements of that talk that appeared in their publication of the conference's proceedings, as "Arranging the Absolute: The Modernist Rupture of History and Urban Space in the Soviet Era," pp. 99–118 in Irina Shevelenko, ed. *Reframing Russian Modernism* (University of Wisconsin Press, 2018). The Office of the Dean in the Dornsife College of Letters, Arts and Sciences at USC provided financial support for publication of this book. I am truly grateful to the external reviewers of my manuscript for the University of Toronto Press, whose comments were both ideally incisive and sympathetic to my project. Stephen Shapiro at UTP has similarly been the kind of sharp-witted and supportive editor an author can only dream about. Matthew Kudelka provided admirably meticulous copy editing of my manuscript. Finally, and most importantly, I thank my wife Lisa, whose loving support for this project sustained it when my own energies nearly flagged.

Note on Transliteration

In this book I use the Library of Congress system of transliteration from Russian (without diacritical marks), save for commonly known surnames such as Trotsky (not Trotskii), Lunacharsky, and so on. Throughout I use the spelling "Kyiv" for the capital of Ukraine, except where the toponym appears in transliteration from the Russian, in which case it appears as "Kiev."

STAGING THE ABSOLUTE

Introduction

Perhaps the most striking aspect of Soviet culture was its energetic symbolic agenda, its relentless drive to convince itself and the rest of the world of the significance of the Bolshevik Revolution and its attendant social and political consequences. The forms this agenda took ranged from the propaganda banners and posters that filled Soviet public space to the "socialist realism" that was its peculiar invention in the realm of literature and the arts to the show trials of the late 1930s, where political opponents of Stalin were accused of lurid crimes against the regime and sentenced to death. Among these symbolic enterprises were the many festivals and ritual displays of "enthusiasm" (to borrow the title of Dziga Vertov's 1931 film extolling the success of the Five-Year Plan) that in the early years following the revolution took over major sites in Petrograd in order to stage political spectacles on them, and that in later years marched across Red Square and through the streets of Moscow, Leningrad, and other Soviet cities. A certain exoticism defines these cultural forms (which may explain our enduring interest in them), not least the public rituals, the contemplation of which can induce a sense of the uncanny in the retrospective observer. It is not just the coordination of robot-like masses of workers, soldiers, and gymnasts as they file past the Lenin Mausoleum, impressive and unsettling as that can be, but also, I would submit, the quasi-religious aura attending the rituals' celebrations of a supposedly modern, atheist, and materialist state.

Soviet rituals of course emerged out of a cultural and historical context. Their design was not invented *ab ovo* but had immediate precedents in the theatrical experiments and utopian plans of the pre-revolutionary artistic avant-garde as well as in traditional Orthodox religious rituals, which the regime co-opted. Even Stalinist rituals, which can seem to push the limits of ostentation and excess, are neither as exotic nor as unprecedented as they might initially seem. As well, Soviet rituals did not represent an isolated or narrowly theatrical initiative within their culture. As this study will argue, they emerged, rather, out of a pervasive mindset in the fin de siècle and early twentieth century that was characterized by a desire to disrupt the immediate course of history in order to install some form of access to a transcendent realm, which meant, to that end, staging the absolute. This mindset found expression (or, another way of putting it, worked itself out) in a variety of forms, from literary works, plays, and treatises on the nature of theatre, to the imposingly present physical events of the large-scale festivals staged in the early years following the October Revolution and, eventually, to the Moscow show trials of the 1930s.

Soviet rituals also drew significantly on practices that go back centuries in European cultural life – surprising as that legacy might seem to a modern observer. It may also seem paradoxical that a study that concerns itself with cultural practices in the Russian twentieth century would look to examine certain Western European medieval rituals; but there are two reasons why this is justified. First, Russian modernists and, after them, Soviet festival planners were seeking quite deliberately to revive the medieval mystery play and related forms of urban spectacle and drama that were more characteristic of Western than Eastern Christianity. And second, dramas like the mystery play had analogues in Orthodox Christian processions of icons and the cross; more significantly, the eschatological mindset that informed Western religious rituals was fully native to Eastern Christianity as well.

The pathways along which these practices were transmitted are clear enough. The planners of early Soviet rituals were typically members of the pre-revolutionary avant-garde who had absorbed a widespread modernist interest (by no means limited to Russia) in reviving pre-modern rituals like the mystery play and the Corpus Christi procession, together with more playful forms like the Italian *commedia dell'arte* and Russian fairground puppet theatre, as antidotes to the traditions of the realist theatre, which had come to be associated with a stultifying bourgeoisie. But in so doing, those Soviet planners also transmitted a set of attitudes – a symbolic logic – regarding the means and ends of transforming urban space; arguably, those attitudes then embedded themselves in Soviet culture. The aspect of the mystery play and related rituals that Soviet planners seized upon with particular enthusiasm (if often intuitively rather than consciously) was the way in which those rituals projected a religious symbolic order outward from the church onto urban space in order temporarily to transform that space into a transcendent realm, the site of the Nativity or Passion. Such rituals staged the absolute by suspending the course of merely present, quotidian events in order appeal to a divine order of meaning, and the Soviet planners set out to do much the same.

A parallel example of rituals designed to instantiate a new political order can be found in the festivals staged in the aftermath of the French Revolution. As it happens, the format of the French festivals, which tended toward staging in the open air, "in the plain," under the "dome of heaven," understood as a "theocentric space, ordered by the radiating gaze of an architect God" (Ozouf 126, 129), did not serve as an important precedent for Soviet planners, whose efforts concentrated almost exclusively on urban space. But like Soviet planners, the "utopian festival dreamer" of the French Revolution enjoyed an "unheard-of opportunity" for planning festivals on a grand scale that would displace traditional rites (in France, deeply embedded traditions of Catholic rituals; in Russia, those of the Orthodox Church) with celebrations of a new set of transcendent meanings such as "the Supreme Being," "Reason," and "the Federation" (Ozouf 8). In a particularly compelling parallel, the festivals of the French Revolution, like their Soviet counterparts, "linked rediscovered liberty with reconquered space"; indeed, these processions were expected to "transform history into space" (Ozouf 126, 153). When the empirical reality of Paris turned out to be capable of throwing up physical obstacles like canals and churches that impeded an ideal procession, this was felt to represent "the unexpected eruption of history into the utopian dream" (Ozouf 152; i.e., this was the reversal or frustration of a staged transcendence).

The particular type of ritual – of public symbolic endeavour – that interests me here is thus one that projects its designs (in both senses of that word) onto the city with a distinct agenda: it seeks to appropriate urban space in the here-and-now, then to subject it to a totalizing gesture through which it comes to represent the whole of human history (the city is treated as a symbol of the world, the cosmos). Its purpose in doing so is – implicitly or explicitly – to disrupt the historical present, to declare its end and usher in some form of transhistorical reality or truth, to propel the entire society or humanity toward a transcendent future. Because the aim of such rituals is always to interrupt the course of history, I call them episodes of "intervention." A note is in order on how I use this term. I intend it as a device for capturing a certain aspiration to disrupt the historical present that I see as pervading both Russian modernism and the Soviet rituals that succeeded it – as well as the medieval antecedents of both. My aim in pursuing the various aspects of this phenomenon is not to present an etiology – a linear, causal argument – about the origins of Soviet rituals. It is, rather, to uncover some of the network of features that define those rituals but often lie hidden beneath their surface. I believe that to assess the culture out of which Soviet rituals arose, we need to consider a broad range of cultural phenomena that partook of the same set of attitudes and aspirations that produced them, whether the connections are immediately obvious or not. In the case of the medieval antecedents revived within Soviet rituals – the mystery plays, Corpus Christi processions, and similar rituals – rather than just take such forms for granted we need to consider as well the kinds of semiotic undertakings they represent. Deleuze and Guattari capture the idea behind my approach well with their metaphor of the rhizome as an alternative to the tree or "arborescent" approach to intellectual inquiry. They write that unlike a methodology emulating a tree or root, which "plots a point, fixes an order," the rhizome is a network of more dispersed and heterogeneous linkages that "establishes connections between semiotic chains, organizations of power, and circumstances relative to the arts, sciences, and social struggles. A semiotic chain is like a tuber agglomerating very diverse acts, not only linguistic, but also perceptive, mimetic, gestural, and cognitive" (*A Thousand Plateaus* 7). A related methodological concept is that of the "mental habitus" put forward by the art historian Erwin Panofsky. Summarizing Panofsky's study of Gothic art – an aesthetic mode that, like the medieval rituals this study considers, is remote from us in time and manifests itself in a variety of forms – the French sociologist Pierre Bourdieu comments:

> The parallelism between the development of Gothic art and the development of scholastic thought in the period between about 1130–1140 and about 1270 cannot be brought out unless one "brackets off phenomenal appearances" and seeks the hidden analogies between the principles of logical organization of Scholasticism and the principles of construction of Gothic architecture. This methodological choice is dictated by the intention of establishing more than a vague "parallelism" or discontinuous, fragmentary "influences." Renouncing the semblances of proof which satisfy intuitionists or the reassuring but reductive circumstantial proofs which delight positivists, Panofsky is led to identify the historical convergence which provides the object of his research with a hidden principle, a habitus or "habit-forming force." (quoted in David Wagner 437)[1]

The cultural practices I examine here, which in one way or another all strive toward a moment of eschatological "intervention," comprise just such a mental habitus. At its core reside texts and practices that include literary and dramatic works, projects for theatrical renewal and pronouncements on the nature of the theatre, and, in particular, ritual celebrations staged in the Soviet era. Despite their surface variety these cultural forms cohere around a set of shared elements. They arise out of an impatience with history as merely present reality and seek to implement in one way or another a desire to disrupt that reality – this is the point of calling the reflex one of "intervention" – by arranging or staging (or at times merely depicting) the installation of a different order, an extrahistorical (at times supernatural) reality the effect of whose advent will be to transform the present. Among these phenomena one also finds a recurring concern with realizing this "intervention" within a specific urban space (the streets of Petrograd or Moscow in particular), which serves as the object of transformation. That imagined transformation, moreover, operates in distinctive ways to take possession of urban space in order to render it up to transformation. It is from this perspective that Mikhail Bulgakov's last and uncompleted novel *Master i Margarita* (*The Master and Margarita*) becomes important to my interests as well. This book is not a study of that novel *per se*, but I use it as a departure point for my various lines of inquiry, which radiate like threads out from its pages. As a satirical commentary on the Stalin era, it draws our attention to that era's quasi-religious (one might even say occult) aura, in particular its claims to have instituted an entirely new phase in human history. But in its self-conscious recycling of literary precedents (in particular, the Faust tale, but also a whole culture of modernist fascination with the idea of the Second Coming) it also points us toward a cultural past of ritual, most immediately as it was embraced by modernism, but through that further to the Middle Ages (where we find a syntax of ritual and a specific appropriation of urban space that was replicated in many ways in the Soviet era). The wide-ranging theatricality of modernism also alerts us to the significance of forms that turn out to display an unexpected affinity with the ritual element, such as puppet theatre and the panorama.

The immediate background for an interest in apotheosizing rituals in Russia lies in the apocalyptic mood that prevailed in the fin de siècle and the longings for transcendence that it generated among Russian modernists. An air of foreboding was widespread in the culture of fin-de-siècle Russia, and it intensified after the debacle of Russia's loss in the Russo-Japanese War and the perceived failure of revolution in 1905. The writings of Russian religious thinkers, Symbolist writers and poets, and other mystically inclined figures of the period recurringly register an apprehensive sense of an approaching end. At the very turn of the century (1899–1900) the philosopher Vladimir Solov'ev published an essay on good, evil, and the nature of war, which he cast in the form of "Tri razgovora o voine, progresse i kontse mirovoi istorii" ("Three

Conversations about War, Progress, and the End of World History"). As one of the characters asserts, the acceleration of progress observable in the world is a sign that the historical process, the history of humanity, is nearing its end (705). Another character confesses that for the past year she has felt some kind of agitation in the air, as if it were the premonition of looming catastrophe. The essay ends with its own tale of advent or intervention, the reading of a "Brief Tale about the Antichrist," which declares that the "twentieth century after the birth of Christ was a time of the last great wars, civil wars, and revolutions" (735) and then recounts, in a style reminiscent of Dostoevsky's inserted "Legend of the Grand Inquisitor" in *Bratiia Karamazovy* (*The Brothers Karamazov*), the appearance of a false messiah in Earth's final days.

Another celebrated example of nervous foreboding, Andrei Bely's modernist novel *Peterburg* (*Petersburg*), is saturated with premonitions of a dire end in the aftermath of Russia's defeat in the Russo-Japanese War of 1905. Its hero is a revolutionary youth who has been given the task of assassinating his own father, a senator. The narrative itself abandons realist depictions of events in favour of a series of fitful, disjointed vignettes in which the hero's red cape flits in and out of the street lights and shadows of the capital. An example that anticipates the confluence of themes that will figure in this study is the poet Valerii Briusov's 1903 "Kon' bled" ("Pale Horse"), which takes its title and central image from the Book of Revelation. Briusov imagines a modern urban scene – the poem was allegedly inspired by an accident he witnessed on the streets of Paris (Pyman, *History of Russian Symbolism* 233) – with its busy streets, buses and automobiles, street lights, and advertisements, which is suddenly punctuated by the sound of hoofbeats as the pale horse of the Apocalypse, whose rider has a fiery visage and bears a scroll titled "Death," briefly appears, then disappears. What is especially relevant about this poem in the context of this study is that it imagines its episode of apocalyptic otherworldly "intervention" taking place within an urban space whose random elements in commotion clearly denote an immediacy of experience: a bustling and otherwise inattentive here-and-now.

The fin-de-siècle atmosphere in Russia can also be seen as part of a broader "crisis of modernity" that arose in a number of European cultures in the later nineteenth and early twentieth centuries, whose most important aspect for this study is its manifest impatience or disaffection with the very idea of history – with the notion, that is, that meaning in human lives unfolds in a sequential present whose path may, in retrospect, turn out to reveal consistent laws of development. In Hegel's thought history may harbour a transcendent final goal, the ultimate realization of *das Geist* in a perfectly rational form of government; but the meaning of human existence for him still lies in its progressive unfolding *within* history. Or, as Alexander Herzen, perhaps Russia's greatest commentator on his historical moment (consider his voluminous *Byloe i dumy* [*My Past and Thoughts*]), writes in in the middle of the nineteenth century, "history has no libretto, and from this one thing alone is clear; that one should make use of life, of the present" (*From the Other Shore*, quoted in Rampton 54).

It is this conviction that erodes over the second half of the nineteenth century. The break registers itself notably in the thought of Marx, who famously declared that he had found Hegel standing on his head and set him back on his feet. What he meant was that he had imposed a materialist rather than idealist view on Hegel's understanding of historical process, but in his chiliasm he also disrupted the continualism and processionism that are hallmarks of the Hegelian thought. *The Manifesto of the Communist Party*, which Marx co-wrote with Friedrich Engels, in contrast is saturated with a sense of history as something already consummated, summarized, and therefore irrelevant to human experience. "The history of *all hitherto existing society* is the history of class struggles," they declare in the manifesto's opening (473, emphasis added). "*All previous historical movements* were movements of minorities, or in the interest of minorities. The proletarian movement is the self-conscious, independent movement of the immense majority, in the interests of the immense majority" (482, emphasis added). The event that will complete this rupture with the corrupt past is, of course, the communist revolution, which will bring about "the forcible overthrow of all existing social conditions" (500) and usher in "an association, in which the free development of each is the condition for the free development of all" (491). The resonant declaration that ends the manifesto – "proletarians have nothing to lose but their chains" (500) – is at the same time the expression of a hope for freedom from history. As Marx comments in a related passage in "The Eighteenth Brumaire of Louis Bonaparte," "The social revolution of the nineteenth century cannot draw its poetry from the past, but only from the future" (597). In his "Uses and Abuses of History" (published in 1874 as part of his *Untimely Meditations*), Nietzsche, too, wrote scathingly about Hegel's efforts to see the victory of historical logic in every event – an attitude, as Nietzsche acerbically observes, that led him to see the summit and end point of the world process coinciding with his individual existence in Berlin – and opposed the "historical person" unable to see beyond a present freighted with meanings inherited from the past to the "superhistorical person" who is able to shift to a transcendent and future- oriented freedom from such burdens.

One of the most explicit, if also eccentric, manifestations of this disaffection with history in the Russian context appears in the thought of Nikolai Fedorov, a librarian in the Rumiantsev Museum by day who blended an almost naive faith in the potential of science with an eschatological vision in which humanity would attain immortality. Like Marx, Fedorov considered the past to be nothing more than a record of oppression, save that in his thought, as expressed in his magnum opus *Filosofiia obshchego dela* (*The Philosophy of the Common Cause*, a compendium of his handwritten notes issued by two of his students from 1906–1913), it is suffering from disease and death that commands attention rather than economic hardship. The history Fedorov sought to disrupt was one in which humans unreflectingly perpetuate a vicious cycle of subordination to the forces of nature by reproducing and thereby creating only more beings destined to grow up and die (one could quote Adorno here: "the essential function of a utopia is a critique of what is present").[2] For him, the moment of disruption would come when humanity recognized the need for the ultimate "common cause" in which procreation would cease and humanity would focus its energies on developing scientific means first for curing disease, then for prolonging life, then eventually even for resurrecting the dead (including by searching the cosmos for the dispersed atoms of the long-ago deceased, in order to reassemble and resurrect their bodies).[3]

Lenin's political works, like the seminal *What Is to Be Done?* of 1902, are largely too mired in the particulars of inter- and intra-party manoeuvring to provide a broader historical perspective. The same may be said of Trotsky's generally more perspicacious *The Russian Revolution*, though that work's Preface does comment that "the most indubitable feature of a revolution is the direct interference of the masses in historical events" – an example of the logic of "intervention" that this study will examine, in that it projects not just the advent of a dictatorship of the proletariat but also the disruption of history that advent will entail. But Bolshevik leaders largely assumed a Marxist perspective on history's course (if not its exact mechanisms, which they problematized by insisting on the need for a political avant-garde to direct the course of events – an attitude that may underlie the need the Soviet state obviously sensed to promote the kinds of rituals of "intervention" that I describe here). Trotsky's remonstration to the Mensheviks as they abandoned the Second Congress of Soviets in October 1917 that they would end up in the "dustbin of history" (*svalka istorii*) potentially means two things at once in the original Russian: history's dustbin, that is, the place where failed endeavours land, or the dustbin that *is* history, the empirically present domain that is about to be swept aside to make way for a different order. Stalinism projected the logic of historical rupture even onto its own Bolshevik past, its impatience with the present expressed in such things as the "great rupture" (*velikii perelom*) inaugurated with Stalin's twin campaigns for rapid industrialization and collectivization in 1929, the declaration that the first Five-Year Plan had in fact been fulfilled in just three and a half years, and so on – impulses captured in the title of Valentin Kaverin's 1932 novel *Vremia, vpered!* (*Time, Forward!*).[4]

Note that Marxism and its Leninist derivatives were by no means the only responses in the Russian context to the turn away from the idea of history. As Rampton notes, the early twentieth century saw a "realignment in Russian public values away from grand historical narratives," which led "several prominent Marxists [to draw] on Kantian philosophy to subject their former conceptions of freedom to radical critiques" (58). Empirical-positivist ideas now entered into competition with metaphysical-religious ones in the early Russian twentieth century (63). These metaphysical interests were to prove surprisingly durable in the Soviet context, even as they perforce competed with the state's aggressive materialism. Another way of understanding the atmosphere of the fin de siècle in Russia, this one culturological rather than philosophical or political, is to view it as an abandonment of an element of public display that had earlier originated in a principle of play – in the sense not of leisure but of quasi-reality, as suggested by Johan Huizinga's *Homo Ludens*. Huizinga describes the nineteenth century as an exception in the course of European history in that it "seems to leave little room for play." In that century, "tendencies running counter to all that we mean by play have become increasingly dominant" (191). "Never had an age taken itself with more portentous seriousness. *Culture ceased to be 'played.' Outward forms were no longer intended to give the appearance, the fiction, if you like, of a higher, ideal mode of life*" (192, emphasis added). The fin de siècle and early twentieth century ushered in a renewed desire to see culture "played" in this sense, specifically as part of an aspiration toward a higher reality.

Impatience with "grand historical narratives" in the public and political spheres in Russia was paralleled in the realm of literature and the arts by the breakdown of the paradigm of realism that had dominated much of the nineteenth century. Disruptions of realist representations of course occur earlier in that era, especially among writers influenced by Romanticism. Nikolai Gogol punctuates the ending of Part One of *Mertvye dushi* (*Dead Souls*) with the appearance of a mysterious and otherworldly troika that flies off into the heavens like the prophet Elijah, leaving behind the drab steppes of the Russian provinces. In his study of veridiction in modern European literature, Ilya Kliger locates the departure from the Romantic paradigm (which held sway in Russian letters until about the 1840s) in the nearly parallel appearance of Hegel's *Phenomenology of the Spirit* (1807) and Goethe's *Wilhelm Meisters Lehrjahre* (1796). Both works reject abstract schemes applied extrahistorically to human experience in favour of narratives in which "temporal progress turns into the medium of constant inquiry." Furthermore, the weight in both texts shifts from "authoritative narratorial discourse, pronouncing eternal verities over a mistake-ridden temporal succession, to that succession itself, now capable of yielding truth immanently" (30, 177). Charles Taylor has described this sense of humankind and its place in the world as an "expressivist vision" of the self, in which the self is understood to be self-defining within the bounds of an empirically given reality (6, 15–16, i.e., with no recourse to or even interest in any transcendent order). But a more consequential disaffection with the realist paradigm in the later nineteenth century can be seen – paradoxically enough – in the works of Lev Tolstoy, who was at once a producer of "grand historical narratives" if there ever was one (e.g., *War and Peace*) and a writer who was convinced, as Morson has argued, that life is most meaningfully lived in small moments, day to day (see his *Hidden in Plain View*). The Tolstoy who fills the pages of *Anna Karenina* with minor details of his characters' lives and physical appearance, who charts the complex, dialectical progress his hero Konstantin Levin makes toward a sense of how one should live, and who insists (as Morson has argued) that life is most meaningfully lived in the present – in the end also registers despair with this entire agenda when he suddenly tells us that true intimation of life's meanings comes only in moments like birth and death that serve as "apertures in this ordinary life through which something higher could be glimpsed" (715). Even the starkly unforgiving description of Anna's last carriage ride to the train station where she will commit suicide registers a certain *unhinging* of realist representation: Anna's tormented inner thoughts mix almost randomly with her impressions of scenes on the streets through which she rides. We are not yet at Joycean stream-of-consciousness narration because Tolstoy brackets the passage as an instance of psychological and moral pathology, just as he does the modernist music Levin hears at a Moscow concert in which "gaiety, sadness, despair, tenderness, and triumph alternated without any rationale, like the feelings of a madman" (687) – but the vector already points that way.

In a now celebrated letter of 1900 to Anton Chekhov, the writer Maxim Gorky claimed that with his story "Dama s sobachkoi" ("The

Lady with the Dog"), published the year before, Chekhov had "killed realism." What Gorky evidently had in mind was Chekhov's almost overly meticulous attention to Tolstoyan details with no reference to any evident overarching scheme of meanings (Shcherbenok 297). This observation has been expanded in scholarship into the claim that Chekhov had "destroyed nineteenth-century literary conventions without replacing them with any alternative" (Shcherbenok 298), a lack that can be seen as proceeding out of a sense that such conventions and frameworks of meaning had exhausted themselves. In other quarters, however, the sense of exhaustion with historical narratives and the realist forms that accommodated them stimulated a brilliant efflorescence of the arts, much of whose attention was devoted to the idea of apocalypse or yearnings for a new (higher) world of spirit. Such aspirations materialized not just in the overt mysticism of the Symbolist movement but also in much of the experimentation of the artistic and literary avant-garde (whose collective impulse is well summarized in the subtitle of Marjorie Perloff's study of "the Futurist Moment" in twentieth-century art: "the language of rupture"). To take just one avant-garde example (others are discussed in chapters that follow), the radical verbal experimentation informing poems by the Russian Futurists, which they called "zaum" (roughly, "trans-sense" language or language "beyond-mind"), has been described as operating out of an "insuperable hatred for language that had existed before [them]," as declared in the manifesto "Poshchechina obshchestvennomu vkusu" ("A Slap in the Face of Public Taste," quoted in Steiner 144).[5] Members of the closely related movement in literary theory known as Formalism, which brashly announced its presence on the cultural scene in the early twentieth century, also sought to treat literature as "a given without origins" (Smirnov, *Epokha 'ostranenia'* 43); they saw artistic form as embodying an atemporal present, a kind of anti-successiveness (Kapinos 475). In this both Futurism and Formalism could be seen as part of a broader aspiration of the avant-garde to clear the ground and be the final arbiters of artistic form: in its early days, Formalism too strove to be the last, eschatological word on what constituted literature (Smirnov 48; Groys, *Total Art of Stalinism*, 19–20).

What makes the case of the Soviet rituals that emerged out of these contexts exceptional is that artists and planners of festivals found themselves with the resources of the new Soviet state at their disposal, including access to urban space to a degree perhaps unprecedented since the Middle Ages. The rituals and public displays that resulted, which have different form and tenor in the early Soviet era than in the later, Stalinist period, have received extensive scholarly attention (in works by Clark, von Geldern, Binns, Petrone, Rudnitsky, Mazaev, and many others). These studies have elucidated well the actors and institutions that produced the rituals, those rituals' aetiology in avant-garde theatrical experiments and theorizations, their co-optation of Orthodox religious rituals, their partial emulation of the *fêtes* of the French Revolution, their self-conscious revival of older forms such as the mystery play – and so on. But I am interested in a different set of questions here. I revisit the history of these festivals with two aims: first, to situate them within (and show them to be emanations of) a much broader mindset in the early Russian twentieth century – on both sides of the 1917 divide – that encompasses such seemingly diverse phenomena as literary works, plays, and writings on theatre as well as forms of popular entertainment like the puppet theatre and the panorama; and second, to examine more closely the historical forms that were revived (or perpetuated) by the adherents of this mindset in order better to understand the symbolic logic that defined those forms and that was transmitted – I argue – through their revival within Soviet culture, in which festivals and rituals (like the Moscow show trials of the 1930s) were key expressive forms.

In pursuit of the mental habitus out of which Soviet rituals arose, I am interested in the factors generating their underlying logic of "intervention," their desire to disrupt the historical present and bring about the advent of extrahistorical meaning. How, for example, are retellings of the Faust legend and its own narrative of "intervention" – which enjoyed conspicuous popularity in Russia in the later nineteenth and early twentieth centuries – related to the puppet theatre and the panorama, which also, as I will argue, embodied aspirations to redefine urban space? Why does Bulgakov's *The Master and Margarita* so pointedly engage with the Faust legend as the focus of its satire on the world of Stalinism? My second line of inquiry delves into the past of this complex of ideas involving "intervention" and the forms in which it was realized. Some of the idea's more important roots have been identified – both modernists and Soviet festival planners, for example, sought to adapt the medieval genre of the mystery play and, perhaps without realizing it, other early forms of ritual as well. But what – and more to the point, *how* – did those forms "mean"? What symbolic economy did these older forms deploy, what syntax of meaning-bearing forms? What residue of the mystery play's origin in liturgy or its totalizing projection of symbolic meanings onto urban space survives in its modern adaptations? Apart from its obvious use as precedent for a narrative of "intervention," what complex of meanings does the Faust legend (or Goethe's drama *Faust*) involve?

Equally important to my inquiry is the question of what meanings these aspirations and practices in the Soviet era turn out to harbour when removed from their Soviet exoticism and returned to a broader context of European cultural history. In pursuit of answers to these questions I examine a wide range of cultural evidence, from literary and dramatic works, theoretical pronouncements on the nature of theatre, and other purely textual material to realized or material objects like performances, processions, *agit-poezda* (Soviet propaganda trains), the panorama, and the puppet theatre. The cumulative result could be considered an exercise in cultural anthropology. What is hypothesized here is the existence of a certain collective cultural consciousness – not as closely cohesive as the grammar of a natural language, but like language belonging at once to no particular person and to all the members of the collective – from which *emanate* these various expressive forms, as manifestations of an underlying but not always fully articulated content. Nor is this consciousness unique to Russia. It has its deepest roots in European culture of the Middle Ages.

In the first chapter of this study I seek to assess the broader mindset of this era in Russian culture by examining the late nineteenth- and twentieth-century vogue in Russian literature for narratives of Second Coming, or, as I term them, tales of "intervention." These works feature imagined returns or advents within the present day of Christ or – its functional equivalent in this context – the devil. Retellings of the Faust legend, which proliferated in Russia in the fin de siècle and continued into the early Soviet era, show that in the apocalyptic mood of that era Russian culture was alive with speculation about supernatural intervention. Because the larger complex involved here habitually implicates urban space, I discuss the significance of spatial concepts to culture in general and then trace the convergent themes of the city and of theatre in the oeuvre of Mikhail Bulgakov (in whose *The Master and Margarita* the devil visits Stalinist Moscow) as a way of showing how one writer's evolution converges with the broader ideas alive within his culture. The concept of the city as both a theatrical stage and the privileged site for a staging of extrahistorical advent thus emerges as something of a quintessence in Bulgakov's works: *The Master and Margarita* completes an idiosyncratic trajectory begun in his earliest works even as it responds to broader tendencies in Russian culture as a whole.

In chapter 2, I examine the Faust legend, both the modern recastings of it that appear in early twentieth-century Russia and the theatrical precedent of Goethe's version, as the pre-eminent example in European culture of the "intervention" narrative. From here I step back to consider what the older forms that shaped the Faust legend (and by extension its modern retellings) actually involved as a symbolic endeavour. I consider the medieval mystery and Corpus Christi play as revelatory of the logic – within European cultural practices – behind the symbolic transformation of urban space, the projection of religious drama onto the urban here-and-now. The close genetic connection between theatre and religious rite is important here (I draw on the work of the medievalist Peter Brown and the theatre historian Marvin Carlson, among others). It is also in this context that the expectation of *judgment*, which so ominously and tragically informs the end point of this study, Stalinist ritual, emerges as an element embedded in the entire symbolic economy of urban transformations. The puppet theatre, which modernists looked to as one of their models for theatrical renewal (think, in the Russian context, of Stravinsky's ballet *Petrushka*) also turns out to be an aesthetic form with cultic roots closely related to mystery plays and their inner logic. The kind of symbolic projection of a sacred city (Jerusalem) onto an extant, secular one that is the essential operation of the mystery play also happens to have been a familiar trope in Russian culture, which historically saw Kyiv as a second Jerusalem and Moscow as the third Rome (after Constantinople). This legacy in effect predisposed Russian modernists and their Soviet successors toward the kinds of transformations of urban space they so concerned themselves with. Finally, I argue that panoramas, which often featured Jerusalem and Rome as subjects, augmented a sense in the fin de siècle that sacred events should be projected onto the city, and that specific panoramas in Bulgakov's native Kyiv influenced his understanding of that city as well as the composition of *The Master and Margarita*.

Chapter 3 takes up the specifically modernist aspiration toward "intervention" that emerged from calls during the European fin de siècle for theatrical renewal in the writings of Wagner, Maeterlinck, Craig, and others and in transformative schemes like Wagner's opera house at Bayreuth and Max Reinhardt's open-air stagings of grand dramas on city squares. Remote from Stalinist ritual and detachedly aestheticizing as they may seem, these projects served as crucial seedbeds out of which later practices emerged, not least as symptoms of the persistent designs on urban space that inform the "intervention" agenda. The intense interest Russian modernists had in Wagner served as a conduit bearing ritualizing impulses into the Russian setting, where they were often taken to eschatological extremes. Here I examine Russian calls for a transformation of the theatre in the early twentieth century, as well as a series of works in which Russian writers attempted to create a modern form of the mystery play (perhaps most clearly exemplified in the composer Alexander Scriabin's unwritten but lavishly hypothesized

Mysterium). I return more specifically here to the modernist interest in the puppet theatre, with particular focus on the Russian interest in the *balagan* or fairground booth (Stravinsky's Petrushka is a puppet who comes to life in one of these). This aesthetic line reaches its apogee in two works by the Russian Symbolist poet Alexander Blok: his 1906 play *Balaganchik* (*The Fairground Booth*), which in keeping with modernist convention suggests the ephemeral theatricality of life (rendered here in the idiom of the *commedia dell'arte* or Petrushka play); and his dramatic poem *Dvenadtsat'* (*The Twelve*) of 1918, which surprisingly (but on a deeper level, in my view, entirely symptomatically) projects the farce of a fairground puppet play onto the chaos immediately following the Bolshevik Revolution in Petrograd. *The Twelve* – which startlingly ends with the appearance of an ethereal Christ out of a blizzard – shows how immanent the idea of the city as the locus of "intervention" was in the Russian cultural mind at the very moment that it entered the Soviet era.

In chapter 4 I turn to the set of specifically Soviet practices – particularly the mass festivals staged in the early years following the 1917 Revolution – that served as a continuation of modernist theatrical projects, or, rather, as a means for their assimilation to a Bolshevik political agenda. Bolshevik festivals have attracted a fair amount of scholarly attention, but the tendency has been to treat them as an aesthetic phenomenon, as reflecting a desire to turn urban space into avant-garde art. I contend they were something more: the manifestation of a political desire to seize and transform urban space in order to stage, in effect, the disruption of history. Early Soviet festivals organized by members of the pre-revolutionary avant-garde, which often consciously perpetuated modernist projects for "intervention" (some of which were explicitly labelled "mysteries"), took place in an atmosphere that was religiously charged (paradoxically so, if one considers the militant atheism of the Soviet regime). They were paralleled by a series of newly instituted rituals that openly adapted rites of the Orthodox Church, such as processions of icons and Processions of the Cross (which in their Soviet inflection become parades of portraits of Soviet leaders and the *agitpoezda* – "agitational" [i.e., propaganda] – trains sent out into the Russian countryside in the late 1910s and early 1920s).

Chapter 5 examines what might be considered the apogee of the trajectory this cultural complex reached in the Russian twentieth century: the solemnification that rituals underwent in the Stalin era, the erasure of elements of spontaneity in them in favour of tighter state control and staging in prominent urban sites like Moscow's Red Square – but at the same time the paradoxical new emphasis in the Stalin era on merriment (one of Stalin's best-known slogans was "Life has become better,

comrades, life has become gayer"). In this context I revisit the cultural
theoretician Mikhail Bakhtin's notion of carnival (outlined in his book
on the Renaissance writer Rabelais, known in English translation as
Rabelais and His World) and consider both its incompleteness (historically, carnival merriment always led to Lenten solemnity) and its own
complex relation to Stalinist thought (despite its purely historical topic).
I further examine Stalinist plans for the reconstruction of Moscow as
extensions of earlier (medieval and modernist) designs on urban space
and argue that the infamous show trials of the 1930s emerged out of
the same cultural logic that exercised the modernist calls for theatrical
renewal: as the ineluctable culmination of urban spectacle in a transhistorical event of judgment.

Chapter One

Narratives of "Intervention" and the Culture of Space in the Early Twentieth Century

Festivals and rituals appear throughout the Socialist Realist literature that served as the essential mirror of the Soviet regime's aspirations, at once celebrating and solemnifying the achievements of the working class under the all-wise guidance of the Bolshevik Party. Fedor Gladkov's classic 1925 exemplar of the genre *Tsement* (*Cement*), for example, features both a solemn commemoration, as a sacrifice to the Revolution, of a worker killed by marauding Cossacks and an ecstatic ceremony at the novel's end celebrating the reopening of a cement factory on the fourth anniversary of the Revolution. Furmanov's 1923 novel *Chapaev* about a peasant military commander whose loyal but wayward energy is eventually tamed by the "conscious" oversight of his political commissar offers as one of its plot's epiphanic moments a theatrical performance by a group of actors who travel with the brigade (and fight the Cossacks when not performing). In a respite from battle they present a play "written right here, in the division," featuring "extremely serious content" (251) about how Red Army soldiers battle with Cossacks and convert some of them to the Bolshevik cause – following which Chapaev himself is prodded to get up on stage and deliver "a brief but colourful speech filled with episodes from his military life" (255). As late as 1957, the Thaw-era filmmaker Mikhail Kalatozov in *Letiat zhuravli* (*The Cranes Are Flying*) alots ritual a place of honour even as he dismantles other elements of the Stalinist aesthetic. A portrayal of the experience of war mostly from the perspective of individual lives rather than the grand scheme of the historical conflict between communism and fascism, it ultimately shows its heroine's private grief to be transcended in a moment of collective celebration at a train station to which soldiers (save her fiancé) have returned, complete with a speech extolling the nation's march toward the communist future delivered from a tribunal by a military commissar. Indeed, in the subtitle to her influential study of Socialist Realism, Clark labels the genre "history as ritual."

The work that captures the mindset behind Soviet rituals with perhaps the most acuity, however, is one that would manifestly not have been accepted by literary authorities as Socialist Realist, was never published in its author's lifetime, and only appeared in the Soviet Union toward the end of that state's existence: Mikhail Bulgakov's *The Master and Margarita* (1928–40). In Bulgakov's novel the devil visits Stalinist Moscow in the guise of "Woland," a "foreigner" who insinuates himself into an apartment as well as the repertoire of the city's Variety Theatre for a display of black magic followed by its supposed unmasking. The thrust of the novel is satirical: Woland and his retinue transect the theatrical/ literary world of Moscow, exposing the corruption and venality that are its true norm.[1] In an ironic chiasmus, the novel's infernal Moscow episodes are paralleled by a series of events set in "Yershalaim" (i.e., Jerusalem), which present a pointedly secular retelling of the Passion and execution of "Yeshua Ha-Nozri" (i.e., Jesus of Nazareth). Supernatural beings interrupt grey and corrupt Stalinist life in the Moscow chapters, while the Yershalaim parts of the novel avoid any suggestion of Yeshua's divinity, recasting the Gospel accounts in a realist depiction carried out in the spirit of nineteenth-century debates about the historical person of Jesus.[2] Across their disparity of manner, however, both parts of the novel promote the myth of the artist and his transcendent text: the master's novel about Pilate cannot be destroyed, and Levi Matevei's (i.e, Matthew's) imaginary account of Jesus's life and death becomes the foundation of a religion that overthrows the Roman Empire.[3]

Far from being the aesthetic outlier it might seem to be – an exotic bloom of fantastic literature on the landscape of Stalinist Socialist Realism – Bulgakov's novel is in fact attentively engaged with its cultural context.[4] Besides taunting the entire Stalinist mentality with its real, rather than professed, manias and fears, it offers incisive commentary on a set of aesthetic and political intentions that defined Soviet culture at its inception and that persisted in even more earnest form into the Stalin era. In particular it reveals the extent to which an aspiration toward *ritualized intervention* had embedded itself in Soviet culture: a desire as it were to orchestrate supernatural intervention in the here-and-now of Soviet urban space in order to suspend history – and then, in the ultimate extent of this logic, to bring about judgment of the present world.[5] The supernatural element was of course unacknowledged by the atheist Soviet state and was a mostly unwitting holdover from the pre-revolutionary era, when, as Livak has argued, what united Russian modernists was a "sense of staring into a spiritual, cultural, and social chasm between past and present [...] The periodic recurrence of this sensibility linked them, in an oxymoronic *tradition of rupture*, to the 'moderns' of early Christianity, who had launched the term *modernus* to denote their break with the pagan past, and thence to the self-defined 'moderns' of the Renaissance, the Reformation, the French Revolution, and so forth" (9–10).[6] Those "moderns" of early Christianity together with their medieval and Renaissance successors also turn out to be strikingly relevant to the culture of the early Soviet era.

It is partly the point of Bulgakov's satire to reinstate this sensibility playfully in the literal form of the devil's visit to Moscow. But staging a scene in which transhistorical judgment could be carried out *was* the palpable aim of certain early Soviet phenomena, and Bulgakov's masterpiece serves as a window onto the complex sources and motivations of this impulse. As Boris Gasparov cogently observes, *The Master and Margarita* can be read as a parable about the 1920s (and, one could add, the fin de siècle) told from the 1930s.[7] Bulgakov himself in general can be thought of as a late Romantic (hence his openness to supernatural themes) who is interested in imagining assorted interventions of the spirit realm or the uncanny into the oppressive reality of Stalinism, a writer of science fiction transformations (in works like "Sobach'e serdtse" ["Heart of a Dog"], in which the transplantation of a human pituitary gland into a dog turns the animal into a vulgar proletarian, and "Rokovye iaitsa" ["The Fateful Eggs"], in which a powerful ray accidentally applied to a shipment of reptile eggs turns them into monsters who advance on Moscow) – one who persistently mixes the sacred and the profane.[8] His most significant works habitually depict the magical transformation of this world and its constituents, usually to satirical effect or leading to the upheaval of Stalinist hierarchies: he writes pointedly metaphysical "carnivals," in the Bakhtinian sense, that upset the philistine materialism of the Soviet world (the Bakhtinian concept of carnival, as will be argued, can itself be seen as a product of Soviet culture). Consider, in *The Master and Margarita*, the characterization of the Moscow chapters in the novel's own Epilogue as "[tales] of an evil power that visited the capital" ("[rasskazy] o nechistoi sile, navestivshei stoliltsu," *Sobranie sochinenii* 2004, vol. 8, 531) – tales that "cultured people" in the capital would prefer to dismiss, though the hard facts of the cinders to which the Griboedov house has been reduced and other effects show that at the very least "someone had spent some time in the capital" ("kto-to pobyval v stolitse," 531). Consider as well that "many changes took place in the lives of those who suffered at the hands of Woland and his retinue" (*proizoshli mnogie izmeneniia v zhizni tekh, kto postradal ot Volanda i ego prisnykh* – the word for "retinue" here, *prisnye*, is an archaism with Biblical connotations, 536–7).

The modern era did not invent the tale of intervention, but in the case of Russia, at least, it energetically revived such tales. They are common enough in the literature of Romanticism, and in the Russian tradition they are particularly associated with the works of Nikolai Gogol – the most salient embodiment in Russian literature of the Gothic, Hoffmannesque line and an important predecessor for Bulgakov, who could be said to have absorbed Gogol's sense of the *grotesquerie* of the supernatural.[9] In Gogol's story "Vii" ("The Viy"), for example, the philosophy student Khoma Brut is ridden over the steppes by a witch (who may have been one of the models for Margarita's midnight ride in Bulgakov's novel) and then forced to read prayers three nights in a row over the corpse of a young woman who turns out to be the same witch. Twice saved by the crowing of a cock at dawn (a staple motif of the "witches' sabbath" theme, cf. Mussorgsky's "Night on Bald Mountain," with its chimes heralding the dawn, and Hella's swift departure at dawn in *The Master and Margarita*), he perishes on the third night when the sanctuary of the church in which the corpse reposes is invaded by a horde of demons (*i nesmetnaia sila chudovishch vletela v bozh'iu tserkov'*, 261). The later "Nevskii prospekt" ("Nevsky Prospect") famously makes demonic interference a defining trait of the imperial capital St. Petersburg – which was itself the legacy of Peter the Great's own project for transforming Russian political reality through the aggressive founding of a new urban space – in a tale that can be seen as marking the point when the "intervention" narrative enters Russian cultural consciousness: the misfortunes that befall the tale's two contrasting heroes (one a dreamy artist who falls in love with a prostitute, the other a lustful army lieutenant who pursues a married German woman) are attributed to the devil, who himself lights the lamps on the city streets at nightfall. Gogol's works are pervaded by a distrust of empirical reality, which always threatens to turn out to be a facade stretched over a world ruled by demons.

There is, however, a variant of this plot type that is still more relevant to the fin de siècle and the early Soviet era because it emerges out of the kind of despair with present reality discussed in the introduction to this study: namely, tales that more specifically imagine the disruption of that reality through the return of Christ. In the Christian tradition, of course, the Gospels are the *ur*-text of divine intervention in human affairs, and secular tales of Christ's unexpected return typically appeal to divine authority by foreshortening, as it were, the time between the present and the Apocalypse – the prophesied second, and final, intervention of God in human history (within the canonical Gospels there is already such a tale: the account in Luke 24 of how Christ appeared, initially unrecognized, to some of the disciples on the road to Emmaus).

Fedor Tiutchev's 1855 poem "Eti bednye selen'ia" ("These Poor Settlements"), for example, crystallizes its sense of Russian dolour under the oppressive reign of Nicholas I in the image of a humble Christ wandering through and blessing the impoverished Russian countryside – invisible to arrogant foreign glances – in what can be considered a poignant failure of historical disruption:

> These poor settlements,
> This miserly nature,
> Longsuffering native land,
> Oh you, land of the Russian people!
>
> The proud gaze of the foreigner
> Will not understand or notice
> That which runs through and secretly glows
> In your submissive nakedness.
>
> Saddened by the cross he bears
> In the guise of a slave the Heavenly King
> Walked your length and breadth,
> Oh native land, bestowing his blessing.[10]

Aleksandr Ivanov's massive (some 18 by 25 feet) and controversial 1857 painting "Iavlenie Khrista narodu" ("The Appearance of Christ before the People"), which shows John the Baptist gesturing before a crowd of onlookers on a bank of the Jordan toward the figure of Christ in the distance, reveals a similar mid-nineteenth-century preoccupation with advent as a key to Russia's predicament. (The same painting served as the prototype for the artist Mikhailov's ambitious canvas showing Christ before Pilate in Tolstoy's *Anna Karenina*.) Another example, in a sentimental and moralizing vein, is Tolstoy's 1885 story "Gde liubov', tam i Bog" ("Where Love Is, God Is Also"). Tolstoy adapted his story from an anonymous publication in the journal *Peterburgskii rabochii* a year earlier that itself was a reworking of the French evangelist writer Ruben Saillens's "Le père Martin" – a lineage that suggests the archetypical qualities of the tale. While reading the Gospels at night a poor shoemaker named Martyn Avdeich believes that he hears Christ telling him to expect a visit the next day. Throughout that day Martyn spontaneously renders a series of kindnesses to people who come to his basement shop, but he does not see Christ – until, in the evening, apparitions of the various people he has helped step forth from the shadows to reveal that in them Christ had indeed visited him (291–2).[11]

In a perceptive study of Bulgakov's Kyivan contexts, Miron Petro-vskii identifies an extensive series of such "Second Coming" works in Russian literature, among them Dostoevsky's *Idiot* (*The Idiot*), the "Leg-end of the Grand Inquisitor" section of *The Brothers Karamazov*, Maksim Gorky's *Na dne* (*In the Depths*), Aleksandr Blok's *The Twelve*, and Vladi-mir Mayakovsky's *Misteriia-Buff* (*Mystery-Bouffe*) (164). The latter two will be considered in more detail in chapter 4, but the most pertinent example of a nineteenth-century predecessor that anticipates ideas ani-mating the Soviet context is Ivan's "poem" on the Grand Inquisitor in *The Brothers Karamazov*.[12] Ivan prefaces his "poem" with remarks on its generic qualities that could be invoked as part of the prehistory of Bul-gakov's own narrative of otherworldly intervention in *The Master and Margarita*. The action of his "poem," Ivan notes, takes place in the six-teenth century, when

> there was a vogue for bringing the heavenly powers down to earth in works of poetry. I'm not even talking about Dante. In France clerks of the court as well as monks in monasteries put on entire plays [*predstavleniia*] in which they brought the Madonna, angels, saints, Christ, and even God himself out onto the stage [...] In Victor Hugo's *Notre Dame de Paris* in honor of the birth of the French dauphin, in Paris during the reign of Louis XI, in the town hall a performance free to all is staged of the didac-tic play "Le bon jugement de la très sainte et gracieuse Vierge Marie," in which she herself personally appears and passes her *bon jugement*. From time to time here in Russia, in Moscow of the pre[-]Petrine era, virtually the same kind of dramatic presentations were made, especially draw-ing on the Old Testament; in addition to dramatic works throughout the entire world there also travelled many plays and "verses" in which it was obligatory for saints, angels, and all the host of heaven to take part. In our monasteries they also took up translations, copies, and even the com-position of such poems – and at what time, that of the Mongol yoke! For example, there is one such little monastery poem (translated, of course, from the Greek) called "The Descent of the Virgin into Hell" [*Khozhdenie bogoroditsy po mukam*], with imagery and a boldness second not even to Dante's.[13]

Ivan actually cites Tiutchev's 1855 poem as evidence of how God occa-sionally responds to the fervent prayers of saints and martyrs asking that he appear to them («Бо господи явися нам», *Polnoe sobranie sochine-nii*, vol. 14, 226), which suggests that Dostoevsky's remarks are not an isolated instance but belong to a broader network of ideas within the culture.[14]

Paradoxically, given the official atheism of the Soviet regime, interest in this kind of plot of advent or "intervention" remained not just alive but even pertinent to early Soviet experience. Il'ia Erenburg's 1921 novel *Khulio Khurenito* (*Julio Jurenito*) takes the form of a mock Gospel whose picaresque hero is at once Christ-like (he is called "Teacher," *Uchitel'*, and he travels across Europe during the First World War and the Russian Revolution gathering a motley group of disciples) and a demonic trickster (a Mexican outsider, his function in the novel is to expose and mock the received beliefs of every society through which he passes). His final days in Moscow are referred to as his "way of the cross" (*krestnyi put'*, 218); in the end, he is murdered for a pair of boots. Erenburg himself may have been influenced by the mock-religious allegory and puppet theatre staging in Vladimir Mayakovsky's 1918 play *Mystery-Bouffe*, which maps a tale of humanity's progress from sin to redemption onto the Marxist narrative of history as class struggle (Jurenito speaks of the "purgatory of revolution," the "comfortable little hell" that Moscow has become, and its "unventilated paradise," *chistilishche revolutsii, uiuten'kii ad, neprovetrennyi rai*, 233; Mayakovsky's play will be treated in more detail in chapter 4). Equally indicative of the importance the "intervention" narrative had in the early Soviet era is the number of works that were either influenced by Erenburg's novel or at the very least share some of its key motifs. Iurii Olesha's 1927 *Zavist'* (*Envy*), for example, fuses the self-conscious blasphemy of Christ in Erenburg's novel with the Dostoevskian precedent of the holy fool. Its protagonist Ivan Babichev is a mock-Christ who goes from tavern to tavern organizing his "conspiracy of feelings" (*zagovor chuvstv*) against the materialist age in a pointed parody of the Gospels as well as in sympathetic reply to Erenburg. His self-assigned title "King of the Vulgarians" (*korol' poshliakov*, 80) echoes the mockery to which Christ is subjected by the soldiers as "King of the Jews," with a crown of thorns. He "preaches" (*propovedyval*, 79), calling disciples to his conspiracy ("Pridite ko mne, ia nauchu vas ... Pridite, tiazhelye gorem", 79–80); he warns a young couple to forsake marriage; and then, according to fantastic rumour, he changes their wine to water, after which he is interrogated by the GPU (as both Christ and Bulgakov's Yeshua are by Pilate). He is even symbolically crucified when, in his disciple Nikolai Kavelerov's hallucinatory vision, his mythical invention, a machine named Ophelia, pierces him with a giant needle and pins him to a wall.[15] Olesha's tale also pointedly echoes the *theatrum mundi* tradition associated with the seventeenth-century playwright Pedro Calderón de la Barca, in which episodes are presented as taking place within the "theatre of the world" – a totalizing gesture that as we will see was symptomatic of a broader network of concerns in the Soviet era (*inter alia*, Mayakovsky's play *Klop* [*The Bedbug*] pointedly appeals to this tradition as well). Babichev speaks of the "parade of feelings" he wants to organize as *drama* to be acted out on the stage of *history* – "Here there should be played out a drama, one of those grandiose dramas in the theatre of history that call forth on the part of humanity prolonged weeping, ecstasies, regrets, and anger" (94; the idea of the historically sanctioned "anger of humanity" parodically echoes Soviet ideology; cf. also Dostoevsky's appeal to works of the sixteenth century that bring the gods down to earth). To his GPU interrogator Babichev he declares, "Many characters have acted out the comedy of the old world. The curtain is closing. The performers should rush to the front of the stage and sing couplets. I want to be the intermediary between them and the audience. I want to direct the choir and be the last to leave the stage … in the eye-slits of the mask history watches us with its flickering gaze."[16] That pre-eminent deflator of ideological pretensions, Ostap Bender, the hero of Il'f and Petrov's satirical novel *Zolotoi telenok* (*The Little Golden Calf*), who leads his band of disciple-followers across the Soviet landscape with the refrain "*I* lead the parade" ("komandovat' paradom budu ia") until he shares a death as tragically bathetic as Jurenito's, can also be viewed as a late-1920s response to Erenburg's hero – as can, arguably, Bulgakov's Woland.[17]

For its part Bulgakov's *The Master and Margarita* engages the Gospel narrative of intervention aggressively, by rewriting it as a realist novel in the Yershalaim chapters. It finds its most important precedent for an "intervention" tale, however, not in the Gospels *per se* or in apocryphal legends of Christ's return but in the Faust legend.[18] In Russian culture of the late nineteenth and early twentieth centuries the imagined Second Coming could involve the devil as readily as Christ – what is significant in this context is that what is involved is *supernatural* advent, intervention from outside of history, outside the course of daily life.[19] Bulgakov was particularly preoccupied with the Faust legend, allusions to which run through several of his works (his second wife, Elena Sergeevna Bulgakova, noted in her diary on 17 October 1935, after she and Bulgakov had enjoyed a performance of Gounod's operatic version, that "for Bulgakov *Faust* forms the constant backdrop of his works and is very nearly the main component in the novel he has been writing this year"; quoted in Chudakova, *Zhizneopisanie* 421). In the early novel *Belaia gvardiia* (*The White Guard*), for example, the sheet music on the piano in the Turbin home is specifically identified as the score to Gounod's opera *Faust*, while the later *Zapiski pokoinika* (*Teatral'nyi roman*) (*Notes of a Deceased* [*A Theatrical Novel*]) – a satirical portrait of theatre life in Soviet Moscow closely modelled on Bulgakov's own experiences – pointedly mimics the Faust plot: a figure identified as Mephistopheles appears just as the hero Maksudov is attempting suicide; he turns out to be a mysterious character named Rudol'fi, who promises to get the novel Maksudov has secretly been writing published in a prominent journal. When Maksudov eventually converts his novel into a play, it opens with music from Gounod's opera *Faust* being played on the piano.

The deeper ways in which Goethe's drama and the Faust legend conditioned meanings in the Russian fin de siècle and early Soviet era will be taken up in the next chapter, but here it is important to note how widespread reworkings of it were in the period, a symptom of that era's apocalyptic atmosphere and the longings for "intervention" that it generated. As Weiner comments, "Russian demonic authors found a more appealing demonology in *Faust*, which Russians have always known and liked better" than other models of demonic literature (50). A new translation of Goethe's drama by A. Sokolovskii appeared in 1902. In 1916 Anatolii Lunacharsky, who became Commissar for Enlightenment in the early Soviet government, wrote a play titled *Faust i gorod* (*Faust and the City*), which at least one reader claims is a target of parody in Bulgakov's *The Master and Margarita*.[20] The play is a quaint adaptation of Goethe's drama to what were then the rapidly developing conditions for revolution in Russia (Lunacharsky insists in his post-1917 preface to the play that it had all been written by December 1916 and not in retrospect, with the October Revolution in mind).[21] Lunacharsky's Faust is the good ruler of a town called Trotzburg who evades Mephistopheles's wiles and is angered by the behaviour of his dissolute son Faustul, who abducts the wife of one of the town's workers. The city's angered proletarians rise up, seize power, and turn the town into a republic. Mephistopheles variously tries to subvert the course of events, but Faust refuses to submit to his power. The city workers dedicate a monument to Faust with the inscription "Urbi Faustae Faustoque urbano" ("For a Faustian City and an Urban Faust"). Faust greets this "moment of happiness," makes a gift to them of the robot he has been tinkering with in his cottage (a *perpetuum mobile* he calls *zheleznyi rabotnik*, "the iron worker") – and dies.

If Lunacharsky's play is a clumsy effort freighted with comic-opera medievalism evidently intended in earnest to harness the Faust legend in the service of Marxist historical hopes, it nonetheless underscores the affinity between the Faust drama and thought about the *city* as the site of intervention ("Urbi Faustae Faustoque urbano"); indeed, in his eventual role as Commissar for Enlightenment (*Narkompros*), Lunacharsky exerted considerable influence on the mass festivals staged in Soviet cities. His Prologue borrows the device of metadramatic framing derived from the *theatrum mundi* tradition and prominently figured in the opening of Goethe's own *Faust*: Mephistopheles sits alone on a cliff, contemplating the vain ways of the world ("They even think they are smart, these little worms"). He promises to show the audience "pictures that will edify at a glance" (*kartinki radi nagliadnogo obucheniia*). In the middle of Faust's study there also stands a huge globe and a throne-like armchair, suggesting the contemplation from above of human affairs (cf. Woland's similar globe in *The Master and Margarita*; Lunacharsky's Faust also wears "a velvet cap with gold embroidery," *rasshitaia zolotom barkhatnaia shapochka*, like the Master's cap). The play is also titled *Faust i gorod* and uses the town of Trotzburg as a metonymy for social relations in the modern state. "The city must become a republic" is the rallying cry offered by one of the organizers of the revolution – and Lunacharsky informs us in his preface that the play was inspired by the scenes in Part Two of *Faust* in which Goethe's hero founds a free city. This is the city as a political entity, as *polis*, but in a symptomatic moment of attention to urban space Lunacharsky lends an architectural aspect to it as well. Early in the play an architect named Dellabella presents Faust with plans for a Babel-like tower as a monument to him:

> a round building on an unprecedented scale, standing on a square stair-case with sixteen steps. The length of each side will be 6,000 cubits. The building will be crowned by a cupola which could easily accommodate the tallest belfry in the town. The interior will ascend as it were on four grand platforms, which will bear upwards to a dizzying height a group of still more grandiose columns transitioning directly into four soaring arcs. It is on these that the cupola serving as the crown of the entire build-ing will rest. There I will put a window 60 cubits in diameter made of glittering multi-colored glass. There will also be a majestic picture of the deity in white robes, who with a mighty gesture of his hand sends down light, motion, and order. The deity will be depicted with the most majestic features the human eye has ever seen on earth – the features of your most worthy majesty, the first of the rulers of this world.[22]

By the end of the play what has actually been built is a pantheon in the spirit of the French Revolution ("in which according to your design will be gathered triumphant symbols of your birth and life: a temple where your best citizens will sleep").[23] What Lunacharsky ironi-cally invokes here, of course, is a memory of utopian biblical structures like the Tower of Babel or the New Jerusalem of Revelation (especially through his use of the archaic unit of measurement *lokot'*, "cubit"); but the monument also anticipates such Stalin-era phenomena as the plans for the Palace of Soviets in central Moscow conceived on a Babylonian scale (on which see chapter 5). It is not coincidence: ultimately, the same memory of totemic structures, the same logic of seizing urban space and transforming it into the site of extrahistorical intervention, is at work.

More immediately significant here is that Bulgakov was not alone in processing Soviet experience through the Faust legend.[24] Among Soviet "Faust" works proper, Emilii Mindlin's fragment *Nachalo romana "Vozvrashchenie doktora Fausta"* (*The Beginning of the Novel "The Return of Doctor Faust"*) reduces the legend to a fantasy on the Romantic theme of happiness, though it situates events in Moscow by opening with an aged Faust living "in one of the alleys off the Arbat" (74). It might pass as a brief footnote to the Soviet "Faust" theme, save that it appeared in the same issue of the journal *Vozrozhdenie* (vol. 2, 1923) that contained Bulgakov's *Zapiski na manzhetakh* (*Notes on Cuffs*) and thus may have helped alert Bulgakov to the possibilities of the theme (Sokolov even conjectures that an illustration to Mindlin's tale by I.I. Nivinskii showing a semi-naked woman posing in front of a mirror inspired the scene in *The Master and Margarita* in which Margarita admires her figure in the mirror after applying the rejuvenating cream Azazello has given her, 525–6).[25]

Aleksandr Chaianov's *Venediktov, ili dostopamiatnye sobytiia zhizni moei* (*Venediktov, or the Memorable Events of My Life,* self-published in 1921, but illustrated by Natalia Ushakova, who gave Bulgakov a copy in 1926; Sokolov 513) would seem to be another unweighty fantasy on Romantic themes – a demonization of love as a way of dramatizing its supposed power over us: the devil appears in Moscow, and the narrator follows him behind the stage of a ballet performance of *1001 Nights* and out onto the streets, where he sees an actress rush from her carriage and throw into a pond what turns out to be a talisman containing her soul (the pond is in Mar'ina Roshcha, as it happens, an area just north of where the events of *The Master and Margarita* unfold). Chaianov's plot manages to be both convoluted and banal, but his tale exploits its Moscow setting in ways that suggest a preoccupation with envisioning the devil's advent within the space of present-day Moscow (*Venediktov* as it happens was one of Bulgakov's favourite novels; Chudakova, *Zhizneopisanie* 346). "I love the nighttime streets of Moscow," the narrator remarks as he leaves the theatre, "I love, my friends, to stroll down them in solitude, not paying attention to where I go" (19). The fog he walks through is a pointedly "Moscow fog" (*moskovskii tuman*, 20), the empty streets are overshadowed by "the gloomy columns of the Apraksin Palace" and "the mass of the Pashkov House" (*mrachnye kolonnady Apraksinovskogo Dvora, gromada Pashkova doma*) – which also serves as site of the culminating scenes of the devil's visit in *The Master and Margarita* (20). Like Mindlin's Faust, Venediktov lives on the Arbat, a street in central Moscow with aristocratic and artistic connotations (22). Following Goethe and anticipating Bulgakov, Chaianov also insinuates a Gospel motif when the narrator's night with the devil draws to its close: "It began to turn light. The third cocks had crowed" (*Stalo svetat'. Tret'i petukhi zapeli*, 22). Nor would it have escaped Bulgakov's attention that the narrator of Chaianov's tale is named Bulgakov.[26]

Andrei Sobol's *Oblomki* (*Fragments*, 1921) deploys its plot of demonic intervention in a far more extensive engagement with the events of the October Revolution. The "fragments" alluded to in the title are various refugees from the civil war who have settled near the Black Sea and dream of escaping Russia. Suddenly an impeccably dressed stranger appears in their midst. He denies being the devil and even explicitly addresses the genre of demonic intervention ("Do devils really appear these days? In Russia you can never tell where humans end and the devil begins"; *Razve cherti teper' poiavliautsia? V Rossii, kogda i tak ne razberesh', gde konchaetsia chelovek i nachinaetsia chert*, 66) – but his surname "Trech" is the Russian word for devil, *chert*, backwards, he seems already to know everyone, he carries a gold-tipped cane (the devil as a dandy is a widespread motif; cf. Svidrigailov in Dostoevsky's *Crime and Punishment*), his cigar is always burning but never goes out, and he promises to help the refugees escape. The escape, however, turns out to be through death, as various of the characters are found dead or disappear. The intervention of the devil thus figures in Sobol's tale as a response to the unbearable violence of history – as it does, arguably, in Bulgakov's Stalin-era novel as well.

One particularly important example of the Faust theme in Soviet literature was never published during its author's lifetime or, for that matter, Bulgakov's, which suggests that the themes it shares with *The Master and Margarita* were neither idiosyncratically Bulgakov's nor a matter of literary borrowing but part of a broader cultural impulse: Osip Mandelshtam's "Segodnia mozhno sniat' dekal'komani" ("Today We Can Lift the Decals"). What links the two works is a sense that events of sudden intervention must play out within a Moscow setting – even more specifically, within the setting of Moscow as the new, Soviet, capital. As Chudakova notes, in 1934 Bulgakov and Mandelshtam lived in the same building on Furmanov Street in Moscow. "These were people of the same generation [...] both belonged wholly to 'urban' culture. One would be justified in comparing their attitude toward the city as a concentration of culture, a bearer of historical memory, and to the theatre as conglomeration of culture, a bearer of tradition"

("M.A. Bulgakov – chitatel'" 174; they also played pool together, a curious image to contemplate; *Zhizneopisanie* 311). The poem is dated summer 1932, a time when Stalinist culture was energetically delineating itself from the Bolshevik era that preceded it (the first Five-Year Plan had been declared fulfilled, and Socialist Realism had just been declared the official aesthetic of Soviet literature) and, as it happens, the period in which Bulgakov was working intensely on his novel. As in a series of sketches Bulgakov wrote in the 1920s, which will be discussed shortly, Mandelshtam's theme is the city of Moscow and its Soviet-era transformations. Beginning with a childishly playful view of the "bandit" Kremlin, whose image on this clear summer's day one could lift like "tracing paper" from the Moscow River, the poem pauses to register a bird's-eye view of the city as a spatial totality – as will be seen, this panoramic reflex is symptomatic: "before us the whole city unfolds" (*pered nami ves' raskrytyi gorod*) like a grand piano when one has lifted its "rosewood lid" – a combination of motifs one could well imagine in a work by Bulgakov. The poet defiantly asks the "White Guardists" if they have seen this Moscow and heard its piano, before stating that he himself will not see "the future" (*griadushchee*) despite following adults "like a small boy" into the rippling waters of the Moscow River (cf. Ivan Bezdomny's ironic baptism in that same river in *The Master and Margarita*). He then declares his resistance to the Soviet regime's architectural pretensions: he announces that he will not enter the new sports stadiums in march-step with youth, nor the "glass palaces on chicken's legs" (a parodic reference to avant-garde architecture via the folkloric figure of the witch Baba Yaga, who lives in a hut on chicken legs). In the midst of this scene of urban reckoning there suddenly appears "Faust's demon," who tempts an old man with touristy appropriations of Moscow space: renting a boat to sail on the river, making a run up to the Sparrow Hills, or "racing across Moscow" on the tram (*na tramvae okhlestnut' Moskvu*) – entertainments for which Moscow, now anthropomorphized as a "nanny" with "40,000 cradles" on her hands, has no time.[27]

Space and Its Cultural Inflections

What works like the tales by Lunacharsky and Chaianov, the poem by Mandelshtam, and in particular Bulgakov's novel (with its projection of Moscow onto Jerusalem) reveal *inter alia* is a distinct sense of urban space. As Genette suggests in "La Littérature et L'Espace," there are some authors who more than others exhibit "certaine sensibilité à l'espace" (44); but as Lotman, one of the most prolific commentators on spatial themes in Russian writers, points out, the "language" in which the author's "model of the world" is expressed is never truly individual but ultimately belongs to the author's moment, era, and socium ("Problema khudozhestvennogo prostranstva v proze Gogolia" 414; or as van Baak observes, literary space in most cases also means cultural space, which is "any property or manifestation of space that can be anthropologically meaningful and as such receive semiotic values," 37).[28] The representation of space in the works of some authors may thus tell us much about the spatial intentions of the culture as a whole – but here some comment on the concept of space itself is in order because in the broadest sense it provides the facilitating and determining framework within which the beliefs and practices with which this study is concerned unfold. It makes them possible to begin with and shapes (constrains, channels) their evolution (and, one notes as an example of how spatial thought conditions our dealings with the world, that "framework" and "within" are themselves spatial concepts).

The concept of space, the way we interpret or experience it, is never absolute or self-evidently given in human perception. To a significant degree it is, rather, an intellectual construct, which is to say it is variable and subject to interpretation. The Greek atomists, for example, believed space to be an infinite void into which things are placed, whereas Newton considered it substantive, a thing existing apart from other things.[29] By the early twentieth century the Newtonian sense of homogeneous space governed by mathematical order had eroded, together with grand historical narratives and the realist aesthetic (one has only to think, in the Russian context, of Bely's subversion of the Russian empire's pretentions to geometrical order in *Peterburg*). Subjectivist tendencies then began to assign "space" an active and contingent role in human experience. In his later work, for example, Edmund Husserl, the founder of phenomenology, argued that the geometrical understanding of space characteristic of mechanistic world views should be bracketed and set aside as yet another construct of consciousness, a concept whose seeming self-evidence is in fact illusory. In its place philosophy should strive toward an absolute sense of space grounded in immediate experience that underlies, but has been forgotten by, geometrical interpretations of the world.[30] This geometrization of the world satisfies a desire for "procuring objectivity," which in turn is served by the "art of measuring," which "thus becomes the trail-blazer for the ultimately universal geometry and its 'world' of pure limit-shapes" (27–8). The resulting view of the world is one in which "things and their occurrences" are not arbitrary but are bound together. "[T]hrough a *universal causal regulation, all that is together in the world* has a universal immediate or mediate way of *belonging together*; through this the world is not merely a totality

[*Allheit*] but an all-encompassing unity [*Allenheit*], a *whole* (even though it is infinite)" (31). For Husserl's successor Martin Heidegger, the realization that this view is not absolute leads to an understanding that space must always be interpreted and constituted anew – a project in effect taken up by Russia's revolutionary culture: in the Soviet era, urban space itself becomes the object of aggressive transformationalist designs. *Being and Time* rejects the Cartesian understanding of space as the external locus of human life – the container in which it is contained – and insists instead that "being-in-the-world" involves the mutual conditioning of existence and world. For Heidegger it is not space that precedes and qualifies things, but things that through their existence define and constitute space (cf. his *Zuhandene Dinge*).[31] Equally at odds with the mechanistic Newtonian view were older folkloric and mythic traditions – *nota bene*, among them ritual forms revived in the culture of modernism – that treated space as heterogenous and as marked by points of greater and lesser value. In their concept of space the festivals of the French Revolution again offer an informative parallel to those of the Soviet era. As Ozouf comments, "belief in the educative potential of space derives directly from the idea of utopia," which in the case of the French expressed itself in "a self-conscious spatial voluntarism" (126).

Soviet rituals expressed a similar spatial voluntarism, one with even more extensive consequences than those of the French Revolution. Whatever the ultimate validity of Heidegger's (or others') challenge to the Newtonian (or Aristotelian or Cartesian) concept of space, in other words, culture at least *functions* in Heideggerian fashion to constitute human experience of the spatial world. As a result, phenomena like literature (which in the broadest sense includes folklore and myth – in essence, the verbal record of human experience) and theatre (whose representational designs must always be realized in space) provide us with an encyclopedia of human conceptions of space; indeed, they have themselves functioned as significant instruments of the hermeneutics of space.[32] In the case of modernist theatrical practices and Soviet spectacles, the spatiality of literature can reflect the culture's most concerted efforts to define its place in the world. The tendency in spatial studies corresponding to this trait has been to treat the literary (or folkloric) work as anthropological evidence for the ways in which a particular culture has constructed mental representations of the world – to penetrate surface motifs in search of underlying archetypes that can ultimately be traced back to mythology and possibly represent some fundamental substratum of human thought (see van Baak 4). Eliade's *The Sacred and the Profane*, for example, uses anthropological evidence to reveal that the primordial human experience was of heterogeneous rather than geometrically homogeneous space. For "religious man" (i.e., for human cultures before or outside of the secularization introduced by the Renaissance and accelerated by the Industrial Revolution) "some parts of space are qualitatively different from the others" and "spatial nonhomogeneity finds expression in the experience of an opposition between space that is sacred – the only *real* and *real-ly* existing space – and all other space, the formless expanse surrounding it" (20). In fact, without the designation of a sacred *centre* to the world, "no *orientation* can be established" and we are abandoned to the chaos that is uniformly profane space (21–2). As Eliade remarks, perhaps not without a touch of mid-twentieth-century angst, "Religious man's desire to live *in the sacred* is in fact equivalent to his desire to take up his abode in objective reality, not to let himself be paralyzed by the never-ceasing relativity of purely subjective experiences, to live in a real and effective world, and not in an illusion" (28). Hence, for Eliade, a fundamental human impulse (or even "ontological thirst," as he calls it, 64) is to organize space by delineating within it a sacred centre and in so doing "repeat the paradigmatic work of the gods" who created the world in the first place (32). "The experience of sacred space makes possible the 'founding of the world'; where the sacred manifests itself in space, *the real unveils itself*, the world comes into existence" (63). The narratives of "intervention" discussed earlier, which imagine the momentary interruption of the empirical (historical) world by the divine, arguably arise out of a similar impulse – a similar "ontological thirst." Russian modernists (Bulgakov among them) and Soviet urban planners alike operated in this realm in which space is viewed as contestable, subject to wilful redefinition – and in need of a sacred centre to be installed within previously profane empirical space.[33]

Eleazar Meletinsky, whose 1976 *Poetika mifa* (*The Poetics of Myth*) constitutes the *summa* of Soviet studies of mythology, argues convincingly for the transmittal of mythic themes, heroes, and narrative devices to literature, which relative to the archaic forms of myth is always a modern form – and his own ideas, like those of Bakhtin or Bulgakov, can to some extent be understood as inflections of the Soviet experience. In Meletinsky's view "the tale, heroic epic, and older theatrical forms" – the latter, as will be seen, important to Soviet culture, including Bulgakov's novel – served as intermediate vessels that preserved mythical material "in embryonic form," enabling its eventual transfer to modern literature. "The entire corpus of classical literature up to the medieval period was larded throughout with motifs inspired not only by archaic myths and cosmologies but also by classical myths" (259). This inheritance appears in realist literature of the nineteenth century largely in the form of "implicit mythification," a combination of archaic elements *per se* and universal forms of thought that are related to and resemble myth without necessarily being derived from it directly (one spatial example he gives is Gogol, in whose works "north," associated with cold and oppressive St. Petersburg or Paris, is opposed in quasi-mythological manner to "south," associated with warm and sunny Italy or Ukraine; 264–5). Most interesting in connection with the Soviet context, however, is Meletinsky's claim that the literature (especially the novel) of the twentieth century is defined by a self-conscious "mythification" (sometimes inspired by scholarly studies of myth, as in the case of D.H. Lawrence's enthusiastic reading of Frazer's *The Golden Bough*) as a reaction against the representational world of the nineteenth-century realist novel (275). In Meletinsky's view, what is particularly at stake in such modernist mythification is the question of how history should be narrated. He cites Joseph Frank's observation in his study of "spatial form" in modern literature that "in the modern novel, mythological time has come to substitute historical or 'objective' time, since action and events, no matter how specifically they are grounded in time, are presented as manifestations of eternal prototypes" (275, quoted in Meletinsky). Or, as he comments with regard to Joyce's *Finnegans Wake*, "Vico, Quinet, and Jung are used by Joyce to organize his material and create an internal structure for a mythological novel whose immediate goal is to represent his version of a universal history" (298). Bulgakov's *The Master and Margarita*, with its satirical portrait of mundane life under Stalinism that is both invaded by supernatural powers and mapped against a retelling (albeit in pointedly "realist" mode) of the Gospels, is a clear example of this impulse to make apparent the eternal or universal underlying the historical moment. And, again, in the case of Bulgakov, part of what is imported via archaic forms is a particular spatial sense of the world, especially of the city.

V.N. Toporov's studies of literary space suggest why a novel like *The Master and Margarita* might have served as a particularly sensitive mirror of its culture's obsessions despite its surface polemic vis-à-vis the era's ideological norms. A partisan of mythic cultures, Toporov sees the Newtonian world view (together with its predecessor, the Aristotelian) as a pernicious attempt to unify space geometrically and thus remove signs of animacy from it ("Prostranstvo i tekst" 229–30) – and he sees the novel as a form of latter-day resistance to this epistemological hegemony.[34] Following the lead of Mikhail Bakhtin, for whom the novel represents the culmination of the dialogic principle in verbal art, Toporov sees the genre of the novel as representing something of an apogee in the history of spatial depictions (as Frank notes, this is *contra* Lessing, who famously argued in "Laoköon" that the depiction of spatial form is the proper task of painting while that of verbal art is the depiction of time; "Spatial Form"): "'Spatiality' celebrates its most complete triumphs in the novel, which from this perspective can be considered both the most complete model of spatial relations in art and the sphere in which 'spatiality' repeatedly finds new reflections and images" ("Prostranstvo i tekst" 283–4). For Toporov this is a direct extension of the value-laden sense of space predominant in myth: "as in the cosmological scheme of mythopoetic traditions, space and time are not simply a frame (or passive background) within which the action unfolds; they are active (and therefore determine the behaviour of the hero) and in this sense may be compared with the plot" ("O strukture romana Dostoevskogo" 238). Moreover, within the tradition of the novel there are, for Toporov, certain writers who display a particularly evident "preoccupation with space" (*prostranstvennaia oderzhimost'*), among them Goethe, Gogol, Dostoevsky, and Bely – all important precursors of Bulgakov in this regard ("Prostranstvo i tekst" 251). And if Toporov's account of the novel and its role in spatial perceptions is accurate, then it should not surprise us that the Soviet novel – whether in its official, Socialist Realist form or in dissenting deformation of that form – played a formative role in that culture's conceptualization of the spaces to which it laid claim.

Toporov is interested in the broadly conventionalized ways in which human cultures assign axiological markers to physical reality such as the opposition between a sacred centre and an alien periphery; or between the compass directions north, which certain cultures deem alien and evil, and south, which they deem native and good; he also explores the ways in which such motifs as "the path," in works of literature ranging from the *Odyssey* to Goethe, provide an organizing axis for the hero's experience of the world. Toporov even finds a "degenerate" (*vyrozhdennyi*) successor to mythological pathways in modern city streets, which "define the network of links between parts of the whole while underscoring a hierarchy of relations (delineation of a main street and the placement on it, or on a square to which it leads, of sacred symbols of the highest order, or of desacralized secular power"; "Prostranstvo i tekst" 267).[35] Thus, he is interested in the ways in which, say, certain novels tend to situate events in what emerges as the sacred *centre* of space and at a sacred *temporal node*, on the boundary between two states of being ("O strukture romana Dostoevskogo" 227). In Dostoevsky's novels in particular, differences in the urban landscape through which the hero must travel on his life journey between high and low, or centre and periphery, become as primally charged with meaning as with myth; or a motif such as "sunset," situated in the west and marking the boundary between day and night, becomes charged with ambiguity (238).[36]

A similar engagement with the spatial concerns of its era is what lends *The Master and Margarita*, especially as a work written in polemical dialogue with the Soviet world from which it emerged, valuable as an index to that world. The particular trajectory of Bulgakov's career is relevant here because it illustrates how one writer's engagement with the spatial themes he found embedded in the literary and theatrical tradition assimilated itself in and responded to preoccupations in the culture as a whole. Like Genette's writer possessed of "certaine sensibilité à l'espace" or Gogol in Lotman's description of him as a writer realizing his own "peculiar way of perceiving space" (*spetsifika vospriiatiia prostranstva*), Bulgakov exhibited a heightened awareness of space from the outset – an inclination that may, among other things, explain his attraction to theatre as a privileged aesthetic space, his predilection for placing life on a *stage*, holding it up for contemplation and response.[37]

Bulgakov's early works express consistent yearnings to escape the backward provinces (*derevnia, glukhaia provintsiia*) and return to an urban centre as the site of civilization. In *Zapiski iunogo vracha*, for example, based on his own experiences as a doctor (published in the mid-1920s but outlined as early as 1919), the narrator has been sent fresh from medical school to his first posting in a Russian province that is so difficult to reach that it is described as "*glush'*" (*Sobranie sochinenii*, 2004, vol. 1, 91), a nowhere.[38] He feels the isolation most keenly as the absence of urban culture, in particular the theatre and the opera (184) – preoccupations of Bulgakov from early on. The keenness with which he felt this geographical separation can be sensed from a letter he wrote to a friend in February 1921 about the premier of his first play (the now lost *Brat'ia Turbiny* [*The Turbin Brothers*]), while he was biding his time in the Caucasus: "And this was the fulfilment of my dream ... but how deformed it was! Instead of the Moscow stage, a stage in the provinces" (quoted in Chudakova, *Zhizneopisanie* 105).

What is significant for the broader concerns of this study is how in Bulgakov's works the privileging of places like Moscow and Kyiv as centres of civilization unfolds into an apotheosis of the theme of the city, especially the city as a site for potential "intervention."[39] The spatial themes of his writings change correspondingly following his move to Moscow in 1921, with the shift heralded in the 1922 "Notes on Cuffs" by the recitation – not necessarily ironic – of the motto of longing from Chekhov's *Tri sestry* (*The Three Sisters*), "To Moscow! To Moscow!!!" (*V Moskvu! V Moskvu!!!*, *Sobranie sochinenii* 1982, vol. 1, 230). For the newspaper *Nakanune* he begins to write *feuilletons* whose unifying task is to chronicle daily life in the post-revolutionary city.[40] As Chudakova notes, in these years to write about Moscow meant, for Bulgakov, to write about contemporaneity, the present day ("Arkhiv M.A. Bulgakova" 57). These impressionistic sketches – which appear under titles like "Notes on Cuffs," "Stolitsa v bloknote" ("The Capital Captured in a Notebook"), and "Moskovskie stseny" ("Moscow Scenes") – with their succession of casually observed street scenes and ironic commentary on social habits, institutional mores, and signs of the new (Soviet) culture – are elaborated in the manner of nineteenth-century "physiological" sketches of cities such as Paris, London, and St. Petersburg. The debt to Gogol is especially palpable.[41] The 1922 "Moskva krasnokamennaia" ("Red-Stone Moscow"), for example, offers a variegated portrait in the manner of Gogol's "Nevsky Prospect" of Moscow on the eve of a Bolshevik holiday. Bulgakov observes a servant girl named Annushka running to the Cathedral of Christ the Saviour, notes the absence of Tsar Alexander III from the pedestal of his monument, and catches a "red specialist" (*krasnyi spets*) buying newly abundant food items in the former Eliseev store. An ordinary Soviet crowd fills the trams, from the windows of which one sees a "brightly-colored masquerade" of "sign shop upon sign shop" in which "there is everything but the hard sign": the motley line-up of the Mosselprom store, the Mosdrevotdel, Vinotorg, the Workers' Theatre, the "Sport" tavern all pass by (*Sobranie sochinenii* 2004, vol. 1, 261). Another "physiological" sketch is "The Capital Captured in a Notebook," whose brief vignette of life in NEP-era Moscow strings together observations on the seemingly endless building repairs taking place in the city, the shells from sunflower seeds that litter the streets, newly imposed fines for smoking, "trillionaire" NEPmen, and a boy on the street who, somewhat surprisingly, is going to school instead of peddling newspapers. The narrator remarks of this motley scene, "Moscow is a pot – in it the new life is being cooked up" (*Moskva – kotel: v nem variat novuiu zhizn'*, 290). "Pokhozhdeniia Chichikova" ("The Adventures of Chichikov") makes the Gogolian reference overt by borrowing the subtitle of *Dead Souls* and recounting a dream in which Chichikov arrives in Moscow to mount a series of scams under the New Economic Policy (he receives advances for businesses that do not exist, registering his companies at an address that turns out to be the Pushkin monument so that when he is investigated nothing can be found – themes that anticipate the picaresque satire of Il'f and Petrov's *The Little Golden Calf* (as well as the devilry of Bulgakov's own *The Master and Margarita*).[42]

At the very least these sketches collectively attest that one of the tasks Bulgakov set himself as a writer in the early 1920s was to define the

essence of *the city* – Moscow in particular, which had been made capital
of the USSR in 1918 and was about to rise to the status of the exemplary
socialist city – and centre of the cosmos, in Stalinist ideology. "I know
1920s Moscow thoroughly. I ransacked it from top to bottom. And I'm
determined to describe it" (*Moskvu 20-kh godov ia znaiu doskonal'no. Ia
obsharil ee vdol' i poperek. I nameren ee opisat'*), Bulgakov announces in
"Moskva 1920-kh godov" ("1920s Moscow," *Sobranie sochinenii* 2004,
vol. 1, 408). But Bulgakov cannot let his depiction rest in the physiological mode's attention to the present moment and its trivia. Beyond
cataloguing the city's variegated surface, the kinds of things observable
by a casual *flâneur*, the sketches reveal other tendencies that were to
define Bulgakov's oeuvre. The first is the ironic reflex, traceable back
to Gogol's "Nevsky Prospect" and its closing injunction to beware that
street because the devil himself comes out at night to light its lamps, of
attributing various vices of NEP-era Moscow to infernal magic.[43] This
does not yet articulate a myth of "intervention," but it prepares the
ground for it. "Moscow Scenes," for example, describes how the host
of a dinner Bulgakov attends, a former government official, has managed to redesign his apartment to suit the Soviet era. He stores flour
in the library, hangs a portrait of Marx on the wall, and "magically"
transforms the original six rooms of the apartment into three, hiding the
library door so well with a screen that "it was as though the library had
disappeared and the devil himself could not have found its entrance" (*i
biblioteka slovno zginula – sam chert ne nashel by ee khoda*; *Sobranie sochinenii* 2004, vol. 1, 308). The men in "gray overcoats and black coats" who
have been trying for three years to requisition the space have yet to
make headway (309). "1920s Moscow" similarly mentions one Zina,
whose ability to find a four-room apartment for three people Bulgakov
calls "supernatural" (415). In a sketch that breaks from its description
of present-day Kyiv, which Bulgakov has revisited, to recall what that
city was like during the civil war of 1917–20, the vertiginous changes of
regime in those years are described as having made it a "city under an
evil spell" (*zakoldovannyi gorod*, 328). Even now the inhabitants retain "a
conviction, born in the year 1919, of the instability of earthly life" (333),
and when malfunctioning fire hoses fail to save a burning building on
the former Tsarist Square it is as if they, too, had been placed "under a
spell" (330). So ready is Bulgakov to resort to this ironic *topos* that he
even applies it to positive phenomena. In "Putevye zametki" ("Notes
from a Journey") he describes the Briansk train station as being so clean
and orderly, in contrast to its state just a couple of years before, that
everything inside it seems "supernatural" (*Sobranie sochinenii* 2004, vol.
1, 318). The running ironic comparison of devilry with Stalinist life in

The Master and Margarita – the complaint that no matter what one wants, be it beer or God, "they are out of it" (*vse nichego net*); the recurring sinister disappearance of inhabitants from Sadovaia Street 302B; the hard currency that "magically" finds its way into Nikanor Ivanovich Bosoi's briefcase, the magical expansion of Apartment 50 to accommodate Satan's ball, which is ironically compared with other "magical" apartment exchanges in Moscow – all of these emerge out of these moments in the early Moscow sketches.[44]

Another descriptive habit of Bulgakov's in the 1920s sketches that can be thought of as related, via the ironic trope of the supernatural, to the depiction of "magical" events involves the projection of events in Moscow or Kyiv onto a biblical frame of reference, typically either the Passion (i.e., the last days of Christ's earthly ministry) or the closely related Apocalypse. At first glance this would appear to be simply another, more or less casual, way of registering irony in the portrayal of the NEP era's many social and economic contradictions ("the NEP-era's grimaces" – *grimasy NEPa* – in a phrase common at the time); but from the retrospective vantage point of Bulgakov's oeuvre as a whole and in particular of *The Master and Margarita* the habit appears consistent and telling – and, as will be seen, represents a reflex that repercussed more widely in the culture as a whole. In "Kiev-gorod" ("Kyiv-City") Bulgakov notes that during the civil war the church attributed the confusion of triple regimes warring over the city (Reds, Whites, and Greens [i.e., Petliura's anarchist band]) to Satan himself. When Bulgakov demurs, an old woman declares him to be "a servant and forerunner of the Antichrist," who is supposed to arrive in 1932 (*Sobranie sochinenii* 2004, vol. 1, 335; recall the fascination with the idea of the Antichrist in fin-de-siècle Russia). A passage in "1920s Moscow," a comic sketch about the housing situation in the capital, anticipates the weightier ironies of Woland's debate with Berlioz on the existence of Christ in the opening scenes of *The Master and Margarita*. When the narrator begins a complaint about how difficult it is to find a decent apartment with the words "In the year of our Lord ..." he is interrupted by the voice from the next room of his *komsomolets* neighbour remonstrating, "He didn't exist!!" "Well," the narrator continues, "whether He existed or not, in the year 1921 when I came to Moscow ..." (414). The more specific event-frame of the Passion intrudes upon "Samogonnoe ozero" ("A Lake of Moonshine"), a sketch about the social ills of home-brewed vodka. "At 10 p.m. on the eve of Holy Easter," Bulgakov reports, "the accursed hallway in our apartment grew quiet ... And at 10:15 in the hallway a cock crowed thrice" (*Sobranie sochinenii* 2004, vol. 1, 341). If the sketches share their wry observations of NEP-era grotesquery with other satirists of the

Soviet 1920s (Zoshchenko in particular), their impulse to relate those observations to biblical narratives is very much Bulgakov's own.

In this connection one of the most striking instances of Bulgakov's sensitivity to spatial themes in the culture of the Soviet 1920s occurs in "Sorok sorokov" ("Forty Times Forty," 1923; the title is a reference to historical Moscow's legendary abundance of churches), which represents something of a culmination, at least for this stage of his career, of his evolving mythologization of the city. Unlike the Gogolian mannerisms of "The Capital Captured in a Notebook" (1922), whose title suggests the provisional nature of its observations, or of "Red-Stone Moscow" (1922), whose street-level perspective on rapidly shifting phenomena allows the recording of only immediate impressions, "Forty Times Forty" presents Moscow in a series a four panoramic views that tend toward an almost eschatological comprehensiveness (they are explicitly labelled *panorama pervaia, vtoraia*, and so on). The first is a mere vignette of three streetlights in a thick fog at night on the Dragomilevsky Bridge – the narrator's introduction to the city when he arrived there cold and hungry in 1921 (*Sobranie sochinenii* 2004, vol. 1, 296). The fourth, reflecting Bulgakov's emerging habit of juxtaposing Soviet reality with the theatre, contrasts the Bolshoi Theatre during a theatrical performance and during a Party meeting (300). But it is the second and third that are most interesting in spatial terms. In the second Bulgakov decides on a grey April day to go up to the roof of the House of Soviets on Gnezdnikovskii pereulok, which he refers to as the "highest point in the centre of Moscow" (*Na samuiu vysshuiu tochku ia podniualsia v seryi aprel'skii den'*, 297). From there he hears the acoustic essence of the place, the sound of socialist Moscow coming to life (298). Underscoring the exceptional nature of his rooftop experience, he describes his return as a descent *from the heights* into *the thick of things*, where he begins to live again, as if the normal course of life had been interrupted: "And having descended into the thick of things from this high point, I began to live again" (*I spustivshis' s vysshei tochki v gushchu, ia nachal zhit' opiat'*, 298). In the third panoramic experience he repeats his visit to the rooftop on a humid July evening; now he sees "chains of lights" on the streets and at last hears the "distinct sound" of Moscow "rattling and humming" (*Moskva vorchala, gudela vnutri*, 298). At the end of the sketch the two rooftop experiences are projected (again, from the quotidian reality of the narrator-writer's everyday existence) onto an anticipatory vision of a still more comprehensive panoramic view: the one available from the still higher vantage point of the Sparrow Hills: "And sitting in my room on the fifth floor, surrounded by antiquarian books, I dream of climbing the Sparrow Hills in summer and from them gazing just as Napoleon did at the radiant forty times forty [cupolas] on seven hills, watching Moscow breath and shine. Moscow – our mother" (302).[45] The perspective anticipates that of Mandelshtam's "Today We Can Lift the Decals," and its aspiration, again, is to grasp the city in its totality; but in this case the perspective comes with a legacy. Via the famously pyrrhic triumph Napoleon enjoyed as he (actually) stood on another Moscow hill (Poklonnaia gora) gazing down on the abandoned city he had fought so hard to conquer, the vision of Bulgakov's narrator echoes with the Temptation of Christ in Matthew 4:8, when the devil takes him to "a very high mountain" and tempts him with a vision of "all the kingdoms of the world and the glory of them" (meanwhile the gestation of this vision in a room piled high with antiquarian books gestures toward Faust's study). A remark offered in the notes to the Ardis volume containing these sketches on the related, but more *flâneur*-like, "Zolotisty Gorod" ("Glittering City"), could well be applied to these scenes from "Forty Times Forty": "The panoramic views here anticipate the analogous passages in the writer's last novel" (424) – in particular, the final Moscow scenes in *The Master and Margarita* in which the devil and his retinue observe the city from the rooftop of the Rumiantsev Museum in central Moscow.[46]

Another important line in the evolution of spatial themes in Bulgakov's works involves the merging of this interest in Moscow as a distinctive space with an orientation toward the world of the theatre, the latter a hallmark of both his oeuvre and the culture in general. Bulgakov's interest in the theatre was persistent and self-conscious.[47] He wrote several plays, opera libretti, and film scripts – the satirical *Zoikina kvartira* (*Zoyka's Apartment*) of 1925; *Dni Turbinykh* (*Days of the Turbins*), reputedly Stalin's favourite play; the 1939 *Batum*, an assimilationist play about Stalin's childhood; and a libretto for *Don Quixote* – and he worked in the theatre for as long as he was permitted by the cultural authorities; moreover, his prose works constantly look toward the world of the theatre – he cannot, as it were, help but think about the theatre, no matter what the ostensible topic, if sometimes only in incidental ways.

This reflex already pervades the 1920s Moscow sketches, where it engenders a persistent attention to theatrical phenomena in the city. For example, the motley sites the narrator observes from the tram in "Red-Stone Moscow" form a "masquerade" – a term that had become synonymous with the theatricality of life among Russian modernists, including in the early Soviet era following the avant-garde theatre director Vsevolod Meyerhold's staging of Lermontov's play of that name in war-torn Petrograd.[48] "Benefis Lorda Kerzona" ("A Benefit for Lord Curzon") describes a demonstration mocking the British foreign secretary in which the procession follows a truck bearing a giant marionette of

Curzon in top hat through the streets, while the real figure of Bulgakov's nemesis Mayakovsky, like an oversized element of street theatre himself, appears on a balcony and, "opening his monstrously large, square mouth, bellows out over the crowd in a cracked bass 'Roar British Lion! Left! Left!'" (a pun on marching commands: *"britanskii lev voi ! / Le-voi ! ! Le-voi!"*; cf. the "broken bass," *nadtresnutym basom*, in which Woland sometimes speaks in *The Master and Margarita*). "The crowd called out to Mayakovsky," Bulgakov remarks, "and Mayakovsky kept hurling words as heavy as paving stones down at them" (316). In "Glittering City" the narrator's visit to an agricultural and trade exhibition ironically promotes the pavilion in which it is held to the "golden city" of the sketch's title, then draws attention to every theatrical element in the displays. A giant portrait of Lenin made of flowers makes its dramatic appearance: "A shadow covers the city and the Moscow River. A partial gloom descends on the exhibition's fantastic flower garden, and in it the portrait of Lenin in flowers looks like it was drawn on a huge canvas" (367; cf. the storm over Jerusalem in *The Master and Margarita*). A crowd gathers beneath the balcony of the Tsentrosoiuz pavilion to watch an "agitational-cooperative Petrushka show" in which Petrushka, member of a cooperative workers' group, dispatches a deceitful merchant (375). The sketch closes with a visit to a packed theatre, where a debate is being held on the topic of "the tractor and electrification in agriculture" (377). The subtext of Bulgakov's description, of course, is sardonic condescension toward this intrusion of decidedly rustic matter into the theatre – save that at the end of the proceedings an ironic note of "magic" enters when the chair of the praesidium holding the debate declares that a people who since the revolution have transformed more than one fantasy into reality will not balk at the fantasy of tractors (378).

The theatricality of Bulgakov's prose, however, runs much deeper than these topical motifs: it inhabits the essential structure of the works themselves. These sometimes appear the products of a playwright *manqué* but in the present context may be taken as signalling Bulgakov's particular sensitivity to theatricalizing tendencies in early Soviet culture in general.[49]

The particular ways in which theatrical and urban spaces interact in *The Master and Margarita* are already anticipated in *The White Guard*, Bulgakov's first novel (published in 1925, although Bulgakov began work on it in 1921), a work therefore revealing of his ideas about novelistic structure and purpose. Theatrical motifs pervade the novel, from the opera *Noch' pered Rozhdestvom* (*Christmas Eve*) heard outside the windows of the Turbin apartment (14), to the sheet music from Gounod's opera *Faust* open on the piano (*Dazhe Tal'bergu, kotoromu ne byli svoistvenny nikakie sentimental'nye chuvstva, zapomnilis' v etot mig i chernye akkordy i istrepannye strannitsy vechnogo Fausta*, 26), to mention of Theatre Street (*Teatral'naia ulitsa*) and its opera theatre (69), as well as Sergei Ivanovich's sardonic reference in a newspaper article to the Hetman's (Petliura's) republic as "comic opera" (*operetka*, 26).[50] Most of the novel's scenes are set within the Turbin apartment and readily lend themselves to stage adaptation – as they did when Bulgakov rewrote the novel in 1925 as the play *The Days of the Turbins*.

When the play premiered in the mid-1920s it immediately became embroiled in polemics. A debate held at the Communist Academy on 5 October 1926, for example, was devoted to the question of whether it should be staged at all, with the setting provoking particular ire: "all the parades, the singing of the International and things like that take place off stage," one critic complained (Chudakova, *Zhizneopisanie* 272, 312). At the very least the debate shows how ideologically charged spatial representation could be in Soviet theatre of the 1920s. The play's irksome sidelining of public rituals, which might otherwise have displayed the regime's own "interventionist" agenda, was the result of its concentration on the scenic space of the Turbin apartment, which Bulgakov calls a "gentry nest" (*dvorianskoe gnezdo*). The play's staging thus emerges as a distinct ideological gesture. Bulgakov's term is an overt (if also ironic) allusion to the "gentry nests" portrayed in the works of the nineteenth-century writer Ivan Turgenev, but it is equally informed by an immediate experience of history, by an awareness of the violence unleashed on the streets outside such homes in the aftermath of the Bolshevik Revolution. But Bulgakov's concentrated attention to the "nest" as a scenic stage also draws on more universal themes. In his *Poetics of Space* Bachelard argues that the ways in which we experience the spatial arrangement of the house in which we are born establish paradigms within our minds that influence all subsequent experiences in life. The everyday objects filling this house, seemingly self-evident to the point of boredom, turn out to provide the framework for the very phenomenology of our existence. For Bachelard, the house in which we were born provides our first experience of being in general. It is "being's first world," "our first universe, a real cosmos in every sense of the word," in this regard preceding even the moment of being "cast out into the world" so central to more anxious doctrines such as Heideggerian phenomonology (4, 5). In Bachelard's view, we carry the experience of our native house through life. "All really inhabited space bears the essence of the notion of home" (4–5). "The house, even more than the landscape, is a 'psychic state,' and even when reproduced as it appears from the outside, it bespeaks intimacy" (72). For Bachelard, moveover, the house even lends its geometry to remembrance, representing a kind of *"theater of the past* that is constituted by memory," in which "the stage setting maintains the characters in their dominant roles" (8, emphasis added). Mircea Eliade, in his *The Sacred and the Profane,* imputes an even broader anthropological meaning to the house when he argues that in most human cultures the house is far from the industrial and indifferent "machine for living in" that Le Corbusier called it. Rather, the "house" precedes even "the temple" in human culture as a structure erected in order to mark the sacred centre of the world and therefore contains within itself a model of that world in its entirety: *"cosmic symbolism is found in the very structure of habitation. The house is an imago mundi"* (53). As such, its depiction pointedly contests Soviet theatricalizations of public space. It is precisely this spatial sensibility that came under intentional assault in the years following the Bolshevik Revolution. The sudden interest in modernist architecture that characterized the early Soviet period is relevant here as well. Taking the modernist vogue for glass architecture to its utopian limits, Russian artists and city planners set about planning to replace old-fashioned edifices with airy glass towers – Le Corbusier's "machines for living" – in which life's functions would be radically redistributed. In a 1925 editorial in *Izvestiia,* the head of Moscow's planning division called for "as much glass as possible" in the cityscape of the new metropolis. The Tsentrosoiuz building at Miasnitskaia Street 39, the only building designed by Le Corbusier actually built in Russia, had a largely open ground level supported by columns (later filled in; Paperny 47) and flooded with natural light by its expansive glass windows. Together with neighbouring buildings (which in the end were also not built) it was to provide a triumphant new entrance to socialist Moscow (see Chadaga 170, 173, 153). For some members of the avant-garde, even glass towers were not enough. As one architect put it, "the very idea of motion presents great possibilities for development" (Krutikov, in Paperny 47). Buildings were now to turn constantly to face the sun, but also to consist of modular units that could be disassembled, with changing distribution of rooms, furnishings, and so on. The model for living was now to be the cabin of a steamship, airplane, or railway sleeping car. As the Futurist poet Velemir Khlebnikov mused, the house would be transformed into a "box made out of curved glass or a moveable ship's cabin, equipped with a door with rings, on wheels, bearing its inhabitants inside" (47). At a still further extreme, the architect Mikhail Aleksandrovich Okhitovich envisioned complete "disurbanization," a shift to living in mobile cells that would be distributed evenly across the landscape (52). It is to these very initiatives that Mandelstam responds when he writes in the poem "Today We Can Lift the Decals," discussed earlier, "Not even as a light shade / Will I enter into any glass palaces on chicken legs" (*V stekliannye dvortsy na kur'ikh nozhkakh / ia dazhe legkoi ten'iu ne voidu*).

What is most significant about *The White Guard* in relation to evolving Soviet conceptions of space, however, is the way it situates the apocalyptic events it portrays in the context of the city, in effect suggesting that their siting within the city defines their global significance. Throughout the novel Bulgakov refers not to "Kyiv," his native city and the locus of immediate events, but to "Gorod," *The* City, almost always capitalized, simultaneously universalizing it and underscoring the boundaries separating it from the surrounding world, as if it were a self-contained cosmos.[51] Through a series of allusive motifs (akin to the religious references already evident in some of the Moscow sketches) he then sustains the interpretive possibility that this Kyiv, "Gorod," is a reincarnation of Jerusalem and hence the site of life-altering transformations: a restaging of the Passion that is – perhaps – simultaneously the Apocalypse (a favourite notion of the Russian fin de siècle and early twentieth century, but here reunited, as it were, with its biblical counterpart as "intervention" narrative).[52] The novel repeatedly emphasizes the miraculous (i.e., transcendent and transhistorical) nature of the events taking place in The City[53] but also via the Faust legend's Brocken Mountain, site of a witches' sabbath, and Mussorgsky's symphonic piece with the same title and theme.[54] At a political street meeting the sun beats down as at the Crucifixion (*Sobranie sochinenii* 2004, vol. 4, 212–14), with crowd and orators, one of whom (a Bolshevik, so assumed to be a Jew) the crowd beats to death (217–18; another Jew is beaten later in the novel, 242). A character named "Nero" alludes to the Roman setting of the Passion (158; however inaccurately, since Nero reigned after Christ), while the name of a colonel in *The White Guard*, Nai-Turs, has no clear ethnic connotations and would seem instead to anticipate the Hebraicisms of the later *The Master and Margarita* (e.g., "Yeshua Ha-Nozri") – and Nikolka Turbin retrieves his corpse from the morgue like Levi Matvei stealing the corpse of Yeshua in the later novel (226; Aleksei Turbin is also described as having been "resurrected" – *voskresshii* – from typhus, 234).[55] A syphilitic patient whom the recovered Turbin treats offers a thoroughly apocalyptic interpretation of recent events in Ukraine, replete with the Antichrist, Trotsky as Satan, the Bolsheviks as angels, and so forth. Petliura is briefly detained in the city prison in cell no. 666 (56) – and the end of the novel quotes directly from the Book of Revelation (20:12), the passage referring to the great white Throne of Judgment in which the book of life is opened and the living are separated from the dead (246) – as this study will argue, a characteristic reflex for this strain in Russian culture.

In Bulgakov's oeuvre, however, it is in his summary work, *The Master and Margarita*, that spatial motifs find their most significant and complex expression – and are most acutely responsive to the meaning of "theatre" and "the city" as contentious matters within the culture as a whole.[56] As in most of his other works, theatrical motifs and settings abound. The pivotal scene in which the hypocrisy of Muscovites is unmasked and their true moral nature revealed takes place in the Variety Theatre, which perhaps does not quite establish the theme, as Petrovskii again suggests, that all life is a theatre, though it gestures in that direction (42). The theatricality of unmasking and repentance (a notion that may look back to Dostoevsky, with his histrionic scenes of soul-baring acted out before a jeering crowd) further informs the dream of Ivan Nikiforovich, who is arrested by the NKVD when the roubles he had taken as a bribe from Woland magically turn into foreign currency. While in detention he dreams that he is in a theatre where an emcee calls members of the audience up onto the stage and induces them to admit that they have been hiding valuables from the Soviet government. Like Preobrazhensky's apartment in "Sobach'e serdtse," the apartment Woland takes over from Likhodeev (the "evil apartment," no. 50 at Bol'shaia Sadovaia 302-bis) could easily be a theatrical stage (even as it participates in another important motif in Soviet literature in the late 1920s and early 1930s, that of the *kommunalka*, the communal apartment). Its miraculous expansion into an enormous hall in the scene of Satan's ball literalizes the instances in sketches like "Moscow Scenes" and "1920s Moscow" in which the transformation of apartments into larger space is described with mock irony as "supernatural" (this in keeping with a tendency noted by Fusso of the early works to indulge in figurative transformations, which in *The Master and Margarita* become fantastical, i.e., "real"; 392–3).[57]

As Chudakova astutely observes, once the Master and Woland leave the novel, its epilogic events enter into a "bad infinity" (*durnaia beskonechnost'*) in which year after year the remaining characters perform the same actions (the former poet Ivan Bezdomny, now a professor of *history* under his real name, Ivan Ponyrev, returns to the same bench at the Patriarch Ponds, the lovestruck Nikolai Ivanovich, whom Margarita had transformed into a boar, gazes longingly at the moon, etc; Chudakova, *Zhizneopisanie* 463–4): in other words, after "intervention" the world returns to *history*, which is nothing but dull repetition.

Most significant of all in the present context, however, is Bulgakov's mobilization – evidently quite intentional – within the novel's Moscow chapters of formerly sacred points on the city's pre-revolutionary landscape.[58] Just as *The White Guard* insists on projecting the turmoil of civil-war Kyiv onto the backdrop of the Passion and Jerusalem, *The Master and Margarita* turns Moscow and Jerusalem into ironic mirror images of each other. If the Jerusalem chapters are pointedly secular (and, *nota bene*, rendered as historical fiction, i.e., in the mode of realism otherwise cancelled by modernism), the Moscow chapters hum with the presence of the supernatural. As Larson has shown, from Woland's first appearance at the Patriarch Ponds to Ivan Bezdomnyi's flight toward an inadvertent and ironic "baptism" in the Moscow River, near the Cathedral of Christ the Redeemer (which was demolished in 1931, while Bulgakov was working on the novel, to make way for a "Palace of the Soviets," which in the end was never erected), Bulgakov "literally and metaphorically builds his story on top of a medieval landscape," insisting on a "medieval paradigm of spatial practice" (82; see also map on 79) instead of the secular sense of space implicit in nominally atheist Stalinist ideology. In so doing he restores to Stalinist Moscow what Eliade calls an "irruption" of sacred space into profane space (26), or what I am calling "intervention." "Bulgakov," Larson comments, "was writing his novel at a time when the Soviet powers were actively engaged in a campaign of the destruction of religious sacred spaces and the creation of their own, materialist, secularly sacred space" (46). Or to paraphrase this statement in the terms of the present study, Bulgakov was a writer who was especially alert to the spatial designs of Soviet culture.

"Intervention" narratives, as this chapter has argued, figure prominently in Russia's culture of the fin de siècle and early twentieth century as expressions of a restlessness or dissatisfaction with present history. In the era's prolific reworkings of the Faust tale and in the mock-gospels of works like Erenburg's *Julio Jurenito*, Olesha's *Envy*, and Bulgakov's *The Master and Margarita* the depiction of "intervention" becomes a vehicle for dissent from Soviet values. But it does so because the same idea formed the core of the Soviet regime's own symbolic agenda. A key index to these shared intentions is their reflexive turn to the phenomenon of the theatre, which here figures less as a quintessential form of artificiality than as a mechanism for totalizing representations whose canonical form is the *theatrum mundi* with its aims to place the whole of human experience on a stage before the viewer. In its physical dimension the theatre also serves as an index to the spatial preoccupations of this mindset, which finds its fullest expression in these texts' imagined projections of meaning onto urban space, especially that of Moscow as the new Soviet capital. The projection of eschatological designs – in both senses of that word – onto urban space was also one of the key ways in which Soviet festivals incorporated an agenda of "intervention" into their own symbolic agenda.

Chapter Two

Faust and the Medieval Roots of "Intervention"

The implications for Russian modernist and Soviet culture of the various episodes of advent so broadly imagined in the fin de siècle become clearer when one considers the theme's historical roots. One conduit to those roots runs through the Faust legend. As we have seen, the Faust tale was popular in fin-de-siècle and early twentieth-century Russia, as it provided a ready-made form for experimenting with plots of "intervention." In the Soviet context these experiments reached their apogee in Bulgakov's *The Master and Margarita*, which so vividly displays the broader concerns of the culture at the time.[1] Although Bulgakov's immediate frame of reference is the 1859 opera by Charles Gounod (e.g., in his conversation with the culturally ignorant Ivan Bezdomny in the psychiatric asylum, the Master asks, "Forgive me, but maybe you've never even heard the opera *Faust*"; Простите, может быть, впрочем, вы даже оперы «Фауст» не слыхали?, *Sobranie sochinenii* 2004, vol. 5, 246), behind it clearly stands the model of Goethe's canonical drama.[2] *The Master and Margarita* shares an extensive series of motifs with Goethe's drama. In addition to the obvious plot device of the devil's appearance in Moscow, there is Woland's magic performance in the Variety Theatre, which echoes the scene in which Faust performs magic in a theatre in Part Two of *Faust*. Then there is Satan's ball, which echoes the courtly masquerade of the *Mummenschanz* in Part Two of *Faust*, which in turn replicates features of Roman allegorical carnival with its motif of royal review of the whole of the social hierarchy (Phelan 148–9). There is also Woland's appearance in various contradictory guises in Bulgakov's novel, drawing on the changing masks Mephisto adopts in Part Two of Goethe's drama (astrologer, miser, inventor of paper currency – which, *nota bene*, is likely the source of the currency transformations in Bulgakov's novel, from foreign currency to roubles and back again, from roubles to mineral water labels). There are the transformations of Woland's retinue; in particular, the "cat" Behemoth recalls Mephistopheles's first appearances in the form of a black poodle, and in older chapbook versions of the tale Mephisto often accompanies Faust in the guise of the black dog Praestiger (Mason 92).[3] In addition, the "witches' sabbath" of a luxurious dinner with jazz music at the Griboedov house in Bulgakov mimics the drinking party in Auerbach's cellar in Goethe; and Margarita's flight to meet Woland and his retinue in a remote landscape echoes Faust's journey to the Walpurgis Night, for which Mephistopheles offers him a broomstick to fly on (Mussorgsky's *Night on Bald Mountain* is a likely intermediate link here; it is intriguing that the *Walpurgisnacht* in Goethe's drama originally included a scene with Satan at the top of the mountain, but he eventually decided not to include it; J.K. Brown 123). What these extensive borrowings suggest is that in addition to the basic plot of *Faust*, Bulgakov drew on its sustained attention to various forms of theatre.

Goethe's *Faust* so readily lent itself to Russian modernist interests because it is itself markedly a narrative of "intervention." The play begins with the Prologue in Heaven (i.e., in a space above that of the natural world) with Mephistopheles being given the power to seduce Faust – an overt reminiscence of the tale of Job in the Old Testament (which itself can be viewed as an "intervention" narrative, in that God enters the natural world of human events in order to test Job; the Book of Job, *Faust*, and *The Master and Margarita* are all tales of human nature tested by supernatural intervention). Mephistopheles enters Faust's world in order to test the limits of human knowledge and susceptibility to base temptation. Moreover, the events in *Faust* begin on the eve of Easter day, thus projecting the drama's own narrative of "intervention" onto the palimpsest of an older, indeed canonical form: the Gospel account of the Passion and Resurrection, together, as will be seen, with the mystery plays that re-enacted these in the medieval era.[4]

The *Faust* precedent also opens a door to a host of still deeper themes having to do with the nature of the theatre (especially as theatre represents, conceives, mirrors, or projects the world), the relation between the divine and the everyday world (especially the world understood as bogged down in the long wait between the Incarnation and the Second Coming), and the playing out of these events within – and their imagined power to transform – a particular urban space. The generic history of Goethe's *Faust* is complex, in ways that are relevant to the work's absorption by Russian modernists: the Faust legend, and especially Goethe's dramatic rendition of it, enjoyed so much popularity in early twentieth-century Russia because in its origins it mirrored the *Weltanschauung* conditions, the tensions between different world views and assumptions about humanity's place in history, that defined the later era. The historical Faust was a certain Johannes or Georg Faustus (or "Sabellicus"), who was born in 1480 in Knittlingen, a suburb of Würt-temburg. He may have studied magic in Kraków, and later, in Würz-burg, he claimed to have repeated the miracles of Christ ("die Wunder Christ zu widerholen"; Scheithauer 14; Mason 2). The subsequent six-teenth century, when the Faust tale became popular, was a time when the devil in general had entered literature as a newly complex character – perhaps because new translations of scripture made the Bible more vivid than it had previously been in the popular imagination (Durrain 77). It was a time when the religious life of Germany was dominated by Mar-tin Luther (Heller 4), on whose preoccupation with the devil Goethe himself commented, noting "the accursed devilled imagination of our Reformer, which peoples the entire visible world with the devil and personifies it as the devil" (*die verfluchte Teufelsimagination unseres Refor-mators, der die ganze sichtbare Welt mit dem Teufel bevölkerte und zum Teufel personifizierte*; quoted in Mason 2; it is not an exaggeration to suggest that this same attitude would resurface in Soviet Russia under Stalin, particularly in the show trials of the 1930s).

There appears to have been at least one sixteenth-century German Faust drama, but the first "Faust book" was the *Historia von D. Johann Fausten*, published by Johannes Spiess in 1587 in Frankfurt am Main (Scheithauer 16). The Faust tale then made its way to England, where it was translated by one "P.F., Gent.," as *The Historie of the Damnable Life and Deserved Death of Doctor John Faustus* (Heller 5). This is the text on which Christopher Marlow based his far better-known *The Tragical History of Dr. Faustus* of 1592. Paradoxically, the Faust tale was popular-ized in German lands not by the indigenous tradition of the sixteenth century but by troupes of English actors in the Shakespearian period who took Marlowe's play with them in their repertoire (performing it in Graz in 1608 and Dresden in 1626, then Prague in 1651, Hannover in 1661, Lüneberg in 1666, Danzig in 1668, and so forth; Palmer and More 240). It was out of Marlowe's drama that the established tradition of German Faust drama eventually evolved (Mason 3).

The Faust drama's run on the German stage was impermanent, how-ever. As German culture entered the Age of Enlightenment its theatre "began to turn away from the mummery, superstition and vulgarity which had come to form such a large part of the play" (Palmer and More 241). In particular, under the influence of Johann Christoph Gottsched, professor at Leipzig and "literary dictator of Germany," the theatre turned emphatically away from medieval and folk elements, toward French models (241). As Jane K. Brown suggests, what happened in

German lands was part of a nothing less than a vigorous suppression in European theatre of the late seventeenth and early eighteenth centuries of allegories, masques, mystery plays, and the like in favour of "character-oriented neoclassical drama and theory of the Enlightenment," for which the precepts of Aristotle's *Poetics* served as guide (Brown 16). In Huizinga's terms, this was the moment when the culture began to abandon its ludic element, its principle of play. In any event the last known performance of the Faust play on the regular stage was in Hamburg in 1770, after which it was relegated to the cultural basement of the puppet theatre (Palmer and More 241; Mason 7).

"Basement" may be relevant as more than a metaphor here. In *The Secret Life of Puppets* Victoria Nelson argues that the erosion of belief in the supernatural from the Renaissance onward – the great shift in cultural attention from the transcendent to the empirical realm – forced the relegation of the Platonic underworld to the grotto (drawings of strange hybrid monsters having been found in the crypts under Nero's Domus Aurea outside Rome when it was excavated in 1480; viii, 2). In Nelson's thesis, the true turning point in Western culture's transition to modernity was marked by a "drastic reinterpretation of reality as a material world in which one's only transcendental link to God is internal" (56), so that the former realm of the divine or otherworldly came to be limited to the imagination, the subconscious, and art, including popular entertainment. A similar – indeed, radical – reinterpretation of the world as material reality was precisely the ideological turn with which Bulgakov (and several other Soviet writers) polemicized.

Thus, when Goethe took up the Faust legend in the late eighteenth century, his turn involved a self-conscious revival of the theatrical culture of an earlier era, much as the modernists after him turned to older forms for theatrical renewal as a way of reversing this hierarchy in the European cultural consciousness. As it happens, Goethe did not read Marlowe's *Dr. Faustus* until 1818, by which point he had completed his so-called *UrFaust* (of the 1770s), *Faust, ein Fragment* (1790), and, best known of all of Goethe's Faust texts, *Faust I* (1808); only *Faust II* of 1832 was written after exposure to Marlowe (Swales 31).[5] Goethe instead knew the tale from "the crude German popular plays which were descended from [Marlowe's play]" (Mason 4), although he may also have encountered the Faust drama as "grossen Maschinenkomödie" following his return from Leipzig to Frankfurt in 1768, and again in 1770 in Strasbourg, where there was a troupe performing it (Scheithauer 22). He also knew it from the puppet theatre of his boyhood (Mason 4; he also had a marionette theatre as a child; Nelson 47), which may have been a conduit for a good deal of the Faust tradition. "The only viable indigenous dramatic tradition in Germany in the early eighteenth century was the puppet theatre, through which Goethe first became acquainted with the Faust legend and which was the only form in which he knew Christopher Marlowe's *Dr. Faustus* until 1818" (Brown 30).

Russian modernist interest in the Faust legend most likely stems from its subsequent revival in Romantic culture. Lessing (the incomplete *Doktor Faust*, posthumously published in 1784), Heine (*Der Doktor Faust*, a *Tanzpoem*, 1846), Grabbe (*Don Juan und Faust*, 1829), and Lenau (1836) all wrote versions (Heller 6). Berlioz's opera *La Damnation de Faust* debuted in 1846 and Boito's *Mefistofele* in 1868, while Gounod's version, the one most familiar to Bulgakov, appeared in 1859 – to name just three of the legend's many musical adaptations. In Russia, Pushkin wrote "Stsena iz Fausta" (1828); A.K. Tolstoi's "Don Zhuan" has a Faustian theme and echoes Goethe's drama; and Turgenev's "Faust. Rasskaz v deviati pis'makh" ("Faust. Story in Nine Letters") appeared in 1856. The Russian adaptations of the legend considered in chapter 1 extend this trend into the early twentieth century.[6] Among later instances, Valéry left an unfinished work titled *Mon Faust*, posthumously published in 1946, while Thomas Mann's *Dr. Faustus* appeared in 1947.

Bulgakov's own affinity for the Faust legend might additionally lie in certain parallels between the philosophical and cultural context in which Goethe wrote his drama and that in which Bulgakov wrote *The Master and Margarita*. Goethe's age was, roughly speaking, one in which traditional religious belief clashed with the scientistic, demystifying, and deist predilections of the Enlightenment – with neither side, however, prevailing unequivocally over the other. It has been suggested that the very material for the Faust legend has its source in "the Renaissance turmoil of a universe centred on God giving way to one centred on Man" (Phelan 248). This break from a deist world view, from a sense of the world as defined from another realm, was moreover, paralleled on the stage by a shift from theocentric to anthropocentric theatre, "from our relations to the divine and the cosmic to our relations to ourselves and other people" (Curtius, quoted in Brown 21). Schanze speaks of the "disconnect between adherents of classicism and romanticism" (*Zweispalt zwischen Klassikern und Romantikern*) in the theatrical practices of Goethe's day (182). Goethe's anachronistic revival of the Faust legend may in turn reveal something about that legend itself: as the archetypal post-biblical tale of supernatural intervention it lends itself particularly well to eras defined by tension between a religious world view, which looks for interruptions of the everyday world by the supernatural, and a scientific or materialist world view, which erases any such presence from a homogeneous world of purely physical – or human – causality. As will be seen, despite its officially atheist ideology, Soviet culture in a variety of ways perpetuated an ambivalent relationship to its own religious past.

The spread of rationalist thought associated with the Enlightenment led most thinkers in the late seventeenth century to regard the Faust tale and its like with increasing scepticism, and this shift has been identified as a primary reason for the tale being relegated to the folk-cultural domain of the puppet theatre (Mason 6). Goethe's relation to this trend was complex, however. On the one hand, his version of the Faust tale is imbued with scepticism toward Christian teachings, and Faust himself has been described as a figure who has "seen through and outgrown Christian revelation" (128). On the other hand, as Mason argues, the "spiritual ground-pattern" of Goethe's life was one in which "the triumphal advance of Enlightenment rationalism came up against its own limits" and "the supernaturalism of Christianity, which had seemed irretrievably doomed, was afforded a fresh lease on life," even if the new forms of mysticism were individualistic rather than centred on a transcendent God (19). A similar ambivalent quasi-religiosity characterizes *The Master and Margarita* and its author – and early Soviet culture in general. Bulgakov for his part can be thought of as a late Romantic or Neoromantic whose plots often involve the intervention of otherworldly forces in the empirical realm (most obviously in the supernatural grotesqueries of *The Master and Margarita*).[7] The son of a prominent Kyiv theologian and nephew of a major twentieth-century religious philosopher, Sergei Bulgakov, Bulgakov rejected his father's strict religious views in favour of a Bohemian lifestyle complete with morphine addiction. But he retained a partisan interest in church questions into the 1920s and consistently displayed an aristocratic disdain for Soviet philistinism and the Marxist-Leninist materialism that served as its rationalization. Furthermore, although there is no question of influence or imitation, the textological history of the two writers' masterpieces is remarkably similar. Goethe's *Faust* was composed piecemeal over several decades and was completed just before its author's death in 1832. There are also textological uncertainties attaching to the "final" text – for example, it is unclear whether the "Vorspiel auf dem Theater" really belongs to *Faust* (Mason 20; Swales 31). Bulgakov worked on *The Master and Margarita* from 1928 until his death in 1940 (in fact, the novel we have is unfinished, even though its plot comes to a conclusion), with little expectation of seeing it published in the Stalinist Soviet Union, given the considerable pressure he faced to conform to Stalinist culture ideologically and professionally. Both works, in other words, are complex and in the end inherently incomplete grand projects that were composed, fitfully, in conditions of philosophical ambivalence.

Like Bulgakov's novel, Goethe's drama manifests a distinct sense of space, one specifically conditioned by a theatrical past. Goethe knowingly invokes the theatrical traditions that precede his version, in particular the metaphor of the world-as-theatre (in the Prologue, which presents the work as a summary allegory of human affairs; the canonical texts in this tradition are Calderon's *The Great Theater of the World* and Act II, scene 7, in Shakespeare's *As You Like It*) but also the related framework of the medieval mystery play.[8] Like those plays, *Faust*, at least in Part One, uses its urban setting to delineate its supernatural drama. It opens in Faust's confining room, which until then has been his "universe" (although the bells tolling the Easter Mass can be heard in it) but then moves out into the city – to the city gate, then to Auerbach's tavern, then ultimately to the cathedral and the wilder places of the witches' kitchen and the Harz Mountains, where the Walpurgis Night ritual is held: a cycle of sites reminiscent of the mystery play's distribution of scenes from the Passion or the Nativity play among symbolic sites of the medieval town.[9]

Goethe's *Faust* is written in the form of a play to be performed in a theatre (at least, hypothetically; the actual staging of its assorted spectacles would be a daunting task). Its ideological complexities are reflected in a heterogeneous composition whose peculiar nature may not be immediately obvious to modern readers. The finished work we now know is in reality a motley organism that was stitched together out of disparate forms: "Knittel" verses (rhyming couplets, later used by von Hofmannsthal in his 1911 play *Jedermensch*), Madrigal verses (Mason 58), Renaissance masques, processionals, operettas (Jane K. Brown 24), mystery plays, and baroque drama (Swales 33). What unites these parts is their orientation toward forms of theatre that are markedly pre-Enlightenment and non-Aristotelian, that tend toward devices of allegorical rather than psychological exposition – and it is these elements that were later to resonate with modernism's own unease with the idea of history and with realist representations. Mason, for example, comments that the opening scene of the so-called *Urfaust* employs the "type of exposition that has still not moved far in the direction of realistic illusionism or psychological subtlety from the practice of medieval biblical and allegorical drama, where the characters ingenuously inform the audience in so many words about who they are and what the situation is" (110). This generic diversity as a form of resistance to Enlightenment aesthetics may have been linked with a certain self-conscious reflection on the nature of theatre in *Faust* – the play's metatheatrical moment. Swales argues that *Faust* both is sited in and reflects on the theatre, which provides its "central existential metaphor"

(33), while Phelan comments that Goethe's revival of archaic forms of allegory (especially in Part Two, for example, the "Mummenschanz," which recreates a form of allegorical carnival from Rome, in which the court reviews the hierarchical social order of the empire – a scheme replicated, one notes, in the satanic ball scene of Bulgakov's novel) led to the now-fashionable view that the entire work is allegorical (148–9). In Part Two, Faust performs magic in a theatre – as Bulgakov's Woland does in the Variety Theatre – which may also be an allusion to the metaliterary themes of Shakespeare's *The Tempest* (Phelan 155).

The nature of the theatre is thus a central rather than merely auxilliary theme in *Faust*. In her compelling analysis of Goethe's theatricality Jane K. Brown points out that when Goethe directed the Weimar Theatre from 1791 to 1817, a period during which he was working on *Faust*, the largest share of his output consisted of masques, libretti for operettas, and allegorical festival plays. For Goethe the stage was meant to provide the viewer with totalizing spectacles like masques (when he staged Shakespeare's *Julius Caesar*, for example, he was mostly interested in the mob scenes; *nota bene*, totalizing spectacle was the aim of Russian modernists and Soviet festival planners as well); the events performed on it were episodic rather than chronologically unified, and ludic or allegorical rather than mimetic (Brown 18). What might appear a disorderly violation of Enlightenment norms represented, instead, a reversion to an entirely different theatrical milieu: that of "world theatre," whose paradigmatic text is Calderón's *Great Theater of the World* but that more broadly represents the dominant poetic of medieval European theatre, whose cardinal feature was a striving to place "human beings in the largest possible context of their relations to the totality of society and to the divine order" (16). To it belong the mystery and Corpus Christi plays, masque, Spanish Golden Age dramas, and Shakespearean comedy, tragedy, and romance, which were acted out in town squares and in streets or were performed in theatres with names like The Globe, and in which supernatural figures, including God, appeared freely on the stage (16). Indeed, the entire purpose of such medieval theatrical forms, and their point of greatest relevance to Bulgakov as well as to early Soviet culture, related to the way in which they facilitated such contact between an the urban here-and-now and the divine order, the manner in which they appeared to bring God, Christ, the Virgin, the devil, and so on into the very streets in which people lived (recall Dostoevsky's comments on this kind of plot in *The Brothers Karamazov*). Brown argues that *Faust* needs to be read in the poetic terms of this "world theatre," and not of the neo-Aristotelian forms that displaced it in the seventeenth century (17). Thus the "Prologue in Heaven" of Goethe's drama draws pointedly on the Book of Job, but does so in a theatrical idiom that "makes God a concerned spectator of the entire subsequent action," so that the play is, "in effect, played before God, just as it is in Calderón's *Great Theater of the World*" (24), in which the world is represented as a theatre and life as a play, with God as director, and representative character types (King, Rich Man, Peasant, Beggar, Child) are told that at the end of the performance they will surrender their costumes to the director, who will judge their performances (indeed, so prevalent was the metaphor of the world as a stage that by the seventeenth century it had become a cliché; 24n15).

Corpus Christi and Mystery Plays

How, then, do these forms actually function in their performative moment? I have dwelt on *Faust* at length here because it serves as the pre-eminent example of a modern work that appropriates and redeploys the symbolic logic of the mystery play and related genres, in particular their tendency toward totalizing spectacles that place human affairs before God, if they do not indeed bring God down onto the stage to intervene in human life. The older forms of theatre that Goethe's *Faust* energetically revives all represent forms of theatre that predate the enclosing of drama within a *camera obscura* wherein spectators suspend their disbelief (in Coleridge's celebrated phrase) and gaze passively on events acted out by others before their eyes. Mystery plays, Corpus Christi plays, and their like reach outside of that neoclassical frame in two dimensions: the dramas they portray purport to originate beyond this earth, in the divine realm, with the point of the drama being the intervention of divine figures and events in earthly life; and they characteristically take this transcendent spectacle out of the enclosed space of the theatre (initially, the church) into the street, the city square, which is thereby transformed into the site of divine manifestation and intervention.

In *Faust* Goethe does this on a conventional stage, so that in his case it is the paradoxical counterpoint of Aristotelian versus medieval theatre that is relevant. Something similar can be said of works like *The Master and Margarita* and Olesha's *Envy*, which merely allude to quasi-theatrical themes within a literary narrative. But in both cases the vector of the work, its quiddity, pulls away from mimetic naturalism in the direction of ritual and mystery. Both carry forward an essential memory of the semiotic of medieval theatre.

It is precisely this semiotic, this symbolic economy, that is preserved within the modernist revivals of earlier theatrical forms and through them transmitted to their Soviet-era successors. Medieval European theatre originated in the "play in church," a form of enactment that on the holidays of Christmas and Easter staged such biblical tales as the Annunciation and birth of Christ, the Last Supper, the Crucifixion, and the Resurrection. These early church dramas derived from the liturgy but preserved a complex relationship to it, and they did so in ways that were determinative for later medieval mystery plays as well as their modernist revivals. It is by considering the phenomenon's deeper cultural roots that we can see where the whole symbolic logic of the modernist interest in staging "intervention" originates. The earliest dramas of this type were Easter plays staged in France in the eleventh century, especially the so-called *Quem quaeritis* plays depicting the arrival of the Marys at the empty tomb on Easter morning, with Christmas plays and their derivatives developing later by analogy with the Easter play, rather than directly from the Christmas liturgy (Hardison 226). What is distinctive about them is their combination of *ritual* elements originating in the liturgy (such as processions, candles, and the ringing of bells; 232) with liturgically non-essential *representational* ones whose function was the verisimilar narration of a tale using such devices as pantomime, stage props, costumes, and dialogue taken from historical sources (in this case, the Gospels; 176). The ritual and representational modes were fundamentally distinct. The former (as for example in the Mass proper) transported the community of participants to an "eschatological world" whose events take place in a timeless present (i.e., absolute time), where they shared the fellowship of the very apostles whose images decorated the nave of the church as well as the angels standing before the throne of God (47). The latter occupied the "plane of history," which is the domain of human events and in which sequential (chronological) time unfolds. It was not entirely divorced from the world of the divine (for example, Christ is sacrificed and dies on this plane) but was ontologically distinct from it (55). The very point of the enactment was the merging of these two modes – or rather, the entry of one into the other in an episode of "intervention." In the broadest sense, in both the Middle Ages and the modern era, what we are dealing with here is the logic of a world view that assumes the existence of two realms, as well as a hierarchical relation between the two in which the first, present world is incomplete, is not final, but will be interrupted by the second, truer realm, whose advent will provoke a resolution of contradictions in the first: a judgment.[10]

To some extent this duality of modes is prefigured in the Mass itself. Gregory the Great observed of the Mass that in it "high things are accomplished with low, and earthly joined to heavenly, and [...] one

thing is made of visible and invisible" (Hardison 36); whereas Amalarius, Bishop of Metz in the ninth century, whose *Liber officialis* is one of
the most informative early documents on medieval Mass and religious
drama, claimed that the Mass combined historical meaning with ritual
or allegorical meaning in a way that rendered mysteries comprehensible to the *simpliciores* (38). Amalarius also claimed that in the singing
of the *Hosanna in excelsis* angelic voices join those of humans so that
"the invisible world impinges directly on the visible" (64). The church
plays that developed out of the liturgy considerably expanded the representational (earthly, human, historical) component but preserved the
liturgical impetus. As in the Resurrection plays developed in the tenth
to twelfth centuries, ritual and mythic elements were not abandoned
but rather were "re-embodied in the modes of representational drama"
(250), while liturgical drama in general was "the outcome of a search for
representational modes which preserve a vital relation to ritual" (252).
The subsequent development of cycles of religious plays (such as those
associated with the Corpus Christi festival) may actually have represented a movement *back* toward the liturgy (286).

Nonetheless the early history of these religious dramas was that of
the outside world finding a way to "burst in[to]" the church interior as
the style of representation became more realistic and the plays began to
include topical references and even elements of farce and the grotesque
(Berthold 251). In Germany, where the mystery play developed somewhat later than in France, the form involved even more realism and
comedy (e.g., the shopkeeper from whom Mary buys myrrh for Christ's
body would fight with his wife, and in some versions the Virgin would
even entertain spectators with her coquetry and dances; Andreevskii et
al., *Entsiklopedicheskii slovar'*, s.v. "*misterii*" 452–4). The play in the church
was not yet Bakhtin's "carnival," perhaps, but it was its forerunner, as
the folk culture of the market square began to contaminate sacred ritual.[11]
In the fifteenth century this comic element spun off on its own as *Fast-
nachtsspiele* of a completely secular nature (452–4). But the contamination
also proceeded aggressively in the opposite direction. The liturgical play
"was brought out of the church and before the portal, to the church square
and the marketplace" (Berthold 228).[12] "The Easter play broke its close
link with the liturgy," and "the church opened its doors and let the play
escape into the busy bustle of the town" (264). Thus released, the mystery
play became an elaborate affair extending throughout the city, often running for several days (for example, in Frankfurt am Main, Vienna, and
Antwerp) and involving groups of patricians, burghers, and craftsmen.
"Wooden platforms and scaffolds were erected on sites specially staked
out, *tableaux vivants* were carried along in procession and went into scenic

action at predetermined stations" (229).[13] As early as 1350 Frankfurt presented an expansive drama depicting events from Christ's baptism in the river Jordan to his Ascension and mixing didactic elements with topical allusions (such as to the plague, which had struck the city in 1349; Berthold 265–7). The repertoire expanded as well, as mystery plays began to portray such diverse biblical events as the creation of the universe, Lucifer's revolt and fall, and the creation of Adam (286).

One of the most important consequences of the overlapping of allegorical and historical modes in early church drama related to how such dramas appropriated and redefined the space in which they were staged. The logic of this appropriation derived from the Mass itself, whose physical components are distributed within the empirical space of the church interior according to their symbolic relation to absolute space. The altar represents Jerusalem – more specifically, the Temple in Jerusalem – as the *sanctus santorum* (Hardison 59). The space to its left is occupied by the Gospel (i.e., the account of Christ's time on earth), while the right side of it symbolizes the Resurrection, so that the move from left to right symbolically accomplishes transcendence. Moreover the altar, as the site of Christ's sacrifice, represents the plane of history in which Christ is sacrificed and dies, while the presbyterium represents the plane of eternity from which the resurrected Christ looks down on humanity (51, 55). The temporal symbolism of the Mass is equally comprehensive and robust. The cosmic drama it invokes imposes a "time compression" that joins the ancient Mosaic prophecies to the New Jerusalem destined to arrive at the end of time (47). Both the Mass and religious dramas yoke their historical episodes in reference to the original sacrifice of Christ, and hence to absolute time (83). The temporal setting of the Easter vigil at midnight on Holy Saturday (an important node in Faustian *Walpurgisnacht* and the demonic escapades in *The Master and Margarita*) was based on an early Christian belief that the Second Coming would take place precisely then (144).

When religious drama exited the church, it projected its spatial symbolism onto the town square, onto the urban space without (Lewis Mumford even comments that the entire medieval city functioned as a stage for the ceremonies of the church; cited in Carlson 19). This marked the ritual's moment of spatial aggression. In such rituals the entire town centre was drawn into a plan of cosmic dimensions.[14] Churches themselves were already oriented along "world axes," with the altar looking toward Jerusalem in the east, and the processions within them moved "east toward the high altar or west toward the altar of the Saviour" and thus were "evocative of world or cosmic journeys." These in turn were "echoed by movements along these same axes in the liturgical dramas – the journey to Emmaus, the race of the disciples to the tomb, the journey of the Magi" (15).

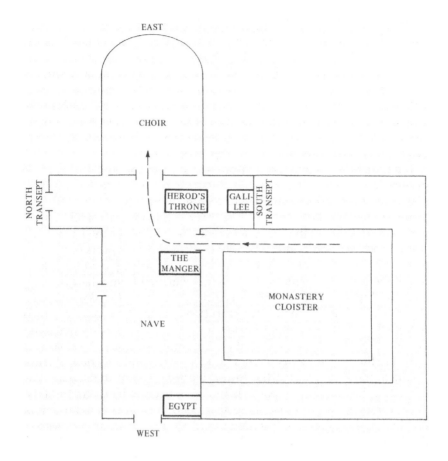

2.1. Diagram of the Church of Saint Benoît-sur-Loire (Fleury) showing possible acting locations for the play *The Slaughter of the Innocents*. From Carlson 16, reproduced from David Bevington, *Medieval Drama*, copyright © 1975 by Houghton Mifflin Company, 54.

On the town square during religious dramas the church itself was considered to represent Jerusalem while adjacent ground (such as the cloister) symbolically became the Mount of Olives (86). Heaven and Golgotha would typically be situated at one end of the square (with the three crosses on a high point, if possible, so as to be visible from afar), with the "mouth of hell" at the opposite end (Berthold 267, 286). In the twelfth-centrury Resurrection play *La Seinte Resurreccion*, for example, specific points on the square were designated as the cross, the tomb, heaven, hell, Emmaus, and so on (Hardison 262–3).

The transformation to which urban space was subjected during these dramas was often extensive and detailed. By the time the mystery play reached its apogee in the fourteenth century (before the Renaissance "killed the taste for mystery plays" [*Entsiklopedicheskii slovar'*, s.v."*misterii*"], just as the Enlightenment later would for the Faust tale), special societies and guilds typically oversaw various parts of the performances, often at considerable expense. The wealthy paid for spaces under the canopy; the mass of spectators watched from wherever they could find space, including the roofs of nearby houses (*Entsiklopedicheskii slovar'*, s.v. "*misterii*"). In the Frankfurt Passion play, for example, which occupied an oval space about 120 feet long, the *loca* of the different players and scenes followed each other: the house of Mary, Martha, and Lazarus, the house of Symonis, Herod's *Carcer* and *Castrum*, Pilate's *Palatium* and *Pretorium*; at the lower, western end of the square was the gate of hell (making it possible for Satan to enter by rising from the Wassergraben, the old moat); here also stood the half-covered fountain for the baptismal scenes. The table used for the Last Supper (*mensa*), the Temple, and the column with the cock whose crowing proclaimed Peter's betrayal – all these were placed in the middle of the open space. The public watched from street level or from the windows of adjacent houses (Berthold 267–8).

It is important to understand how different the symbolic import of these arrangements was from a mere outdoor staging of the drama, something along the lines of "Shakespeare in the Park" – and here one could follow Éric Buyssens, who in his 1943 *Les langages et le discours* remarks that operatic performance (for our purposes, theatre in general) is the richest object available for semiotic analysis of a culture because of the way it combines word, music, gesture, dance, costumes, and social relations (cited in Carlson 5). Performance in urban space includes the culture's designs on the cosmos as well.

As Hardison points out, the division of episodes within a play like *La Seinte Resurreccion* was based not on the plot but on the physical arrangements required for its *mise en scene*, so that both setting (the

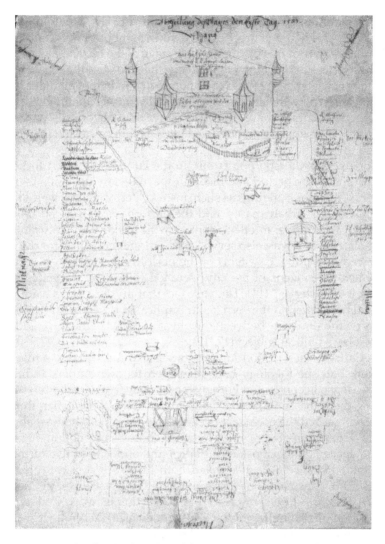

2.2. Stage plan for the first day of the 1583 Passion play in the Lucerne Fischmarkt. Heaven is placed against the permanent building at the top, where the action begins. Other structures – the largest are the temple on the right side of the marketplace and the Hell-Mouth (upside down in this drawing) at the lower left – for various later scenes are scattered about the open area. Characters are listed next to their stations. Description from Carlson 18. Image from Franz Liebing, Die Inszenierung des zweitätigen luzernes Österspiels (1869). Used with permission from ZHB Luzern Sondersammlung (Eigentum Korporation), BRd.27.1.1.

town square) and narrative were absorbed into the ritual enactment (262–6). Such staging, moreover, involved a symbolic order fundamentally different from that of "the Protean stage of the Elizabethans, which can be a palace at one moment, a tavern the next, and the rebel camp a few minutes later. Rather, it is the bounded container of all that exists." The mystery play instantiates "geometrical" rather than "geographical" space, events that are universal rather than historically particular (272; all this, again, is later mobilized within modernism and then transmitted to early Soviet culture).

Moreover, as Carlson points out, in the late Middle Ages and early Renaissance – the period in which European theatre developed – there were no "theatre" buildings as such; instead, performances were staged within existing urban spaces, and the performances were specifically designed to arrange, in effect, contact with the divine: "this fabric of symbols, rich as it was, also served as a setting, a container for the even more central symbolic systems of the performed rituals of the church, by which the citizens of the city were led to a direct participation in the divine mysteries" (14). The very fact that mystery plays were written and performed in the vernacular implicated urban space as well by stressing the similarity between the physical world of the town and that of the play's biblical subject (17, 19).

As Carlson's description suggests, a sense of space played a role here as well. Patristic theology had developed its own understanding of cosmic space in contention with elements of ancient Greek philosophy, among them the "volumetric" concept central to Aristotelian thought (which regarded the cosmos as a receptacle filled with bodies) and the Stoics' very different opposition between "body" and "nothingness" (in which space is the extension of bodies, the opposite of the surrounding void; Torrance 8–9). It rejected both in favour of a concept, centred in the Incarnation, of space not as a "receptacle which contains material bodies" but as the place of "interaction between God and the world," an intermingling of the two domains (24). Yet in the Christian West, after Aristotelian philosophy became ascendant once again in the twelfth and thirteenth centuries – the very period, one notes, in which the mystery play developed – the receptacle concept of space persisted and gave rise to the idea, particularly relevant to the Sacraments and Orders, that supernatural grace could be *contained in* ecclesiastical vessels and handed on in space and time by means of them (25). This led the medievals to think of the presence of God in pointedly spatial terms, as something that could be imported bodily into empirical reality. For all that the general theological point behind medieval religious drama was the concept of the Incarnation, in actuality the mystery play and related forms, with their emphasis on the sudden and miraculous advent – the *intervention* – of the divine into the life of the town square, were particularly inflected with this stubborn remnant of Aristotelian thought.

A good example of this complex of designs is the Corpus Christi procession, a relatively late phenomenon (first celebrated in Liège in 1246), in which the eucharistic host is paraded through town or village on the Thursday following Trinity Sunday. As pointed out by the medievalist Jacques Le Goff, who suggests the foundational importance of the Corpus Christi procession in the development of Western European public rituals in general, prior to the Corpus Christi procession only those admitted to Holy Communion (in the Middle Ages, by no means all believers) saw the body of Christ. "Now it was displayed to everyone in a magnificent and glorious procession" (70). The Holy Sacrament made a "regal" entry, "followed by the people of the town who were themselves on show surrounding the body of Christ" (70), and it was in fact the Corpus Christi procession, which established perhaps the single most important precedent for ritualized "intervention" of the divine in European public space, that became the model for later royal processions. "The physical and mystical body of the king was paraded under a canopy," argues Le Goff, "because the Holy Sacrament had already been so displayed. The Incarnation came first" (71). The public display of divine mystery in the Corpus Christi procession, moreover, "confirmed quite decisively the choice made by Western Christianity" to *display* its mysteries in what Old French called *monstrance* (in urban space, one could add) rather than adopt rituals of absence or secrecy, as the Eastern Church chose to do, concealing its mysteries behind the iconostasis (71). In his study of the Corpus Christi play V.A. Kolve similarly observes that the essence of the cycle's story was that it staged the three advents of God in human affairs (the Creation, the Incarnation, and the Salvation) because "the moments judged to be the most important in human history are those in which God openly and decisively intervenes" (58–9).

The intermingling of the sacred and the profane in the lives of medieval Europeans was to some extent a commonplace, a "part of a style of life"; yet as Peter Brown has shown, during the late Middle Ages when the mystery play and related forms of drama developed, the line of demarcation between the two underwent a transformation from a state of more or less constant co-presence to one in which each occupied a more carefully delineated sphere (317, 320). The eleventh and twelfth centuries in particular were a transitional era in which a whole series of social, legal, and clerical practices were undergoing dramatic change (303). The need, in effect, to *parade* holy presence through the streets of medieval cities may have been a reflex on the part of the church in this atmosphere of competition from a rising secular autonomy. Like Goethe's *Faust* and Bulgakov's *The Master and Margarita* that followed it, and for that matter Soviet public rituals as well, the intentional intrusions of the supernatural into the daily realm that define the mystery play and Corpus Christi processions may thus have arisen in response to the ideological uncertainties of the age – they were a way of using a drama of "intervention" to push back against the empirical realm and the pressures of its secular, everyday order of affairs.

Brown also comments that "unlike paganism and much of Judaism, the Christian communities were prepared to invest individual human beings with supernatural powers or with the ability to exercise power on behalf of the supernatural" (176). This led to humans in Christendom being viewed as potential *loci* of the supernatural. The western parts of the Roman Empire tended to regard this capacity as limited – to the clergy, if not to the bishop – whereas in the east it was essentially open to anyone (179). Both west and east subscribed to a "stark discontinuity between the human and the non-human," but in the west the holy man (as point of "intervention" of the supernatural in the material world) was "deeply inserted into human society" (191–2). In the east, on the other hand, the holy man removed himself from society – to the desert, where the angels were (181) – all the more powerfully to "intervene" in that society when he did appear within it. Brown describes the kind of advent the holy man represented as a "very ancient trait": "it is the world of the *epiphaneia*, of the sudden appearances of the gods. It is not enough that the divine should exist, it must be seen to exist, in the occasional flash of clear vision" (182–3). This notion of *epiphaneia* well describes the logic of "intervention" at work in such medieval rites as the Corpus Christi procession and the mystery play, and it was the attempt to revive something similar that characterized modernism's later infatuation with revived versions of such rites, as well as, I argue, a variety of Soviet cultural practices intended to stage an epiphany of extrahistorical meaning on the very real streets of Moscow, Petrograd, and other Soviet cities.

Nor were these practices limited to Western Europe. In Russia, which, *nota bene*, did not experience any secularizing Renaissance prior to the twentieth century (which meant that religious rituals were more immediately present in the cultural consciousness there than in the West), the presence of the mystery play goes back to semi-dramatic plays (*deistva*) adapted from Greek works (*Entsiklopedicheskii slovar'*, s.v. "*misterii*"). Consider, for example, the "Palm Sunday procession on a donkey" (*shestvie na osliati, v verbnoe voskresen'e*), an early seventeenth-century re-enactment of Christ's entry into Jerusalem during which a procession was mounted from Uspenskii Cathedral in the Kremlin out through the Redeemer (Spasskii) Gate to St. Basil's Cathedral on Red Square, including four men carrying a luxurious saddle for the patriarch to sit on, a chariot drawn by two horses in which was placed a tree decorated with apples and figs, accompanied by young boys singing "Hosanna!" and placing pussy willow branches instead of palms in the procession's path, and a white horse symbolically dressed as an ass. At the cathedral the patriarch, symbolizing Christ, mounted the horse holding the Gospels in one hand and a cross in the other. He was then led by the tsar himself to the cathedral (Evreinov, *Istoriia russkogo teatra* 62–5). Mystery plays adapted from Polish works were also widespread in Ukraine, such as the seventeenth-century *Dialogus de passione Christi* with a prologue in Polish and five scenes in Russian. In the first half of the eighteenth century the southern Russian church borrowed liturgical passions from the Polish Catholic church (one, on the life of Aleksei the godly man, was even staged for Tsar Aleksei Mikhailovich; *Entsiklopedicheskii slovar'*, s.v. "*misterii*"). Bulgakov, a native of Kyiv, may well have been aware of this legacy – and in any event, as we have seen in chapter 1, his pronounced use of such Moscow sites as the Patriarch Ponds and the Cathedral of Christ the Saviour (dynamited in 1931, while Bulgakov was working on his novel), which paradoxically become the site of devilry in *The Master and Margarita*, mobilizes a very similar sacralization of urban terrain. (As Larson comments, "Bulgakov was writing his novel at a time when the Soviet powers were actively engaged in a campaign of the destruction of religious sacred spaces and the creation of their own, materialist, secularly sacred space," 46.)

Judgment

Impressive as they undoubtedly were, these theatrical performances set within medieval urban space were not intended as mere spectacles or even only as lessons in morality or theology for the *simpliciore* (important as that function was). Through the intervention of divine forces in the here-and-now – which they did not so much represent as bring about – they were intended as transformational events, and the transformation they intended – of the urban space where they were staged, together with the spectators who watched them – typically had to do with the notion of *judgment*. As Bakhtin remarks, this is also a moment of totalization or comprehension: "The underworld is a peculiar image of summary, an image of the end and consummation of individual lives and fates. At the same time it is the final trial of a particular human life in its totality, a trial at whose basis lay the *higher criteria* of the official Christian worldview (religious-metaphysical, ethical, social, and political)."[15]

Berthold observes that "not only the great mystery and Last Judgment plays, but all the legend and miracle plays throughout the Western world drew heavily upon the contrast between damnation and redemption" (256). "The Passion as such was displaced by *Le mystère de la Passion*, the mystery of the Passion – a spectacle originating in divine service and at the same time firmly anchored in theological interpretation, with heaven and hell constantly present in every word and image" (276–7). In Brussels and Bruges the *Geselle von de Spele*, or craftsmen's acting associations, counselled their audiences from the platforms of their movable stages to heed their conscience and examine their way of life (261). In the little town of Nymwegen, "on Corpus Christi day, a stage cart rolled into the market square, and a trial was performed, in which the Virgin Mary interceded for sinful mankind and wrestled from the devil the poor souls that had fallen into his power" (261). Both Goethe's version of the Faust legend, in which Faust is ultimately rescued from his contract with Mephistopheles, and the more typical "chapbook" medieval version (to which Marlowe's play also adheres), which moralizes about Faust's damnation, have their source in this kind of medieval drama (so too – via *Faust* – does the plot motif of the Master's equivocal salvation at the end of Bulgakov's novel).

A closely related phenomenon in the Middle Ages involved allegories and morality plays (as we will see, an initiative conspicuously revived in the Soviet era). One very early example, Prudentius's *Psychomachia* of the early fifth century, portrayed the struggle of personified virtues and vices (Ecclesia, the Prince of This World, the Wheel of Fortune) for the soul of man. In later plays (the genre became especially important in the fifteenth century, particularly in France and England), allegorical figures become the active protagonists in the plays themselves: characters such as Heresy, Peace, Justice, and so on were part of a "personification of the conceptual world" that reflected an effort to look behind things and discover the essence of morals (326). Some of these allegories were fairly simple declamatory affairs performed on stage (such as a play written by students of the Paris Collège de Navarre in 1426 to celebrate the "bona magistra" of Reason), but often they involved large casts and elaborate sets and were performed, like mystery plays, on the cathedral square (of particular note was the 1425 *Castle of Perseverence*, whose spectators crossed a moat to enter a walled area whose various compass points held actors representing God, the Devil, the World, the Flesh, and so on, who walked through the crowd to play their part at a central tower where the "soul of man" was being tried – and eventually saved, by Mercy; 329–31).

Yet another hybrid of the sacred and the profane in the history of theatre bears mention here, and it is particularly significant because it arguably lies at the heart of all subsequent Passion plays. Hermann Reich, a scholar of the *mimus*, a dramatic form popular in ancient Rome that travestied the gods, comments that when it appeared, a religion like Christianity, "whose Redeemer uncomplainingly suffered the most ignominious death of common criminals[,] was bound to be scorned by the populace" (quoted in Berthold 208). Reich even suggests that Jesus's flagellation by the Roman soldiers and Pilate's presentation of him to the crowd with the words *Ecce homo* were directly derived from the *mimus*: "the soldiers who placed the crown of thorns on the head of the King of the Jews ... were performing a typical derisive scene from the mime repertoire, such as was popular among the Roman armies and included both the king and the vanquished subjects as a fixed type" (208).[16] In other words, central episodes in the tale of Christ's martyrdom, the basis for the mystery play, thus turn out *already* to have been theatrical events. Among Russian writers, Dostoevsky had a particularly keen, if largely intuitive, sense of this derivation – and it is significant in this context that Dostoevsky, one of the most vivid depictors of space in Russian literature, is also one of the most inclined to represent space in theatrical terms (usually melodramatic). In his novels suffering often appears commingled with farce; the given character's pain is typically acted out before a jeering crowd. One thinks most immediately of Marmeladov in *Crime and Punishment*, who delivers his pathetic life story to Raskolnikov while drunk in a tavern, surrounded by jeering habitués of the place – and who calls out to them, «Се человек!», that is, "Ecce homo"; or Katherina Ivanovna, who coughs her consumptive lungs out on the streets of St. Petersburg, having literally turned her miserable children into street performers, despite her insistence that "[i]t's not some kind of 'Petrushka' show we're performing on the street here, we are singing a noble romance" (*Ne 'Petrushku' zhe my kakogo-nibud' predstavliaem na ulitsakh, a spoem blagorodnyi romans*, 330); a tragically slapstick Punch-and-Judy show is essentially what they present. Most directly evocative of the Gospel subtext, there is also the horse Raskolnikov dreams of in chapter 5 of part 1, whose desperate efforts to haul an impossibly heavy load under a hail of blows provide a drunken peasant crowd with lurid entertainment (one thinks here of another tale merging divine intervention with sinful mirth, that of the Golden Calf the Israelites worship as Moses brings them the Ten Commandments).

Two closely related developments in medieval European theatre were
the processional and the wagon stage, which evolved primarily out of
Corpus Christi processions (the feast of Corpus Christi was instituted
by Pope Urban IV in 1264; 259), in which the religious rite of devotional
procession through the Stations of the Cross merged into processional
pageant and street theatre. The wagon play had its roots in tourna-
ments and street pageants arranged in honour of the sovereign (e.g.,
John Lydgate's allegory welcoming Henry VI to London in 1432; 263),
which themselves were was the precursors of the allegorical *trionfi* of
the Renaissance (259).[17] Sometimes the wagons were stationary and the
spectators moved from scene to scene, sometimes the wagons moved
through the town performing before successive audiences. Kolve notes
that the York Corpus Christi play involved forty-eight wagons moving
through twelve stations throughout the town (269). Also mixing church
interior and urban exterior was the medieval French genre of the *sottie*,
an example being Pierre Gringoire's *Jeu du prince des sots et de la mère
sotte*, which was performed on Shrove Tuesday in 1512 in Paris and
contained a sharp polemic against the church, "a panorama of the age
in fool's guise" (Berthold 321; in this connection it is hard not to think of
Peter the Great and his *Most Drunken Synod* – and of the entire Petrine
era, with its aggressive redefinition of Russia's cultural identity – as an
important precedent for Soviet rituals). Farces and Shrovetide plays of
pointedly profane character were also performed on street stages, using
the same theatrical forms as the Corpus Christi and legend plays (321).

Elements of this symbolic practice endured beyond the time when the
theatre for the most part moved back indoors, into buildings dedicated
exclusively to performances. On the one hand, theatres internalized the
event of "intervention," which had been the focus of religious rituals
formerly carried out in the town square. "The church or temple has
perhaps the closest systematic architectural relationship to the theatre,"
Carlson remarks, "since it involves the meeting of a secular celebrant
with a sacred celebrated" (129). As a result, action within the modern
theatre still occurs "in a mystic space created by the confrontation of two
worlds – the uncanny, dangerous, and fascinating space of the archetyp-
cal *illus tempus* inhabited by our representative shaman/actor and the
duller and safer world of everyday reality from which we observe him"
(David Cole, *The Theatrical Event*, quoted in Carlson 129). On the other
hand, not all elements of the theatre abandoned the street when theatre
became a separate institution and moved, together with polite society,
indoors (27). "From the Renaissance onwards, city streets and market
places continued to serve for the ancient forms of civic entertainment
– the parades and processions, the mountebanks and medicine shows,

the acrobats, farceurs and mimes whose descendant[s] may still be seen today in the clowns, mimes, fire-eaters and jugglers found in such popular urban gathering places as the square before the Beaubourg in Paris" (26–7). These urban spaces did as well, one might add, for the fairground entertainments and puppet theatre that so appealed as an aesthetic model to the Russian modernists and their Soviet successors.

Puppet Theatre

Another theatrical form relevant to the episodes of divine intervention that were central to medieval theatre, one that Goethe incorporated into *Faust* and that was later taken up by the European and Russian modernists, is the puppet theatre. One explanation why the Faust legend found refuge in the puppet theatre when Enlightenment values displaced it from the German theatrical stage might be that, as a performance, it simply had nowhere else to go. But it may also have been the case that something in the culture of puppet theatre was particularly receptive to it and that in "descending" to the puppet-theatre repertoire, its tale of supernatural intervention had in a sense returned to its home. It persisted there even as the Faust legend came back into high-cultural vogue in the late nineteenth century (writing in the 1930s, Palmer and More note that puppet-play versions of the Faust tale maintained their popularity well into the nineteenth century – "in fact, one can see performances still," 241). Goethe himself seems to have thought of the drama in terms reminiscent of the puppet theatre (anticipating perhaps Russian modernist interest in the *balagan* as a source of primal energies). „Shakespeares Theater," he commented, „ist ein schöner Raritätenkasten, in dem die Gesichte der Welt vor unseren Augen an dem unsichtbaren Faden der Zeit vorbeiwallt." (Schanze, who quotes this passage, then explains that *Raritätenkasten* "meint eine Vorführung auf dem Jahrmarkt, eine Art von frühen Kino," 52–3.)

With its miniaturized figures and embeddedness in popular culture the puppet theatre would seem to be the antithesis of the grand machinery of the medieval mystery play. But it has a metaphysical heritage of its own, and it turns out, perhaps unexpectedly for modern minds, to have been something of a reservoir for spectacles foregrounding divine intervention. Puppet theatre in fact has its deepest roots in religious spectacle. The very word "marionette" (*marionetka* in Russian) comes from a diminutive for "Mary," reflecting that puppets were often used in medieval mystery plays portraying the Nativity. Puppets themselves originated in the ancient world as objects of worship in temples and only later migrated out into the secular world (thus following a path later repeated by mystery plays themselves). In medieval Europe the Western Church was particularly tolerant of puppet theatres, allowing them to represent such sacred events as the Annunciation, the Nativity, the Resurrection, and so on. At the same time the marionette theatre tended also to incorporate set pieces of biting satire on worldly institutions (intrigue at the Vatican, the foibles of local rulers, etc.). In England, Punch continued his topical political satires even under the Puritans, a combination of the satirical and the sacred that is reminiscent *inter alia* of *The Master and Margarita* – one could think of satire as the other side of the kinds of "transformation" aimed at in mystery plays, in the sense that it works from below to scourge the world and cleanse it of its moral failings, to make way for the advent of the divine. (Mayakovsky's play *Mystery-Bouffe* conspicuously draws on this aspect of the puppet theatre, as will be seen in chapter 4; also reminiscent is the tendency of the marionette theatre – for example, in France – to parody literary fashion as well, such as neoclassicism.) Unlike its light-hearted French counterpart, which often portrayed romantic affairs, the German puppet theatre where Faust found a home tended to deal in more sombre plots having to do with metaphysical phenomena such as unrepentant sinners (e.g., Faust, or Don Juan; *Entsiklopedicheskii slovar'*, s.v. *"marionetki"*).

In Russia the most significant traditional form of puppet theatre was the *vertep*, which, like mystery plays in the eastern Slavic lands in general, was associated with the western territories of Ukraine, Belorussia, and Poland (and therefore may have been familiar to the Kyivan Bulgakov). Related to the German *Christschau* and Polish *szopka*, the *vertep* typically depicted the Nativity of Christ (the shepherds, wisemen, Herod, who gets dragged down to hell by devils, etc.). It derived from Western European mystery plays and took root in Poland around the seventeenth century, where it was usually performed by seminary students, who travelled the countryside with their miniature theatres.[18] In the early eighteenth century it was imported into Ukraine as part of a broader wave of Polish Catholic influences. It was initially produced by students at the Kyiv Academy (*Entsiklopedicheskii slovar'*, s.v. *"vertep"*). Initially simply a crêche displaying the Nativity scene at Christmas, the *vertep* evolved into a puppet Nativity drama in the church, then into a travelling puppet show that exited the church into the town square eventually to be carried on a tour of neighbouring villages, with its own band of musicians and accompanied by liturgical chants, up until the *maslenitsa* feast marking the beginning of Lent. (Like puppet theatre in general, the *vertep* thus replicates the history of church drama; Freidenberg 41.) The northeast Russian and Muscovite offshoot of this was the *raek*, a combination of the *vertep* puppet theatre imported from the south together with the native Russian visual tradition of folk woodcuts or *lubok*, in which puppet action was replaced with scenes painted on glass, narrated by the *raeshnik*. As its name indicates, the *raek* (*rai* in Russian means "paradise") derives from the German *Paradeisspiel*, which depicted the fall of Adam and Eve, though eventually little remained of that origin (*Entsiklopedicheskii slovar'*, s.v. "*marionetki*").[19]

Like the mystery plays themselves, the *szopka* and the *vertep* did not hold out for long against the temptation of secular themes; in fact, the dualism of sacred (ritual) and profane (representational) modes – which, as we have seen, inhabits the very origins of medieval theatre – was reflected graphically in the structure of the *vertep* theatre itself (Bogatyrev 396). *Vertep* plays were typically staged in a two-tiered box or little house (*domik*), with two stories and a mezzanine. The action would take place on balconies in *front* of this house, a somewhat peculiar arrangement that leads Freidenberg to suspect there is something especially significant about the architecture (41). The top of the structure was reserved for the religious dramas that were the ostensible focus of the *vertep* performance; the bottom was given over to decidedly secular and even farcical themes – folk-comic *intermedia* featuring the stock characters of Herod, the devil, a Zaporozhian Cossack who speaks with the devil as an equal, squabbling gypsies – essentially, as Freidenberg points out, Petrushka plays – all served up in a macaronic patter that mockingly distorted Great Russian and Polish speech (41; *Entsiklopedicheskii slovar'*, s.v. "*vertep*"). This spatial logic was absorbed with striking clarity, one should note, by Bulgakov in *The Master and Margarita*, in which events are strictly divided by chapter between Moscow and Jerusalem scenes (with the ironic transposition of divine intervention to contemporary Moscow, while Jeruslaem, which ought to be the site of the sacred, is portrayed with markedly desacralizing realism; see Petrovskii 141, and his suggestion that the same structure is also realized in the earlier *Belaia gvardiia*, 144).[20] The replication of *vertep* architecture within the structure of Bulgakov's novel, which thereby subordinates the Stalinist world to its scheme, was almost certainly not happenstance. Bulgakov's godfather N.I. Petrov wrote articles about the *vertep* theatre for the journal *Kievskaia starina*, and *vertep* performances were still common in the Kyiv of his youth (Petrovskii 142).

In her essay on the semiotics of the *vertep* form, Freidenberg makes still stronger claims about the significance of the puppet theatre – for example, that as a cultural practice it is connate with theatre as such – and thus alerts us to the sacral element embedded in that very form. The *vertep* and marionette theatre as well as the Russian *raek*, she claims, all derive from the *aedicula*, an elevated miniature shrine set within a larger temple and containing the image of a god. The temple, with its image of a god inside (often shrouded in darkness), has the same form as the puppet theatre: both are *cystai mysticai*, secret holy chambers or baskets serving as repositories of a deity (the ancient Greeks had a *naiskos*, a niche for the statue of a god, whose form merged with that of the tombstone and in ritual processions was often carried on a wagon; similar objects in Freidenberg's view are the Ark of the Covenant in Judaism and the tabernacle in Christianity).[21] Religious processions, Roman *trionfi*, and burial rites, as well as the rituals shared by many cultures that symbolically re-enact the transit of a deity across the heavens, are all extensions of this inner shrine, and all partake of the logic we have seen earlier, for example, in the Corpus Christi procession: that of parading a *receptacle* of the deity through the streets of the town. As chapter 4 will argue, the *agitvagony* of early Soviet festivals also derived from this practice. Greek tragedy was itself "born on the cart of Thespis," which was hauled about during the festival of Dionysius (moreover, with a two-tiered structure like that of the *vertep*, with heroes below and gods above; Evreinov in his *Istoriia russkogo teatra* suggests that the early Russian ritual of the *sviatochnyi kozel*, which he still was able to observe in "half-pagan Belorussia," in which a *ded* parades around a "goat" – in reality a young boy in a goat costume with a human face – was the exact parallel of the high priest in the ancient Greek goat rituals believed to be the source of tragedy; 29, 30, 32). For Freidenberg all this architectural symbolism works to "place a sign of semiotic equivalence between the deity, the table, the heavens, and the tomb"; "the temple and the theatre are completely identical in their material forms, in the manner in which they reproduce one and the same drama [*dramena*] about godhood, and in the original [*pervonachal'nykh*] ways in which they realize this idea." *Vertep* in Freidenberg's view is thus simultaneously a miniature theatre and a temple, a device for linking heaven and earth, deity and death. Moreover, in the modern era it was the fairground booth – the *balagan* beloved of Russian modernists – that preserved these features in their least altered form: "The *balagan* of the fairground, which preserved the Petrushka puppet theatre and the *raek* longer than did mediaeval churches, transmits this idea in its pure form" (41–3) – and one notes that Freidenberg was a scholar writing within Soviet culture and that her ideas (in this case, about situating deity within the empirical world), like those of Bakhtin about carnival, can be seen as inflected by it.

As Victoria Nelson further shows, puppets played an important role in the world of antiquity, especially that of ancient Egypt, although cultic use of puppets persisted throughout the Mediterranean world into late antiquity and was absorbed into Christianity in the form of, *inter alia*, the veneration of saintly relics. For the ancients, the puppet – and for the ancient Egpytians, the mummy – was important as a human simulacrum capable of attracting and retaining within itself a soul (*Secret Life of Puppets* ix). Indeed, it was felt that in their immobility, dolls and mummies were closer to the divine body "because their static and unchanging nature imitates the permanence of the immortal" (38). Puppets in the ancient world – "god-statues" – were understood as points of access to the supernatural; their cultic use as a form of theurgy was meant to facilitate the "drawing down of the divine into the material world" (35, 39). Thus, for example, in the early twelfth century in Spain, Abraham ibn Ezra, the great commentator on the Torah, "interpreted the golden calf as a legal way to bring down astral powers into matter," while the uncanny sixteenth-century legend of the golem in Prague was preceded by an older one that drew on a mystical tradition of achieving contact with God by making a micro-*anthropos* (52).

Cities

Some comment is in order, at this juncture, about cities themselves, which serve as both backdrop and object of all this symbolic activity. The ultimate precedent for bringing urban space into contact with the divine is Jerusalem – "the essential place on earth for communication between God and man," as Simon Montefiore puts it in his "biography" of the city (xviii). Bulgakov's pairing of Jerusalem with Moscow in *The Master and Margarita* is startling but also culturally apt and ultimately not his idiosyncratic choice. It is startling in that the Stalinist world in which Bulgakov lived and wrote was, at least nominally, aggressively atheist (the quasi-religious aura of Stalinist rituals and "cult of personality" is another matter). But his use of the Jerusalem setting is apt because ever since since the conversion of Kyivan Rus' to Christianity in AD 988, Jerusalem has served as the implicit ideal of Russian cities in their aspiration to sacred status: Kyiv was a "new Jerusalem," and in Metropolitan Filaret's sixteenth-century doctrine Moscow was the "third Rome" – but in the Christian era Rome's sanctity derived from its status as a "second Jerusalem." Even Peter the Great's capital St. Petersburg asserted parallels with Jerusalem (cf. the "Jordan Staircase" leading from the Winter Palace to the Neva River in St. Petersburg), and Jerusalem arguably inhered even in Stalinist Moscow's utopian intentions (which architecturally appear to invoke a strange mixture of Babylon and Rome; see chapter 5). Jerusalem itself, moreover, is not simply the fundamental referent of the mystery genre; it is itself saturated with theatricality. Throughout much of its history, especially in the Christian and Muslim eras, Jerusalem has been seen as simultaneously real and celestial, the site of past Revelation and future Apocalypse, always simultaneously the sign of something else. Festivals involving theatrical re-enactments of the Passion and tours of its sites began as early as AD 380, under the Emperor Theodosius I (Montefiore 152) – and when mystery plays were staged in Jerusalem the symbolism became especially vivid. Christ's entry into the city was re-enacted "in its original locations, beginning with the descent from the Mount of Olives," with the result that "historical and liturgical space, as well as historical and liturgical time, symbolically coincided" (Hardison 86–7). By the twelfth century Jerusalem had entered an "intensely theatrical age in which every technique was used to heighten public feelings through display" (Montefiore 227). There were even complaints that Jerusalem was being reduced to a "theatre of mysteries and miracles" (300).

In addition to orienting itself toward Jersualem symbolically and spiritually, beginning with the reign of Catherine the Great and continuing through the fin de siècle Russia took a geopolitical interest in the city. Nicholas I wanted to "save the holy places for the Russian God" (Montefiore 341) – a desire that partly motivated Russia's involvement in the Crimean War. Gogol, too, made a pilgrimage to Jerusalem, and once there succumbed to "Jerusalem syndrome" (341), as did Rasputin after him (385–6) – all of which is to say that Jerusalem was much more present in late nineteenth-' and early twentieth-century Russian cultural consciousness than we might otherwise assume. In the later nineteenth century the Grand Duke Konstantin Nikolaevich also visited the city. In fact, his visit may have been especially important for Bulgakov because he subsequently wrote a stage adaptation of the Passion titled "Tsar' Iudeiskii," which premiered in Kyiv on 29 October 1918 (Petrovskii 118).[22] There is no direct record of Bulgakov having seen the play, but he had a copy of it in his library (with commentary by "K.R.," the signature the Grand Duke used), and one scholar even suggests that Woland's remark that he was present at Pilate's interview with Yeshua is a veiled reference to the play, a key scene of which takes place in Pilate's palace (122, 126).[23] Kyiv in 1918 would have been a particularly receptive place for such a premiere, not only because of the city's apocalyptic mood during the civil war (as we have seen, a key theme in Bulgakov's *The White Guard*), but also because the city's symbolic resemblance to Jerusalem was taken for granted by its residents: both cities are situated on hills and have Golden Gates, and caves, as well as a lower city and an upper city (parallels already important, as we have seen, in Bulgakov's own *The White Guard*; 276). It is telling in this regard that revolution for Bulgakov thus connoted Jerusalem. The Kyiv of Bulgakov's youth even featured a panorama of Golgotha sited in a pavilion (specially constructed by an architect named V. Rimskii-Korsakov) on St. Vladimir Hill (Vladimirskaia gorka) and thus implicitly projecting the Crucifixion onto the city beyond (it had been created for an exhibition in Vienna in 1892, then moved to Kyiv after a fire; it also travelled to Odessa, where, as it happens, a young Valentin Kataev also saw it; 273–4). It was eventually replaced by a panorama by Jan Styka of Christians being tortured in Nero's circus in Rome – thus cementing the Jerusalem–Rome–Kyiv triad (174).[24] At the end of *The Master and Margarita*, in the scene on the roof of the Rumiantsev Museum, as Woland's entourage surveys the city of Moscow they are about to leave, Azazello symptomatically remarks, "I like Rome better" (*Mne bol'she nravitsia Rim*; *Sobranie sochinenii* 2004, vol. 8, 357).[25]

Panoramas

A related cultural object that drew the attention of modernists was the panorama, which also brings together the city and an implicit memory of the mystery play. Now largely forgotten, panoramas once figured prominently in the visual experience of urban Europeans in the nineteenth century (the first was constructed in Leicester Square, in London, in 1792 by one Robert Barker, who invented the term). Panoramas both expressed and shaped perceptions of the world. It has been suggested that they met a human need for overview, for an apperception of a totality of events (Oetterman 5). As Bulgakov's "Forty Times Forty" *feuilleton* shows, he knew panoramas well enough to think of representing Moscow in their terms, perhaps as a memory of the Rimskii-Korsakov panorama in Kyiv; the scene toward the end of *The Master and Margarita* in which the devil and his retinue appear on top of Pashkov House is particularly evocative of a panorama.[26] Chudakova notes that "the image of a large city viewed from a high and remote vantage point appears several times in Bulgakov's works, beginning with the first Moscow *feuilletons* and stories" and including the image of Kyiv – "Gorod" – in *The White Guard*: "the City smoked and hummed and lived, like multitiered cells in a hive" (*Kak mnogoiarusnye soty, dymilsia, i shumel, i zhil Gorod*; "Arkhiv M.A. Bulgakova" 129, 129n185; as we have seen, Mandelstam's "Today We Can Lift the Decals" also exhibits this reflex of panoramic description of Moscow).[27] Again, my claim is that Bulgakov's appeal to the panorama is not idiosyncratic but reflects his awareness of deeper tendencies in the culture as a whole.

If the impetus behind the panorama was modern and technological – it has been suggested that panoramas specifically replicated the

2.3. Nadar in his balloon over the city of Paris. Lithograph by Honoré
Daumier, 1862.
Shawshots/Alamy Stock Photo.

overview newly available to aeronauts (Oetterman 11–12) – it is nonetheless striking how frequently they featured Jerusalem and Rome as
subjects (so that the Kyiv examples discussed earlier were quite typical). It is as if their totalizing representation of the city had struck a
chord with some deep memory of the mystery genre and its sublimating
appropriations of urban space.[28] When a smaller-format panorama was
developed for display at local fairs, it was termed "Theatrum Mundi"
(223–4), as if its purveyors sensed its aesthetic affinity with the mystery play, namely, a striving to place "human beings in the largest possible context of their relations to the totality of society and to the divine
order"; Jane K. Brown 16). Pierre Prévost's panorama of Jerusalem
opened in London in 1819; another, by Frederick Catherwood, opened
somewhat later, before it travelled on to New York in 1838 (Oetterman
114, 154). Probably the best-known panorama on a Jerusalem theme
was Bruno Piglhein's "Jerusalem with the Crucifixion of Christ," which
opened in Berlin in 1886, then again in Munich in the 1890s; copies of it

appeared in Köln in 1896. In America – where there had already been a Jerusalem panorama in St. Louis in 1841 – "Jeruslaem and the Crucifixion" appeared in New York in 1886 and Philadelphia in 1890 (241, 247, 276, 343). As for Rome, there was an early nineteenth-century example in Magdeburg, which then travelled to Breslau (Oetterman 200); Berlin had both a panorama of "Ancient Rome with the Triumphal Procession of Emperor Constantine" and "The Burning of Rome in [AD] 64."

Panoramas thus embodied not only newly available technological means for comprehending urban space – the ability to survey it from the air – but also a deeper memory of the symbolic designs of the mystery play and related genres. They were central to the culture of the nineteenth century, out of which the archaicizing designs of the modernists as well as their Soviet-era successors emerged. Walter Benjamin sees the high point of their diffusion as coinciding with the introduction of the Paris arcades, that arch-embodiment for him of bourgeois ascendancy (Benjamin 5). "Announcing an upheaval in the relation of art to technology, panoramas are at the same time an expression of a new attitude toward life" (6). In Benjamin's view the panorama, like the arcades, combines impressive technological achievement with dubious political effects: the designers of panoramas strive for a "perfect imitation of nature," developing such effects as changing daylight. "In their attempt to produce deceptively lifelike changes in represented nature, the panoramas prepare the way not only for photography but for <silent> film and sound film" as well (5, angle brackets in original; cf. Goethe's description of Shakespeare's dramas as "Raritätenkasten," a marketplace form that Schanze calls "a type of early cinema," *eine Art von frühen Kino*, 52–3). Benjamin also links the burning down of Dauguerre's panorama in 1839 with his subsequent invention of the Dauguerrotype: for Benjamin photography is significant in that it "greatly extends the sphere of commodity exchange" (6).[29] But in its attempt to "bring the countryside into the town" the panorama is also an expression of the city dweller's "political supremacy over the provinces" (6). Benjamin further quotes Marcel Poëte's claim that "the vogue for panoramas […] corresponds to the vogue for cinematographs today" (530). What the panorama enables in particular is a (specious) mode of seeing: "not only does one see everything, but one sees it in all ways"; "the interest of the panorama is in seeing the true city – the city indoors" (531–2). The panorama, in other words, emerges in the nineteenth century as an instrument for totalizing appropriations of urban space, whose tendency moreover is often to project sacred meaning onto it – an impulse carried forward into modernist theatrical experiments and Soviet public rituals as well.

The Faust legend that attracted so much sustained interest among Russian modernists served as an important precedent for a plot involving "intervention"; it also, in the metatheatrical aspect of Goethe's version, transmitted memories of older theatrical forms whose very point was the staging of the absolute, the interruption of the empirical (and in that sense historical) present in order to invoke sacred presence and meaning. The whole syntax, if it may be thought of in such terms, of forms like the mystery play and Corpus Christi procession – memory of which is preserved in the otherwise modern agendas of the French Revolution and Soviet festivals – evolved out of this impulse. The puppet theatre and panorama, two other forms taken up by the modernists whose relation to medieval rites might not be immediately apparent, turn out also to share the totalizing devices of the medieval forms (diminutive, in the case of the puppet theatre; transcendently comprehensive, in the case of the panorama) as well as their orientation toward sacrality. Behind all these forms stands the phenomenon of the city, the spatial domain appropriated as the site for transformative agendas and, via memories of Jerusalem, the iconic embodiment of divine intervention. These memories played an especially vital role in Russia, which since its conversion to Christianity in AD 988 had staked its claim to transcendent significance – to its centrality in the divine cosmos – on its two capitals' (Moscow and St. Petersburg) putative links to Jerusalem and Rome.

Chapter Three

Modernist Dreams of "Intervention"

The history of medieval theatre, with its religious elements, mystery rites, stagings of divine presence on the city square, and so forth, is relevant to the Soviet era not just as a preconditioning part of its distant aesthetic past. It also formed a set of assumptions about the essential matters of human life and the ways in which they should be portrayed – in particular about humanity's relation to history – assumptions that were transmitted through the aesthetic interests and experimentation of Russian modernism. Russian interest in staging "intervention" in the fin de siècle and early twentieth century was also influenced by parallel developments in Western European modernism, in particular by the writings and theatrical projects of Richard Wagner. Across Western Europe in the fin de siècle, modernists rejected the naturalistic theatre as bourgeois and stultifying and sought renewal in aesthetic forms that might revive the more vibrant and essential artistic practices of the ancient and medieval worlds. As Posner describes it, the forms to which modernist directors turned for renewal encompassed "ancient Greek theatre, especially as viewed through the lens of Nietzsche, the *theatrum mundi* metaphor of Spanish Golden Age theatre, the simplicity of the Shakespearean stage, the conventionalized vocabulary of Noh and Kabuki, and popular forms previously thought too base for serious consideration: fairground entertainments, puppetry, and commedia dell'arte" (2–3). Theatre was singled out as the target for this anti-realist drive because, as Michel Aucouturier suggests, it revealed the limits of realism in general (10). The motivating ideas, however, were not merely aesthetic. Modernist calls for theatrical renewal also expressed an impatience with history, with the capacity to find meaning in immediate events.

The aesthetic (musical) practice and accompanying theorizations of Richard Wagner played a particularly important role in this movement.

In Wagner's writings the emphasis falls not only on aesthetic and spiritual renewal but also on the transformation of physical space as a means to achieve it – specifically, the theatre at Bayreuth, which was to be the site of the eventual *Gesamtkunstwerk* uniting all the arts; but also (as in the related work of Reinhardt and Fuchs) on urban space itself, which was to serve as the site for dramatic rites leading to a radical apotheosis. Wagner's concept of the *Gesamtkunstwerk* and, to a more limited extent, his efforts to realize it in productions at Bayreuth had their roots in political events, and in his belief that the unification of the arts would follow the unification of Germany in the mid-nineteenth century (Goethe, too, had wanted to combine all the arts), as well as in utopian political ideas drawn from Bakunin, Feuerbach, and Proudhon (in the *Gesamtkunstwerk* the audience would be forged into a collective participant in cultic ritual). His thought about the theatre takes the form, characteristic of modernism, of a postlapsarian lament out of which arises a call for utopian revival. He rejected the current naturalistic theatre as mere frivolous entertainment (including in particular French theatre as a form of blatant commercialism, especially the operettas of Jacques Offenbach; see Koss 40), and he sought to revive something similar to what he believed had constituted the tragic drama of the ancient Greeks; or, alternatively, the great pilgrimage churches of the Middle Ages (on which see Carlson, *Places of Performance*).[1] Nietzsche's treatise on the "birth of tragedy from the spirit of music" emanates from the same retrospective interest.

The desire to arrange "intervention" through such revivals was central to Wagner's aims.[2] In "Art and Revolution" (1849) he argued that "art" as such had reached its apogee in Greek tragedy – a religious festival in which "the gods bestirred themselves upon the stage and bestowed on men their wisdom" (47) – and that this form had been displaced by philosophy, and then by Christianity, which taught alienation from the world (21). The "splintering of the common tragic artwork," he argued in "The Art Work of the Future" (also 1849), had been a cataclysm that paralleled "the shattering of the Greek religion" and "the wreck of the Grecian nature-state" (166). After their "initial communion" in Greek tragedy, the "three primaeval human arts" of dance, tone, and poetry had gone their separate ways, and their apparent synthesis in opera was nothing more than "the mutual compact of the egoism of the three related arts" (132, 149, 153). The future artwork, however, would revive Hellenic art and transform it into a universal form that would be an "immediate vital act," in contrast to modern theatre's mode of existence as a mere product of culture, the private property of an artistic caste having no effect on public life ("Art Work of the Future" 73, 182). The separate arts would organically reunite in "the highest conjoint work of art," which is "the Drama" (184), and this would accomplish the "universal fellowship of all mankind" (166, 184; the conclusion that these ideas were influenced by the failed revolutions of 1848 and a consequent disaffection with "history" is hard to avoid). The performer in such a drama will portray the very "essence of the Human Species," and the place on which "this wondrous process" will come to pass is the theatrical stage, which will represent, in what one notes is an encompassing gesture reminiscent of the panorama and *theatrum mundi*, the "wide expanse of the whole world" (185, 193). Even at this rapturous height, however, an ominous note sounds that, however remotely and indirectly, looks forward to Stalinism's own use of "interventionist" dramas. Wagner claims that "the last fulfilment of man's being, the demonstration of his full ascension into universalism" in this Drama will be attained in the celebration of "the noblest thing that men can enter on" – man's death (199).

A generation later, Georg Fuchs, whose theatrical activity at Darmstadt directly paralleled that of the Russian modernists, similarly argued that the origins of drama lay in "die Kult, die festliche Geselligkeit" (*Die Revolution des Theaters* 29). In Fuchs's view German theatre in particular arose out of the mystery play and *Fastnachtspiele* but then went astray in the sixteenth and seventeenth centuries when it began to imitate such "amusements" as ballets performed in baroque palaces (30). It followed that theatre could only be renewed by a return to the *Festspiel*. Following Wagner, Fuchs believed that such a renewed theatre would unite all art forms (and he comments, interestingly in this context, that in its unruly form, *Faust*, Part One which he staged, and which he considered to have a "peculiarly modern style" – contains the seeds of future German drama; 157, 191). At Darmstadt, spectatorship was supposed to mean participation in an epiphanic revelation of life.

One important extension of the Wagnerian (and more broadly modernist) impulse to reform the theatre was the vogue that arose in late nineteenth- and early twentieth-century Europe for staging performances in urban space – in parallel, as it happens, to the mass spectacles then being mounted in Soviet cities. In 1920, for example, Max Reinhardt staged Hofmannsthal's *Everyman* (*Jedermensch*) on the square before the cathedral in Salzburg; then in 1924 he staged *The Merchant of Venice* on the Campo San Travaso in Venice and *A Midsummer Night's Dream* in real woodlands – performances during which, as one scholar notes, the setting *became* the things it represented (Carlson 28). Les' Kurbas, who staged some of the early Bolshevik street spectacles, had been influenced by Reinhardt while a student in Vienna (Rudnitsky 108).

For Carlson this practice was nothing less than the direct progenitor of early Soviet festivals: "The two traditions of Rousseau's interest in great civic festivals and Hugo's in the connotations of certain historical spaces merged in the great dramatic spectacles staged in Russia soon after the Revolution" (32).

The Ritual Impulse in Russian Modernism

In early twentieth-century Russia interest in the theatre was more than esoteric. In the minds of leading cultural figures, at least, the question of the future of the theatre – "what form it would take and what place it would have in public life" – was, as one historian of the Russian theatre puts it, "one which preoccupied the minds of leading thinkers and writers in the period between the two Russian Revolutions of 1905 and 1917. It was as if Russia's historical fate depended on solving the problems of the theatre" (Rudnitsky 9). In this allegorizing sense the stage lent itself to being seen as the site of eschatological transformation.

The theatrical and literary world of fin-de-siècle Russia was taken by much the same impulse toward theatrical renewal that swept through Western Europe. In part this was the result of the considerable influence Wagner exerted in Russian cultural spheres in the later nineteenth and early twentieth centuries.[3] Wagner was well-known in Russia, having conducted there as early as 1863. His ideas subsequently became the focal point for heated debates among music critics: as a musical phenomenon, he represented a modernist wedge being driven ineluctably into the conservative musical establishment of Russia, which in the domain of opera inclined strongly toward Italian and French models (he also managed to become a *"particular bête noir"* of that anti-modernist, Tolstoy; Bartlett 52). He had also met and had extensive conversations with Bakunin in Dresden during the Uprising of 1849 (Kamiński, vol. 2, 115), as well as Herzen, who expressed admiration for his essay on "The Art-Work of the Future." The first Bayreuth *Festpsiele* in May 1876 was noted in the Russian press and attended by several prominent Russians (Barlett 6,12, 40, 45). It was the vogue for various aspects of Wagner's world view – its perceived eroticism, its turn toward mythological subjects, the daring "formlessness" of his musical works – among the World of Art group and the Symbolists, however, that exerted the most influence (60, 66). "The Art-Work of the Future," which first appeared in 1849, was translated into Russian in 1897. Meyerhold staged a modernist production of *Tristan und Isolde* at the Mariinsky Theatre in 1909 (95). The Symbolists, especially Viacheslav Ivanov, at whose weekly literary gatherings (the celebrated "Wednesdays" at "the Tower," his home in Petersburg) Wagner became something of a focal point, saw Wagner as the embodiment of a "Dionysian" artist (cf. Ivanov's statement in "Predchuvstviia i predvestiia," an essay published in 1905 in the journal *Zolotoe runo*, that "the inner ineluctable path of Symbolism has already been laid out and anticipated [in the art of Wagner]," 90). The poet Ellis went so far as to declare that the entire meaning of Russian Symbolism found expression in Wagner (118, 184). The poet Aleksandr Blok's library includes a heavily underlined copy of Wagner's *Art and Revolution* (first published in Russia in 1906; Kleberg, "'People's Theater'" 181). But perhaps the most revealing of Blok's underlinings in the present context is the one he made in his copy of *Oper und Drama*, in which Wagner states that Goethe's *Faust* represented a watershed in the development of drama, the innovative nature of which consisted precisely in "Das Drängen des Gedankens in die Wirklichkeit" (the thrusting of thought into reality) – a form of "intervention" in which Wagner believed the future of drama lay (212). Nor did interest in Wagner diminish in the years immediately following the October Revolution. Lunacharsky, the Commissar for Enlightenment in the early Bolshevik government, embraced Wagner's ideas concerning the theatre as "socialist," and the avant-garde director Platon Kerzhentsev's enthusiasm for mass festivals was directly inspired by Wagner (227–8). Among the first works published by Narkompros in Petrograd in 1918 was Wagner's *Art and Revolution*, with a foreword by Lunacharsky (Kleberg, "'People's Theater'" 181).

Wagner's ideas thus served as an important conduit for ideas about "intervention" in the Russian context. When the Wagnerian impulse migrated to Russia, it took two principal forms. The first was metatheatrical writings, which assimilated Wagnerian ideas while fusing them with native impulses toward utopian speculation, if not outright planning, and it is this line in particular that later was to merge with early Soviet initiatives. The second involved a series of modernist artistic texts, especially plays, that sought to realize Wagnerian forms of transformation on the stage, however provisionally.

Russian metatheatrical writing energetically developed Wagnerian ideas by calling for the transformation of the theatre into a site for spiritual events, in particular for rites whose purpose would be to bring actors and spectators into contact with a spiritual otherworld, usually with eschatological connotations (i.e., the transcendence of, or escape from, history, if history is understood as the dull continuance of empirical reality). One of the earliest calls for theatrical renewal in Russia came in the poet Valerii Briusov's "Nenuzhnaia pravda" (1902), which denounced the "imitation of nature" in realist theatre and called for "a theatre of artifice" (*uslovnyi teatr*, 364). Briusov specifically lamented the misguided tendency in Russian theatres of the fin de siècle, especially the Moscow Art Theatre, toward increasingly realistic stage decoration. Such efforts can never really succeed, he argued – the viewers always know it is not real snow or wind they see on the stage. Stylized hints at setting, such as were common in ancient Greek and Elizabethan theatre, would better facilitate the viewer's access to the drama's "higher truth and more profound reality" (*vysshaia istina, glubochaishaia real'nost'*). A still more extensive notion of what the new theatre should be emerged in the writings of the Symbolist poet and theoretician Viacheslav Ivanov, who contended that Wagner and Nietzsche together had outlined the principles for an entirely new form of art, appropriate to the new era that was poised to succeed the bourgeois ascendancy and positivism of the nineteenth century. For Ivanov, however, both Wagner's and Nietzsche's conceptions, and Wagner's actual theatrical experiments at Bayreuth, remained incomplete. Ivanov looked forward to the full realization of the new art in Russia.[4]

Like Wagner, Ivanov viewed the contemporary theatre as the ruins of a former unity, a mere spectacle given over to an imitation of life (*mimetizm*) and acted out before a passive crowd of isolated individuals ("Esteticheskaia norma teatra" 276). Wagner and Nietzsche, however, had shown the way toward a "new organic epoch," an "absolutely new cultural era" that would witness "the merging of artistic energies in synthetic forms of art" ("Predchuvstviia i predvestiia" 89, 91). Drama unfolds before us in time, Ivanov argued, and in doing so manifests an energy that is aimed not just at providing us with beautiful images but also at "becoming an active factor in our spiritual life, at bringing about in it a certain inner event" (93). Symbolism had already sought to overcome the Romantic split between dream and life (86), but what Wagner's art anticipated in particular was Symbolism's evolution into a form of myth-creation (*mifotvorchestvo*) through which the (Russian) collective would attain self-definition (*istinnyi mif – postulat kollektivnogo samoopredelenia*; "Predchuvstviia i predvestiia" 90).

The lost ideal for this form of art – and this is where Nietzsche and his "Birth of Tragedy" enter in – was ancient Greek tragedy, in which the chorus played a vital role and those in attendance were not a passive audience but participants in a religious rite (indeed, as he states more than once, an orgiastic and Dionysian one).[5] Deeply influenced by Nietzsche, Ivanov nonetheless sought to revise him by overcoming his anti-religious views and emphasis on individualism: Nietzsche's understanding of Greek tragedy had been purely aesthetic, whereas Ivanov saw tragedy as essentially religious and sought "a revival of religious mystical feeling in it" (Kleberg, "Vjačeslav Ivanov and the Idea of Theatre" 58–9). The history of the theatre is one in which the previously conjoined elements of such rites – which Ivanov identifies as the dithyrhamb, the chorus, and the hero – went their separate ways, leaving the theatre as mere spectacle ("Predchuvstviia i predvestiia" 94). In the reborn art forms of the new era, however, theatre goers would come together not just to view a spectacle but to "perform an act – in communion" (*deiat' – soborno*). Spectators would merge in a choral body, "much like the mystical commune [*obshchina*] in ancient 'orgies' and 'mysteries'" (95). For Ivanov, theatre in this mode was "fully capable of replacing religion and the Church for a humanity which had lost its faith" (in *Borozdy i mezhi*, quoted in Rudnitsky 9).

The notion of the ancient Greek chorus is pivotal for Ivanov. "The crisis of the chorus," he remarks in "Esteticheskia norma teatra" (1916), "is the crisis of the choral basis of the theatre and of theatre in general" (273), and in the earlier "Predvestiia i predchuvstviia" he cites the ideal of the "choral word" (*khorovoe slovo*), which would embody in "the boundlessness of cosmic ecstasy the dionysian spirit of humanity" (98). The "inner anomaly" of Wagner's art lies in his having excluded both dramatic acting and "an actual chorus" (*real'nyi khor*) from his operas – though Ivanov grants that Wagner's operas and Beethoven's Ninth Symphony, with its choral fourth movement, nonetheless point the way to the future forms of art.

The new forms of theatre that Ivanov anticipates are thus meant to realize a choral drama involving both actors and spectators in a Dionysian rite whose effect will be collective self-awareness, for "out of the dionysian sea of orgiastic perturbations [*volnenii*] arises the apollonian vision of myth" (99). Moreover, in keeping with the broader modernist impulse I am examining here, Ivanov's vision of how to arrange such a rite has a distinctly architectonic and spatial cast. As Michael Wachtel has shown, Ivanov's understanding of ancient Greek theatre was significantly influenced by the findings of the German archaeologist and architect Wilhelm Derpfeld. It is owing to Derpfeld's research, for example, that we know that ancient theatre featured a round stage designated for dance, and that on it was burned the sacrifice to Dionysius, to whom the chorus sang its dithyrambs.[6] It was Derpfeld, too, who proposed building theatres that replicated this ancient form, with a significant part of the proscenium given over to the chorus (Wachtel 139, 141–2). Ivanov thus predicts in "Predchuvstviia i predvestiia" that the architecture that realizes the art of the future will not be static; rather it will be "that dynamic and fluid architecture whose name is Music" (91). The reference to music would seem a shift into abstract metaphor,

but Ivanov's further commentary makes it clear that he has both architecture and music in mind (possibly drawing on Goethe's notion of the
parallels between the two: "architecture is frozen music" – a phrase
attributed to Eckermann's *Conversations with Goethe in the Last Years
of His Life*). Just as in "primitive eras" all creative activity was affixed
in a single architectural style and all creative streams flowed into the
"sacred receptacle of the temple [*khram*]," so will all creative activity in
the future arise in "the spirit of music" and flow into its "all-encompassing
bosom" (91). Ancient art was religious, he remarks, *because* its architecture was "hieratic"; architecture declined together with the decline
of the temple as the site of fetish (91). In other words, all this reform
is useless for Ivanov if art does not find a physical site, a receptacle,
to facilitate the moment of transcendent contact or "intervention" (cf.
Freidenberg on the cultic role of such structures in antiquity, and recall
the monument described in Lunacharsky's play *Faust and the City*). The
cultural forms of the new epoch must, he claims, bring about profound
changes in architectonics; to be convinced of this one only has to realize how in ancient times the chorus and procession (*khor i khorovod*)
dictated to architecture the motifs of the circle and circular enclosures,
as exemplified, for example, in circular colonnades (91). Ivanov's own
prescriptions remain vague – he argues that there should be a small
chorus that is involved in the dramatic action but also a "grand chorus"
symbolizing the "entire collective" (*obshchina*) and reserved for solemn
cadences so as to act with "massive grandeur" and the weight of "collective authority" (91). Moreover he finds the nearest model for such
a chorus and its role in a "divine and heroic tragedy" in the medieval
genre of the mystery play (*misteriia, bolee ili menee analogichnaia sredneve-
kovoi*, 100), which he regards essentially as a reincarnation of ancient
Greek forms (e.g., in "Esteticheskie normy teatra" he states that "in
mediaeval rite [*deistvo*] there once again flourishes a collective element
appropriate to its religious nature," 273). As will be seen in chapter 4,
similar motives would resurface in Soviet designs for urban space – in
some of which Ivanov participated directly.

A particularly energetic infusion of the Wagnerian influence in Russia came in the form of a collection of essays published in 1908 under
the title *Teatr. Kniga o novom teatre*. The essays are unanimous in their
Wagnerian rejection of "the bourgeois idea of theatre as a form of
entertainment" (*burzhuaznaia ideia ob uvlekatel'nom kharaktere teatra*), as
Lunacharsky puts it in his contribution (*Teatr*, "Sotsializm i iskusstvo"
24). The rebirth of tragedy accomplished by Wagner has served as an antidote to bourgeois "satiety" (*sytost'*), remarks A. Gornfel'd (*Teatr*, "Duze,
Vagner, Stanislavskii" 76), while the director Vsevolod Meyerhold aims

his critique at the notion of "theatre as spectacle," in which the viewer only passively experiences events (*Teatr*, "Teatr [K istorii i tekhnike]" 141; Briusov more dryly notes "the shortcomings of the realist theatre in recent times"; *Teatr*, "Realizm i uslovnost' na stsene. Nabroski i otryvki" 206).

Equally prominent in the collection is the Ivanovian expectation – though it is not shared by all the authors – that once it sheds the trappings of "bourgeois" realism, the theatre will be transformed into some form of religious rite, especially one involving viewers as a collective of participants rather than mere observers. An artistic, constantly creating cult (in the Russian sense of religious ritual) will transform churches into theatres and theatres into churches, Lunacharsky muses. He then predicts that "a theatre formed from society [*obshchestvennyi teatr*] will serve as the site for collective stagings of tragedies intended to elevate the soul to religious ecstasy" (22) – a chilly foreshadowing, if one chooses to view it that way, of the Stalinist show trials. Gornfel'd similarly remarks that in *Parsifal* Wagner brings the viewer to a state of religious ecstasy (73), thus accomplishing a return to the originary principles of the theatre. Theatre emerged from ancient religious rituals, he asserts, and to a significant extent preserved the principle of choral action inherent in every religious cult (69). Gornfel'd's pre-eminent example from the European Middle Ages is the Oberammergau mystery play, an essential part of spiritual life in which there was no sharp division between viewers and performers (70). For Georgii Chulkov, Wagnerian theatre represents a "tragic" attempt to escape the dull confines of eighteenth- and nineteenth-century European theatre and create a religious theatre instead – tragic, because for Chulkov Wagner left his audience in a passive state, still separated from the stage and therefore incapable of participating in the kind of religious act that would have taken place in the "pre-Aeschylean epoch" ("Printsipy teatra budushchego" 173, 175). S. Rafalovich identifies medieval mystery plays as an "interval" in the evolution of European theatre when it managed to take a step back to "originary religious theatre" ("Evoliiutsiia teatra [Kratkii istoricheskii sintez]" 186). When mystery declined and the dramatic art was "expelled out into the street" from the church, it became purely intellectual and artificial (188).

As in the case of European modernism, a preoccupation with architecture and urban space informs Russian thought about theatrical reform in this era. In Aleksandr Benois's "Beseda o balete," an artist argues, over the objections of a balletomane who has had enough talk of God and *sobornost'*, that ballet in fact harbours within it a liturgical moment (*liturgichnost'*) of its own that might enable a still fuller realization of "genuine religious mysteries" (what kind these will be can be decided later, Benois suggests; 85, 92). In a reflex characteristic of this strain of modernism, Benois's thought again turns toward architecture: in this case, the Gothic cathedral as a space that brought about direct encounters (*litsom k litsu*) with God. His ideal is not a theatre that would displace the church but one with an even wider mission that would absorb the church within itself (93). For Fedor Sologub, too, the vision of a theatre transformed into religious mystery has architectural consequences: the task before those who work in the theatre, he argues, is to bring spectacle as close as possible to a collective act, to mystery and liturgy ("Teatr odnoi voli," in *Teatr* 151). Once there, the theatre will become the locus (*poprishche*) of collective/cathedral activity. Sologub's wordplay involves the dual meaning of *poprishche* as "field of activity" but also, more literally, as the "threshold of the sanctuary" in a Russian church; and of *sobor* as meaning both "collective" and "cathedral" – meanings also combined etymologically in the Greek roots of the English "synagogue": for Sologub, theatre will become at once the domain of cultural life in which collective activity becomes possible *and* the threshold to a new theatre of mysteries. Similarly, Meyerhold – who generally eschewed religious notions in favour of his theory of "play" as the basis for theatre – goes so far in his contribution to the *O teatre* collection as to suggest that "the religious question can be resolved within the theatre" ("Teatr. K istorii i tekhnike," in *Teatr* 134). His model for theatre as a religious phenomenon is the plays of Maeterlinck, in which one unfailingly discovers mystery, be it in the form of "quiet tears" or "ecstasy calling for a universal religious act ... toward the bacchanalia of the great triumph of Miracle" (135). Even Maeterlinck, he concludes, can be staged from an ecclesiastic point of view (*tserkovnost'*, 140).

Despite its name, the composer Aleksandr Scriabin's *Mysterium* at first glance seems only tangentially related to the modernist impulse toward the staging of supernatural intervention that has been discussed here. The work was never realized, though it was supposed to be the culmination of all his previous compositions. Scriabin evidently knew little or nothing about medieval precedents in the genre of the mystery play when he began outlining plans for his own *Mysterium* around 1901, though he later tried to draw the connection (de Schloezer 159, 162, 180). Nonetheless the ambitious plans he outlined for his *magnum opus* incorporate much the same logic of "intervention" that we have seen elsewhere in Russian modernism, and likely for the same reason, namely, that he was responding to Wagner's transformative projects at Bayreuth. Scriabin's initial plan had been to compose an opera, but this evolved into the dream of surpassing Wagner's idea of

Gesamtkunstwerk – which he considered a purely mechanical synthesis of art forms – by developing the form of an "abstract philosophical drama" (162, 174, 253).

As a utopian project, Scriabin's *Mysterium* characteristically eluded definitive form (with the exception of the *Acte préalable*, which was scored and was supposed to be preliminary to the *Mysterium* proper; 163), but the thoughts and notes on the project that he developed over several years revolve around certain core ideas. Like the other modernist projects we have seen, the *Mysterium* was intended first of all to destroy conventional theatricality – the division between stage and audience, actors and passive spectators – and replace it with a liturgical act in which all present would be active participants, "votaries in the sacrament of theophany" (185, 267).

Scriabin's initial idea was to use the *Mysterium* to bring about the "unification of mankind in a single instant of ecstatic revelation" (161), which was at the same time to effect the "ultimate transformation of mankind in death" (171) and, as if this were not enough, the "collapse and transfiguration of the entire cosmos" (181). The performance was to bring about nothing less than the end of time (Mitchell 50). For content Scriabin tended to draw on the theosophical doctrines of Mme Blavatsky, arranging for representations of various stages of spiritual evolution or even at one point the evolution of the human race as the gradual realization of Spirit (de Schloezer 263; see also Mitchell 80); other scenes were to represent moments of ecstasy in each of the senses (257). The various parts of the drama were to be staged over seven days, or multiples of seven days (263), in a temple specially built for the purpose in India (178). The drama was also to be performed in Sanskrit, or possibly a language of Scriabin's own invention, because he felt modern languages to be degenerate and unsuited for such a grand rite (259; see also Mitchell 78–80 on the planned staging).[7] But beyond these eccentricities Scriabin's plans for the *Mysterium* replicate principal components of the modernist project for "intervention." The cosmic collapse he imagines can be seen as a radical form of disrupting history. Scriabin, too, focuses on the spatial aspects of his drama: he believed that theatre was the spatial expression of humanity's need to find a new incarnation (186), and for the performance of his *Mysterium* he outlined plans for a theatre transformed into a temple, with an altar at the centre (294). He also concerned himself with its geographical siting: India, which following Blavatsky he believed to be the spiritual home of mankind. The whole point of the drama was to arrange a universal reunion of humanity with the divine, an event of "intervention" whose agent Scriabin believed himself to be (180). His drama was also to be not a particular instance of art but an "Omni-art" capable synthesizing all existing forms of artistic expression (251).[8] Moreover, he reinforced these plans with the same reading of theatrical history we have seen in Wagner and other Russian modernists. The liturgical rites from which theatre arose had been degraded, he believed, by the turn toward representation and play that produced theatre as such, until medieval mystery plays had sought to return to the religious origins of theatre (190–1). Evidence for the true "omni-art" that existed at the dawn of humanity had survived in elements of the ancient Greek drama, in which music, poetry, and dance were closely integrated (251).

The avant-garde director Vsevolod Meyerhold's extensive writings on theatre also deserve consideration here, not least because they served as an important pathway for modernist aspirations in the early Soviet era. They generally rehearse the modernist themes of crisis in the present-day theatre and the need for a radically different type of theatre with frequent references to Wagner and his idea of the "theatre of the future," for example, in his comments on the staging of *Tristan und Isolde* in the Mariinsky Theater, and to Fuchs, with his Munich *Künstlertheater* (Meierkhol'd, "K postanovke 'Tristana i Izol'dy' na Mariinskom teatre. 30 oktiabria 1909 goda," *Stat'i. Pis'ma. Rechi. Besedy. Chast' pervaia. 1891–1917* [hereafter *SPRB*] 149, 152). The present Russian theatre has fallen, Meyerhold laments, and has been reduced to either political tendentiousness or banal entertainment ("1909 g.," *SPRB* 176). The root of the problem lies in the post-Renaissance stage itself, which he derisively describes as nothing but a "box with a 'window' cut out of one of its walls facing the viewer" (""K postanovke 'Tristana i Izol'dy,'" *SPRB* 153–4) – and which, incidentally, he blames for the "incomprehension" (*nedoumenie*) of theatrical convention evident in the celebrated scene in Tolstoy's *War and Peace* in which Natasha attends the opera, which the Formalist theoretician Viktor Shklovskii offered as a prime example of the device of *ostranenie*, the "making strange" that he saw as the essence of art (154). In the present day (i.e., the early twentieth century), this failure of theatre to realize its authentic forms finds expression in the popularity of cinema, which Meyerhold interestingly sees as the expression not of technological modernity but of a retrograde vogue for mimesis, an "infatuation with quasi-naturalism" (*uvlechenie kvaziestestvennost'iu*; in "Balagan," *SPRB* 222). Cinema, one might paraphrase, leaves the historical present undisrupted. Authenticity is to be found, rather, in the historical forms of theatre that established it as an autonomous artistic activity by manifesting a certain quality of theatricality (*teatral'nost'*) rooted in the principle of play (*igra*).[9]

For Meyerhold the line bearing this healthy alternative into Russia can be traced to the introduction of *commedia dell'arte* during the reign of

Anna Ioannovna (1730–1740) and its subsequent development into the "fairground booths of the central Russian region" ("*1909 g.*," *SPRB* 182). He finds tentative efforts to create a new theatre in an array of contemporary phenomena, from Ivanov's efforts to resurrect ancient theatre (e.g., in his 1905 play *Tantal*)[10] to Blok's importation of Italian folk comedy in his play *The Fairground Booth*, Kuzmin's stylization of medieval drama, and Bely's and Remizov's efforts to return to the original genre of the mystery play (in their 1903 *Prishedshii* [*He Who Has Come*] and 1908 *Besovskoe deistvo* [*Demonic Act*], respectively) – but unlike Scriabin and other proponents of theatre as religious ritual, he insists on the primacy of theatrical *play* in any such revival (though Huizinga might remind him that play is closely bound up with ritual and that "ritual grew up in sacred play"; 159, 173). Until the creators of neomysteries leave the theatre, he warns, theatre and mystery will interfere with each other ("Balaganchik"; *SPRB* 209). He credits Scriabin with being the first to confront the dilemma of having to choose *between* theatre and mystery, and comments that "the ways of mystery and those of theatre are not joined" ("Puti Misterii i puti Teatra nesliianny," *SPRB* 249). Even while rejecting other modernists' calls for religious rite, however, Meyerhold shares their concentration on urban space. Disputing Benois's claim that "cabotinage" will ruin revitalized mystery in the theatre (*SPRB* 213), he insists that not even mystery can avoid elements of genuine theatricality, and as evidence for this he points to the historical exodus of the mystery play from the church out onto the town square. "Having sensed its helplessness, mystery began to absorb elements of folk culture embodied in the mime and had to exit the nave of the church – out across its threshold and the cemetery – onto the town square" (*SPRB* 210). Contemporary theatre should combat the dull, naturalistic theatre of "life" by giving itself over to jugglers (*SPRB* 215) and learning from the puppet theatre, in which what the public sees is pointedly *not* identical to what it knows of life (*SPRB* 216). If the principles of the *balagan* have been kicked out of the theatre, he asserts, they can be found again in cabarets, Überbrette, music halls, and theatres-Variétés (*SPRB* 223).[11]

Russian Modernist Projects

In addition to theorizing prolifically, Russian modernists produced a series of works that sought to realize these calls for theatrical renewal. One especially potent context for their experiments was the eschatological climate of the fin de siècle, which encouraged speculation on an imminent apocalypse – the final "intervention" that would resolve the tribulations of history – as well as intensified interest in the Passion, the cardinal example of "intervention" in European culture (the conspicuous orientation toward Gospel texts in Bulgakov's *The Master and Margarita* is, in part, a retrospective stocktaking of these expectations). As noted in the Introduction, Solov'ev published his *Three Conversations* on war, progress, and the end of world history, to which he appended the *Short Tale about the Antichrist* (*Kratkaia povest' ob Antikhriste*, 1899), and between 1895 and 1904 Merezhkovsky brought out his trilogy *Christ and Antichrist* (Nikolesku 41). In 1894 Rozanov published his commentary on Dostoevsky's "Legend of the Grand Inquisitor" – as we have seen, a prescient "intervention" tale in its own right. Outside Russia, Ernst Renan published *The Antichrist* in 1876 and Ibsen his play *The Emperor and the Galilean*, set in the reign of the last non-Christian emperor of Rome, Julian the Apostate, in 1873 (43). Around 1915 the composer Vladimir Rebikov planned to write (but never completed) a mystery titled *The Antichrist* that would carry its audience through the "egoism of matter" to the "victory of Spirit" (Mitchell 52).

Moreover, in early twentieth-century Russia a number of artists and groups attempted to enact some literal form of mystery; they included a Petersburg group calling itself the Order of Universal Genius Brotherhood, which sought to initiate worship through collective creative action; and Moscow's House of Song, which attempted in 1912 to produce a collective mystery based on a 1903 translation of a seventh-century text by the Indian poet Bhavabhuti (50–2). Among the artistically more significant examples of this trend is Bely's unfinished mystery play *The Antichrist* (*Antikhrist*). Written around 1901 in a mood of tense apocalyptic expectation – the appearance of the Divine Sophia was then being awaited (Nikolesku 37, 42) – the play indulges apocalyptic anxieties in a plot centred on an instance of realized "intervention." Set in a vague allegorical landscape of "temple," "city gates," "court," "lake," and so on, and saturated with references to the biblical Apocalypse ("abyss," "seraphim," etc.), Bely's draft nonetheless makes clear its orientation toward the situation in contemporary Russia. A figure identified simply as "He Who Is to Come" (*Griadushchii*) suddenly appears, surrounds himself with adepts, and announces to a population eagerly awaiting the Messiah that he will usher in a kingdom of bliss. One of his high priests, however, has doubts about his authenticity and declares him to be the Antichrist (he has been having dreams in which he sees the real Christ, who does not look like the imposter). The Antichrist has seraphim attack and kill him, then plunges the world into war ("the final battle of mankind"), which establishes the kingdom of the devil. The imposter's true identity had actually been revealed in the drama's opening scene, in which a mother shows up seeking forgiveness for her wayward son, who later confronts her and throws her into an "abyss." A subsequent conversation among spirits of the air reveals that he is in fact a prodigal monk who has involved himself in black magic and been seduced by the devil (there is an obvious indebtedness to Goethe's *Faust* here, as well as, possibly, to Chekhov's story "Chernyi monakh").

Especially notable among this farrago of themes is the anxiety that lodges in the play's ambivalence between longing for a new world and fears of total calamity and evil. The intensity of this ambivalence, palpable even in the short and incomplete draft Bely left, can serve here as an index to the modernist desire to have *that* world intervene in *this* one, here-and-now. *Past' nochi. Otryvok misterii* (*The Maw of the Night: Fragment of a Mystery*, 1906) – which Bely wrote in response to the revolution of 1905 (Nikolesku 67) – again juggles motifs of apocalyptic foreboding with those of mystical expectation. The play portrays a band of Christians in their last redoubt, on a mountain plateau where they have been hiding for three years (as Livak notes, "The Christian filiation of the intelligentsia's utopianism was acknowledged by its modernist heirs, many of whom cast themselves, at some point in their careers, as members of an apocalyptic community," 160; this orientation forms the basis of Slezkine's entire history of the Soviet era). Despite gathering gloom they meet each evening for prayers with incense, during which an elder emits his own glow. The aging prophet explains to the young girls gathered around him that the current age of darkness began when the "temple of glory" was profaned by an evil tsar and fell into ruins. Suddenly the old man straightens up and begins to radiate bright light. He declares that the forces of darkness are approaching. A mother castigates him for spreading gloom and tempting them to "this dark island." Her child, whose tender hands she says are destined for crucifixion, throws a handful of the prophet's "light" at his mother, whose dress is then covered with golden circles of light and flowers. But he then says he is afraid, and the drama ends as a voice in the darkness declares, "Woe!" (*Gore!*).

Apocalyptic motifs of the world's ending mixed with vague gestures toward a mystic cult that might inaugurate a new era similarly inform Fedor Sologub's audaciously titled *Liturgiia mne* (*A Liturgy for Me*, 1907). Set nowhere in particular, the drama portrays a ritual that mixes more or less Christian elements (there is a pure youth who is ready to sacrifice himself and offers his blood to be drunk) with neo-Greek ones (a chorus, groups of virgins dressed in white). The motifs of the world's end come in the form of fleeting reference to an evil dragon that has been defeated and a temple built in opposition to him, but in the end no more specific message is offered than that the pure youth (*otrok*, who is linked at the end with the symbol of the Orthodox six-pointed cross) is in all and in every one, and that we should love him.[12] The clearest hope for "intervention" comes when youths bearing votive candles recite "Pridi, / blazhennyi uteshitel'! / Svershi tainstvennyi obriad" ("Come blessed Comforter! / Perform the secret rite," 10), while in his moment of advent the adolescent saviour seems to anticipate Blok's *The Twelve* of 1918: as the ritual starts, the stage direction reads, "A monk with a white tulip in his hand appears. He is wearing only a short toga fastened with a belt of yellow silk" (16).[13]

A work that brings us closer to the Soviet context – especially via its ironic and carnivalesque treatment of the mystery genre – is Remizov's *Demonic Act*. The play was first performed on 4 December 1907 in the V.F. Kommissarzhevskaia Theatre in Petersburg, directed by F.F. Kommissarzhevskii, with music by the poet Mikhail Kuzmin and sets designed by Mstislav Dobuzhinksii. An allegorical drama in three acts, it features a pair of devils who try but fail to take possession of the soul of a righteous monk (*podvizhnik*). The monk is protected by a guardian angel until Death finally claims him. The theme of demonic rampage can be viewed as an instance of "intervention" in its own right and anticipates Bulgakov's novel. If Bulgakov was aware of Remizov's play he might have noticed the Hebrew (or quasi-Hebrew) names of the devils – Aratyr' and Timelikh – as well as the fact that the action takes place on Easter Eve, a calendrical siting that sets Remizov's play squarely within the tradition of the mystery genre and Passion plays. Like those in Bulgakov's novel, the devils are mostly comical figures, at once inept and given to pithy folk retorts, such as calling Death "a cemetery whore" (*kladbishchenskaia shliukha*, 89). At one point they are accompanied by equally comic – or carnivalesque – "masks" (as Remizov designates them in the list of *dramatis personae*) of an ox, bear, mare, and wolf (cf. the tradition of including animal personages, such as the poodle in *Faust* and Bulgakov's own cat Behemoth). Other conventional elements of the mystery genre that Remizov reproduces, as Bulgakov later would, are the *besovskoe deistvo* itself, a scene at the end of Act Two in which a group of demons sings in a terrifying choir, circling faster and faster outside the righteous monk's cave (63), and the swift end to their schemes, which comes when lightning strikes the cave, a light shines, and the traditional Easter greeting "Khristos voskrese iz mertvykh" ("Christ is risen from the dead") resounds. The setting of part of the play in hell – a staple of Russian Passion tales in particular (cf. *Khozhdenie bogoroditsy po mukam*) – also looks forward to Mayakovsky's *Mystery-Bouffe*: it is the same dramatic device and genre at work, the same cultural logic of a mystery play self-consciously revived in order to disrupt the present and render it open to the absolute. *Besovskoe deistvo* also brings the modernist interest in eschatological themes into contact with the genre of the *balagan*. Janet Kennedy draws a parallel between Remizov's play and the devils tending flames of hell in the paintings mounted over the showman's booth in Benois's design for the carnival showbooth in Stravinsky's *Petrushka* (the canonical example of Russian modernist appeal to the fairground tradition), as well as with the more general "diabolical element" in the ballet (60). In fact, she remarks, "there is evidence that when working on *Petrushka*, Benois still vividly recollected Remizov's play, in which the action – as in Petrushka – takes place at Shrovetide" (61). Further evidence for this link is the devils guarding the door of Petrushka's chamber in Benois's stage designs for the ballet, which she suggests may have come from Dobuzhinsky's set for Remizov's play. The 1925 Copenhagen production also featured a comet on the theatre curtain, which had no relation to the scenario of the ballet and "can only be explained as a strong indication of the profound impression made on Benois by *Besovskoe deistvo*" (62).[14]

A bridge between the motifs of Remizov's plays and the constellation of concerns in the early Soviet era can be found in Evreinov's *Samoe glavnoe* (*The Most Important Thing*), written four years after the October Revolution, in 1921. In effect a theatrical manifesto and modernist allegory of aestheticism, the play makes essentially no mention of politics at all (apart from brief references to socialism as a redistributor of roles in life) and seems to unfold in a world in which the revolution of 1917 has not taken place (perhaps not surprisingly: this is a covert debate about what "saves" the world). The "most important thing" of the title turns out to be the realization that life is theatre, that there is no real boundary between theatre and life, and that the present day amounts to a revived *commedia dell'arte* in life as well as theatre. The slim plot revolves around a provincial theatrical troupe that signs a contract with a mysterious visiting entrepreneur to assume roles and put on a "performance" among the petit-bourgeois residents of a boarding house with the apparent aim of dissuading a young student from committing suicide (with lots of comedy involving romantic intrigue along the way). Its centre of gravity, however, lies in the mysterious person of the entrepreneur, who appears in a succession of guises: first as a female fortune teller, then as one "Dr. Fregoli," the theatrical entrepreneur, then in the play-within-the-play as Schmidt, an insurance salesman, then during a *maslenitsa* celebration as Harlequin and a monk, while the cast list informs us that he is in reality "Paraclete" – the Greek name for the Holy Spirit. Evreinov deploys this character as a trickster who invades whatever world is at hand (a provincial theatre, a petit-bourgeois boarding house) in order to introduce another, more authentic theatre, specifically in the form of revived *commedia dell'arte*). A Mephistophelean devil equipped with preternatural knowledge of human desires whose own motives remain opaque (the theatre director tells him, "You are a strange man, Dr. Fregoli, and listening to you one doesn't know whether you are serious or joking," 35), he induces the provincial actors to sign a contract with him, then speaks German, like Bulgakov's Woland, when in the role of Schmidt, an insurance salesman (moreover, in a mock incantation, declaring, "*Ein, zwei, drei*, and everything is transformed!" when they are moving furniture to make way for the *maslenitsa* carnival in the boarding house, 110; cf. Korov'ev's German counting in accompaniment to a magic act in the Variety Theatre in *The Master and Margarita* – both instances clearly reminiscent of *Faust*). Moreover, the actors believe him to be a wealthy American with some kind of scheme (the play thus inscribes itself in the line of Faust works discussed in chapter 1).[15] But as the *raissoneur* of the play's aesthetic statement he is a Christ-like figure (however ironic) who has come to save the world. Toward the end of the play he remarks, in the guise of a monk, "Let the judgment take place [*pust' sovershitsia pravosudie* – as we have seen, the impulse toward judgment is an embedded reflex in mystery plays] and may I be punished for the pity which prompted me to save you all … The path of Paraclete always leads to Golgotha … that's in the nature of things" (131). The message this spirit bears into the world is that "illusion in life is more durable than illusion on the theatrical stage" (124); that "All life's a stage" – the familiar passage from Shakespeare's *As You Like It*, recited on a gramophone record played by Schmidt during the festivities in Act Four (105); and that *commedia dell'arte* has been resurrected, for life as well as for the theatre (Harlequin's declaration toward the play's end, 136).

What is striking about Evreinov's play is how much of the modernist revival of medieval theatre and Passion play context it invokes: when the theatre director asks "Dr. Fregoli" if he really thinks he has found the way to save the world (*put' k spaseniu mira*, 37 – later specified as "the actor and his magical art," coming down from the theatrical stage to enter the world – itself a mini-plot of "intervention," 69), Fregoli responds that he has come into the world to testify to truth (*istina*). The director then asks, "But what is truth?" – and the stage directions instruct him to look at Fregoli inquisitorially (*ispytuiushche*) "like Pilate looking at Christ" (37). When the actors ask "Fregoli" why he would stoop to hiring provincial actors for his scheme he replies that "the Great Teacher's disciples did not ask him why he sought them in Galilee rather than in Jerusalem" (67); that is, this is a moment of "truth's" incognito intervention in the world, akin to that of Christ's appearance on earth. Moreover the play the actors are rehearsing when "Fregoli" hires them is a stage adaptation of Sienkiewicz's *Quo Vadis?*, itself a tale of "intervention" whose title comes from the apocryphal question posed by the apostle Peter, who, fleeing Rome and likely crucifixion, meets Christ on the road – returned to earth ("intervention") to undergo a second crucifixion because Peter flees his own. The crowd of mummers (*riazhennye*) at the *maslenitsa* festivities includes both *commedia dell'arte* characters and figures from the *Quo Vadis* play, a mixing of fairground booth and Passion that recalls, possibly intentionally, Blok's *The Twelve*, with which this play is arguably in dialogue (e.g., at one point during the rehearsal of *Quo Vadis* white paper roses are showered down on the actors). Nor does the play fail to invoke *Faust*, with its sense of human deal-making and searching for another reality. The German "Schmidt" is reminiscent of Mephistopheles; indeed, at one point one of the characters starts humming Mephistopheles's theme from Gounod's opera (prompting Schmidt to comment that "that's from a different opera," 99), and the record placed on the grammophone after Shakespeare's *As You Like It* is one of Faust and Margarita's duet from Boito's opera *Mefistofele* (one could also note the possible parallel between the fireworks – *bengal'skie ogni* – the director sets off at the end and the master of ceremonies Bengalskii in the Variety Theatre in Bulgakov's novel).

Modernist Interest in Puppet Theatre

As part of their search for "primitive" dramatic forms and their interest in aesthetic "play" as an antidote to naturalistic representation and the bourgeois culture it was felt to represent, modernists across Europe in the late nineteenth and early twentieth centuries often turned to the puppet theatre – a form whose cultic roots were discussed in chapter 2. Puppetry, marionette plays, mime, and shadow shows were revived in Germany, Austria, France, Italy, Spain, Poland, and Russia, especially in cabarets – themselves a product of fin-de-siècle culture (Segel, *Turn-of-the Century-Cabaret* 66; see also his *Pinocchio's Progeny*). *Ombres chinoises* were the predominant attraction at Le Chat Noir in late nineteenth-century Paris, while at the Caran d'Ache the shadow play *1808*, consisting of episodes from the Napoleonic campaign, complete with interludia as in a mystery play, was popular (Segel, *Turn-of-the Century-Cabaret* 31, 70). Shadow shows and puppetry were also popular at Els Quatre Gats in Barcelona, and puppet shows on political topics were popular in Berlin and Kraków (160, 249). In Vienna, Egon Friedell and Alfred Pogar's *Grotesque in Two Scenes*, which in its day toured widely, was a parody of

Goethe (205–6). Alfred Jarry's *Ubu Roi* was originally conceived as a puppet show (211). The Letuchaia mysh' (Bat) cabaret in Moscow featured "living doll" routines, in which live actors posed in a tableau, which then came to life with dancing, songs, and dialogue only to return at the end to its inanimate state (Segel, *Pinocchio's Progeny* 58, 73).

Like the mystery play and ancient Greek theatre, puppet theatre appealed to the fin de siècle because of its seeming opposition to conventionally realistic "bourgeois" theatre. Puppets, dolls, marionettes, and their like re-enchant the world, restoring a sense of play and wonder as an antidote to the "materialist-practical age" (Oskar Schlemmer, quoted in Koss 215). The puppet theatre's diminutive, pointedly artificial, toy-like aspect lent itself to a playful aestheticism that would have been impossible in realist drama. It was also associated with the folk culture of the lower classes, who in this way offered a detour around the bourgeoisie and its realist tastes, and which had its natural locus in the town square or in the *déclassé* domain of the fairground. If the mixture of foolery and mysticism evident in venues like Le Chat Noir in Paris (Segel, *Turn-of-the-Century Cabaret* 73) seems to anticipate some of the paradoxical tonality of Evreinov's *The Most Important Thing* and Bulgakov's *The Master and Margarita*, a still more specific parallel is suggested by Moscow's Letuchaia mysh' cabaret, whose puppet and "living doll" shows often parodied dramatic works recently performed at the Moscow Artistic Theatre (Segel, *Turn-of-the-Century Cabaret* 261–2). One notes, too, that one target of Evreinov's parodic *Chetvertaia stena* (*The Fourth Wall* 1915) is Fedor Kommissarzhvskii's production of Goethe's *Faust* at K. Nezlobin's theatre in Moscow in September 1912 (299). Further evidence, if any were needed, for the imminence in Russian minds of the Faust precedent is the fact that the Brodiachaia sobaka (Stray Dog) cabaret in St. Petersburg was actually conceived as a Faustian tavern, with a "fantastic huge fireplace" (305); and it was here on 6 January 1913 that Kuzmin's playfully self-conscious Nativity play *Rozhdestvo Khristovo. Vertep kukol'nyi* (*Christmas: A Puppet Play*) was staged.

Modernist interest in the puppet theatre owed much to a Romantic precedent – Heinrich von Kleist's 1810 sketch "Über das Marionettentheater" ("On the Marionette Theatre"),[16] in which the narrator encounters a dancer and expresses surprise at having seen him several times at the puppet theatre, which he dismisses as a "vulgar art form." On the contrary, the dancer responds, marionettes are free from affectation because they lack intent and are able to allow their bodies to react only to the laws of physics affecting their centre of gravity. They dance more gracefully than humans, who have more mass to move around. If the puppet's unconscious but graceful line of movement could be imitated by a human dancer, it would be "the path taken by the dancer's soul." "In the organic world," the dancer further remarks, "as thought grows dimmer and weaker, grace emerges more brilliantly and decisively. [It] appears most purely in that human form which either has no consciousness or an infinite consciousness. That is, in the puppet or in the god" (quoted in Nelson 62–3; one already notes here the longing to rise above the "organic world" that later reappears as modernism's desire to escape history).

A particularly important conduit for the modernist reprisal of Kleist's ideas (which he "undoubtedly knew"; Segel, *Pinocchio's Progeny* 55) was Edward Gordon Craig. Craig was well-known in Russia, having been invited in 1911 to work with Stanislavsky on a production of *Hamlet* for the Moscow Art Theatre (Rudnitsky 13). In his discussion of "the actor and the Über-marionette" in his *Art of the Theatre* Craig uses puppets as an occasion for promoting the aestheticism and anti-realism characteristic of much fin-de-siècle modernism. He begins by declaring the contemporary theatre to be in a "wretched state" (2); he then declares that if it is to embrace its true aim, which is art, it should begin by "banishing from the Theatre this idea of impersonation, this idea of reproducing Nature" (i.e., what Meyerhold would call "naturalistic" theatre, 75). He further laments the exaggerated "personalities" paraded on the stage by star actors, who by drawing attention to themselves obscure the underlying ideas of the author – the true artist, in Craig's view. The remedy for this would be for actors to become puppet-like, "Über-marionettes," whose strictly regulated movements would make it possible once again for them to serve as "the faithful medium for the beautiful thoughts of the artist" (84; he cites as his aesthetic ideal Flaubert's notion of the God-like artist who is everywhere in his creation but nowhere visible, 77).[17]

In his contribution to the *O teatre* collection, Meyerhold comments that the Belgian playwright Maurice Maeterlinck similarly embraced the ideal of the marionette because for him actors on the contemporary stage had become too expressive, too extrovert, and were thereby robbing plays of inner mystery, which puppet-like acting could restore (125). Maeterlinck himself echoes Craig's disparagement of realistic representation:

> The poem traditionally was a work of art and bore those oblique and admirable distinguishing marks. But then the representation comes along and contradicts it. It causes the swans on the pond to fly off; it flings the pearls into the abyss. It sets things back to exactly where they were before the poet came on the scene. The mystical density of the work of art has evaporated. In contrast to a poem, theatrical representation produces roughly

the same effect as if you extended a painting into life ... in contrast to the mystical rapture you had previously experienced, you would suddenly find yourself to be like a blind man on the high seas. ("Small Talk: The Theatre," in *On the Art of the Theatre* 296; cf. Craig's notion that actors get in the way of the author's "beautiful ideas")[18]

For all the enthusiasm modernists had for puppets and the puppet theatre in the fin de siècle, a distinct ambivalence nonetheless informed their attraction to them, perhaps because of the inherent liminality of the art form. On the one hand, as a diminutive object the puppet is an element of play, offering liberation from bourgeois normality through a return to childhood, a flight to lower-class forms of entertainment associated with an urban milieu. On the other hand it represents an ontological threat: the anthropomorphic puppet mirrors but also competes with and even threatens to displace us. What attracted the modernists to this form was precisely its facility for drawing attention to aesthetic boundaries, for pointing up the difference between performance and reality, between the patently fabricated puppets and the persons they were supposed to represent, even between the "childlike" aspect of the play – and death. As Lotman suggests in an essay on the cultural significance of puppets:

> [W]hat makes the puppet special is that, even as it crosses over into the world of adults, it carries with it memories of a childlike, folkloric, mythological, and playful world [...] That it can be compared with a living being enhances the deathly aspect (*mertvennost'*) of the puppet [...] The motifs of bringing a dead semblance to life and turning a living being into an immobile representation are universal in mythology [...] The puppet turns out to reside at the intersection of the ancient myth of the statue brought to life and the new mythology of dead machine life [...] Thus in our cultural consciousness did two faces, as it were, of the puppet were formed: one lures us into the cosy world of childhood, the other is associated with pseudolife, dead motion, and death pretending to be life. The first looks to the world of folklore, fairy tales, and the primitive. The second reminds us of the machine quality of our civilization, alienation, and duplicity. ("Kukly v sisteme kul'tury" 378–9)[19]

Rainer Maria Rilke's 1921 "Puppen" ("Puppets"), an essay written after a visit to the life-sized wax figures made by a Munich puppeteer, registers a similar ambivalence. For Rilke the doll's combination of human appearance with inhuman nature is unsettling, and in our childhood triggers our first sense of disunity with the world (since the doll cannot talk back, and a child's conversation with a doll can only be a conversation with itself). The wariness toward machine culture in Lotman's commentary also figures vividly in Walter Benjamin's celebrated *Arcades Project* (*Passagenwerk*, 1927–40). After noting the charms of tailor's dummies by Karl Gutzkow and of a puppet show at the Ombres Chinoises in which a "demoiselle" danced while generating still more puppet-demoiselles, Benjamin shifts to a negative mode, quoting Paul Lindau on the horrors of the "automatons" that dolls are as well as J.-K. Huysmans on the grotesquerie of disassembled shop mannikins in the Rue Legendre, "a whole series of female busts, without heads or legs, with curtain hooks in place of arms" (*The Arcades Project* 694).[20] Benjamin then quotes a passage from a letter Marx sent to Engels in which he speculates that the Industrial Revolution proper began when the mechanisms of automatic devices (clocks, in this instance) were transposed onto manufacturing machines, thus creating automatons that had no need for "the human hand" to make their goods (695–6).

In the broadest sense, this unease can be seen as emanating from the cultic origin of puppets discussed in chapter 2. If puppets engender an uncanny disenchantment with the world, their very liminal quality – the source of our unease about the puppet theatre – may also contribute to an awareness of their cultic potential, in which also resides their potential for disrupting quotidian reality. In chapter 2 we saw the role puppets historically played as ritual objects, points of contact with the supernatural, and devices for bringing it into the material world. What ultimately happens to this trait in the modernist revival of the puppet theatre is that the cultic moment of "intervention" becomes a device for interrupting *history* as the realm that determines meaning in human lives. Victoria Nelson notes that in the nineteenth and twentieth centuries the notion of the supernatural was relegated to popular entertainment (8; a shift noted earlier in the Faust legend's "descent" from the stage to the puppet theatre). Indeed, in her account the true turning point in Western culture's emergence into modernity came with the "drastic reinterpretation of reality as a material world in which one's only transcendental link to God is internal" (56). Puppets thereby become a reservoir of "repressed religious" belief (20), a function in which, in fact, they draw on a much earlier history of transcendent connotations. In ancient cultures, god-statues gave access to the spiritual world, enabling "the drawing down of the divine into the material world and the simultaneous raising up of the human soul during life to the transcendental land" (35). In ancient Egypt dolls and embalmed bodies were closer to the divine body "because their static, unchanging nature imitates the permanence of the immortal (38; there is something of this notion in Kleist's view of puppets). In early twelfth-century Spain Abraham ibn Ezra "interpreted the golden calf as a legal way to bring down astral powers into matter" (51), while behind the golem legend of Prague stands an older mystical tradition of achieving contact with God by creating a micro-*anthropos* – just as the Neoplatonists believed in calling down astral powers into mnemonic statues (55).

Puppets thus appealed to the modernists as a potent way out of the present and its representational forms. Even Craig, once he has outlined his aestheticist reading of puppets, moves beyond it toward a cultic reading. The puppet, he remarks, "is a descendant of the stone images of the old temples," and "the marionette appears to me to be the last echo of some noble and beautiful art of a past civilization" (82). The function of this marionette in the revived theatre that Craig imagines will not be to "compete with life" but to "go beyond it" in order to establish contact with nothing less than the afterlife. Its ideal will be not the naturalistic body but "the body in a trance – it will aim to clothe itself with a death-like beauty while exhaling a living spirit" (84–5). If the forms that appear on the stage are still taken from empirical reality, their "colour" should come from "that unknown land of the imagination, and what is that but the land where dwells that which we call Death?" (89). In support of this vision Craig appends an invented history reminiscent, in its orientalism, of Scriabin's plans for the grand theatre-temple that would house his *Mysterium*. Puppets, he asserts, are "the descendants of a great and noble family of Images, images which were indeed made 'in the likeness of God'" (90). They originated in India in a (fanciful) "ceremony" (he does not provide further anthropological specification) that celebrated existence but also, more sombrely, the second existence that will follow death; in fact, he comments, the first actors were women who, not fully understanding this ceremony, decided to imitate it and staged a "poor parody" of its puppet-hero. The revival of the theatre that Craig hopes for will be signalled by the return of this "Über-marionette," at which point "it will be possible for people to return to their ancient joy in ceremonies – once more will Creation be celebrated – homage rendered to existence – and divine and happy *intercession* made to Death" (94, emphasis added).

Maeterlinck too ponders the marionette or something like it as an alternative to realism, precisely because it straddles the ontological divide between living and dead. "It is difficult," he continues,

> to predict by what class of lifeless beings humans onstage ought to be replaced, but it seems to me that the strange impressions that we experience in waxworks museums, for example, should have been able, long

ago, to set us on the track of a new art, an art of the dead. We would then have onstage beings without destinies, whose identity would no longer erase that of the hero. It also seems to me that any being that has the appearance of life without being alive calls for extraordinary powers, and it is within the realm of possibility that these powers may be of exactly the same nature as those to which the poem calls for [sic]. Is the terror inspired by these beings, who are similar to us, but visibly endowed with a dead soul, due to the fact that they are absolutely devoid of mystery? Is it due to the fact that they are not steeped in eternity? Is it terror, born precisely from the subtraction of terror that surrounds every living being, and that is so inevitable and so customary that its absence frightens us, just as a person without a shadow or an army without weapons would alarm us? Is it the allure of our ordinary clothes on bodies without destinies? Are we terrified by the gestures and words of a being similar to us, because we know that these gestures and these words, by a monstrous exception, have no echo and have been chosen by no eternity? Is it because they cannot die? – I do not know; but the atmosphere of terror in which they abide is the very atmosphere of the poem; these are consequently the dead who seem to speak to us in venerable tones. It is thus possible, after all that the soul of the poet, no longer finding the place destined for him, occupied by a soul as powerful as his – since all souls are equally powerful – it is possible that the soul of the poet or of the hero, no longer refuses to descend for a moment, into a being whose jealous soul does not come to forbid him entrance. (*A Maeterlinck Reader* 299)

In this light it is no surprise that for all the puppet show's affinity for satire and topical themes, the mystery genre was in fact never far from its repertoire – a tacit acknowledgment, again, of the form's cultic potential. The French Symbolist Maurice Boucher wrote full-length mystery plays (*mystéres*) for Henri Signoret's marionette theatre in Paris, the Petit-Théâtre. Among shadow plays were *La Marche à L'Étoile*, a Nativity play, and *The Temptation of St. Anthony*, set in modern-day Paris (Segel, *Turn-of-the Century-Cabaret* 72). Even Hanns Freiher von Gumppenberg's parody of "mystery-mongering" by "Ibsenites and Maeterlinkians" (in Segel 163) testifies to the prominence of the mystery genre in these venues.

The diminutive size of the puppet theatre may have also played a role in modernism's awareness of its thematic capacities. Its small stage and actors facilitated the perception that what it portrayed was not a fragment of the "real" world but an *entire* world in itself: hence its ready association with the *theatrum mundi* tradition (Clayton, *Pierrot in Petrograd* 10). Clayton also cites an interest in *Kleinkunst*, in "the miniaturization of culture" originating in German *Jugendstil*, as one impulse behind the Russian fascination with *balagan* in the early twentieth century. Segal also characterizes cabarets as "an experiment in *Gesamtkunswerk* in miniature" (*Turn-of-the-Century Cabaret* 20). It was also the puppet theatre's diminutive size that inspired the French Symbolist Maurice Boucher to write full-length mystery plays (*mystéres*) for Henri Signoret's marionette theatre in Paris, the Petit-Théâtre. Segel argues that the existence of the puppet-theatre inspired Boucher to attempt to "transfer the popular turn-of-the-century neomystery play to the diminutive arena of the puppet stage." In the introduction to his *Mystéres païens* Boucher himself explained that such phenomena as the appearance of St. Michael, the miraculous flowering of lilies and roses, and the transfiguration of a martyr "are more appropriate to our small stage than to conventional theaters where the personality of the actor, too real and too familiar, destroys all impression of the supernatural" (quoted in Segel, *Pinocchio's Progeny*, 79, 83).

The most renowned example of the puppet theatre that so fascinated Russian modernists is Stravinsky's ballet *Petrushka*, which transposes an entire tradition of the genre and its *commedia dell'arte* roots that goes back some distance in Russian culture.[21] As early as 1869 in his "Raek" (the name for a type of puppet theatre that is the diminutive of the Russian word for "paradise," *rai*). Mussorgsky had stylized the rhymed patter with which the barker (*raeshnyi ded*) would lure passersby to his peep show. Blok's 1906 *The Fairground Booth* (on which more below) recreates a fairground puppet booth as the scene of its action, and beginning in 1913 preservationists in St. Petersburg revived *balagan* performances on the Field of Mars (Clark, *Petersburg* 92). At the height of modernist theatrical experimentation Evreinov, Meyerhold, and Tairov all devoted extensive commentary to the puppet theatre in their theoretical works and drew on its techniques in their directing (Bogatyrev 11).[22]

In Russia as in Western Europe, interest in puppet theatre (as well as the related genre of *commedia dell'arte*) was part of the general rejection of realism in the late nineteenth and early twentieth centuries. As an exaggeratedly aestheticized genre (at least when compared with the realist dramas that had preceded it) and, in its puppet version, a toylike and miniaturized form, the *balagan* lent itself to Russian modernists' interest in metatheatrical themes, to stagings of a play-within-the-play and other foregroundings of theatrical convention – that is, to demonstrations of "theatricality as such" (Clayton, *Pierrot in Petrograd* 159–60). But in Russia, as Clayton suggests, the *balagan* was also embraced as nothing less than a program for changing the world (6, 8):

This Russian version of the *théâtre forain* had as its main figure Petrushka, in whom it was easy to see a Russian version of the *paillasse (paiats)* or fool (*shut*) Petruccio/Pierrot/Struwelpeter. Thus *balagan* becomes a key word in Russian versions of commedia dell'arte, called in Russian *ital'ianskaia komediia masok* (Italian comedy of masks). In addition to its direct meaning of the fairground show (and the booth in which this was held), the word had come to be a general term of opprobrium for any manifestation of disorder or scandal, rather like the English "farce." (10)

Interest in the puppet theatre, as in the cabaret, was another aspect of the general "theatricalization of Russian life in the early twentieth century" – itself a response to "the greater social and political unreality around [artists and intellectuals]" (Segel, *Turn-of-the-Century Cabaret* 320). Echoes of the modernist fascination with the *balagan* reverberate in Bulgakov's *The Master and Margarita* as well. Gasparov notes that the black magic performance in the Variety Theatre is simultaneously a parody of the miracles Christ performed and a Black Sabbath – the place itself symbolically functioning as both temple and *balagan*. Moscow in the novel itself becomes the site of a demonic orgy (*besovskii shabash*) – its "interventionist" mode – and thus an expanded *balagan* ("Iz nabliudenii nad motivnoi strukturoi," 46–7).

One additional factor that made the puppet theatre particularly important in Russian in contrast to Western modernism was its even closer association with the city, its decidedly urban identity – and together with that its association with the lower classes that were soon to become the object of Soviet state attention. As Bakhtin suggests, the city historically serves as the prime site for disrupting the established order of the world: "in the Middle Ages and even into the Renaissance unofficial folk culture had its own special territory: the town square, and its own special time – holidays and fair days. This holiday square [...] constituted a special second world within the official mediaeval world" (this is Bakhtin's celebrated notion of "carnival"; *Tvorchestvo Fransua Rable* 166).[23] In Russia the Petrushka play in particular was associated with urban settings. Kelly notes that, notwithstanding attempts by some scholars to claim origins going back to the seventeenth century (Olearius records a puppet performance in Moscow in 1637) or even earlier (the *skomorokh*, a kind of medieval jester in Russia), the best available historical evidence suggests that the Petrushka play first appeared in Russia in the 1840s – in the capital St. Petersburg, gateway for Western influences in Russia – rather than deep in the culturally traditional countryside (50, 78). Unlike the marionette theatre, an indoor genre, the glove-puppet Petrushka play was always performed "outdoors, in fairgrounds, courtyards, streets, squares, the marketplace" (58). As such it also tended to focus "the conflicts and differences of the inner areas of cities," especially St. Petersburg and Moscow, so as to serve as a carnival genre (in Bakhtin's sense of a reversal of cultural hierarchies) manifesting "a high degree of social and sexual aggression" (84, 106).

Russian urban holiday entertainments in general represented a domesticated version of forms imported from the West (Italian *commedia dell'arte*, German organ-grinders grinding). In St. Petersburg they overflowed fairgrounds and occupied squares and regions of the city specifically delineated for them (Senderovich and Shvarts, "'Verbnaia shtuchka" 94). The attractions included Shrovetide sleigh rides, swings and merry-go-rounds, *balagan* theatres and circuses, puppet theatres, panoramas, and booths selling sweets and toys (94). During holidays like Shrovetide, Mars Field in St. Petersburg was filled with *balagan* theatres (95). This whole culture of urban folk entertainments (*gorodskie narodnye gulianiia*) belonged to an older form of theatre native to city squares, in which the populace itself took part (the *zazyvala* would work the crowd while Petrushka engaged in dialogue with him; 96). As Gasparov suggests, the motley entourage that descends on Moscow in Bulgakov's novel also derives from this culture – and one notes that part of the merry grotesquery defining Petrushka is other characters' reference to him as "Monsieur" (a corrupted *mus'e* in Russian, 100) – just as Woland's companions address him.[24]

As it happens, an important precursor of the Petrushka show in Russia was German and Austrian puppet-theatre comedies based on the Faust legend, another way in which the Faust text entered Russian cultural consciousness.[25] As we have seen, among theatrical directors Evreinov adapted the Faust theme – suggesting, again, the intertwining relevance of these various phenomena: the Faust legend, the mystery genre, and puppet theatre (on Everinov, see Senderovich and Shvarts, "Starichok iz evreev"). Moreover in Russia the puppet theatre of the early twentieth century retained closer ties to its cultic religious origins than it did in Western Europe because it remained rooted in the *vertep*, *raek*, and *balagan* traditions and was relatively free of the influence of secular Western European marionette theatre, whose ties to medieval mystery are indisputable but more deeply buried (thus by the time a German marionette theatre opened in the late eighteenth century in St. Petersburg, a vigorous provincial fairground tradition already existed).[26] Perhaps because of the closeness of this cultic memory, in Russia the diminutive stage and actors of the puppet theatre still more readily facilitated the perception of what it portrayed as not a fragment of the "real" world but as an *entire* world in itself – with the suggestion hovering over every performance that the *balagan* onstage, with its emphatic disorder, scandal, and farce, mirrored political and social disorder outside; thus, perhaps, ultimately the *balagan* even came to serve as a general sign for the overthrowing of power (Clayton, *Pierrot in Petrograd* 14, 235). At the same time its essential insubstantiality – the fact that on the fairground it could be folded up in an instant – lent itself to an eschatological view of that world: a miniature view of the world as a whole, which quickly passes away (similar apocalyptic connotations are mobilized in Blok's *The Fairground Booth* as well as Nabokov's *Priglashenie na kazn'* [*Invitation to a Beheading*], which pointedly looks back to Blok's play).

The significance of the puppet theatre for Russian modernism, especially its fusion of urban setting and eschatology and its ready accommodation of episodes of "intervention," becomes particularly apparent in the works of Aleksandr Blok, which played an important role in conveying the mental habitus of "intervention" to the Soviet era. Blok's *The Fairground Booth*, for example, explicitly embraces the puppet theatre as a medium for metatheatrical commentary on life (Lotman, "Blok i narodnaia kul'tura goroda" 196). Although it was designed for performance in a conventional theatre (it was first staged by Meyerhold, who used it as an opportunity to deploy his concept of "biomechanics" by having the actors behave like puppets, on 30 December 1906 in Kommisarzhevskaia's Dramatic Theatre in Petersburg), *The Fairground Booth* looks to the urban entertainment of the fairground for its model. Like its near contemporary, Stravinsky's 1910–11 ballet *Petrushka*, it exemplifies the modernist interest in folk entertainment as an alternative to theatrical conventionality, implicitly turning to "primitive" forms for renewal. The vector of its meanings thus points outward, from the conventional theatre, which it works to dismantle, to the street.

The action in the play is intentionally simple and naive, a fusion of the *commedia dell'arte* genre with the puppet theatre of Russian fairgrounds. Pierrot pursues his fiancée Columbine, who is lured away by Harlequin; but when Harlequin tries to possess her, she falls into the snow. Harlequin then laments the world's indifference to the "springtime fête" he had wanted to arrange – and leaps out the window. There is a ball at which a clown is struck with a stage-prop sword and profusely bleeds cranberry juice. The play ends with Pierrot in his traditional pose alone on a stage from which all decorations have disappeared, lamenting the loss of Columbine and his own *ennui* ("Mne ochen' grustno. A vam smeshno?"). Even this insubstantial action is repeatedly punctuated by farcical episodes. When Columbine first appears, a group of mystics sitting around a table decide, in a parody of the era's apocalyptic expectations, that she is Death, because on her back there is a *kosa* (a pun in

Russian, because the word can mean either "braid" or "scythe"; the pun is even commented on in the play – and there is another, on "Pierrot," which sounds like the word for "pen," *pero*; Blok, *Sobranie sochinenii*, vol. 3, 18).[27] The "author" of the play also repeatedly interrupts it in order to disclaim responsibility for the course that events have taken.

In part what Blok is doing in the play is settling scores with Symbolism. For contemporaries, the love triangle it portrays transparently reflected a real-life subtext, the relations between his wife L.D. Mendeleeva-Blok, Andrei Bely, and Sergei Solov'ev, the latter two of whom were offended by the play (Orlov 129). The comical "mystics" who ponderously deliberate over the events in the play parody the mystical pretentions of the Symbolists, with whose cult of the "Beautiful Lady" Blok had grown disenchanted, as well as the "death-obsessed theatre of Maeterlinck" (Clayton, "The Play-within-the-play" 76). But the play's meanings go far beyond its author's personal crisis. Its aesthetic point lies in its assertion of the puppet-like artificiality – *kukol'nost'* – of reality. In this regard the title can be taken as a synonym for "life," that is, the idea that life is nothing but an insubstantial and farcical puppet show characterized by insufficient authenticity. Pierrot calls Columbine his "cardboard bride" (*kartochnaia nevesta*), the clown (*paiats*) who bleeds cranberry juice flops puppet-like over a railing, the distance into which Harlequin leaps when he jumps through the window turns out to be painted on paper (*Dal', vidimiaia v okne, okazyvaetsia narisovannoi na bumage*, read the stage directions; *Sobranie sochinenii*, vol. 3, 19).

Blok's metaphor of "life as puppet theatre" is of course consistent with the Symbolist belief in otherworldliness: apparent reality turns out to be insubstantial because behind it stands another, more authentic realm – but what is significant here is that this reality is contained *within* the form of the puppet theatre. In *The Fairground Booth* Blok plays on the proximity of puppet theatre to ontological thresholds: the puppet-theatre conceit effectively asserts an eschatological ramping up of the events. At the culminating moment, the scenery "suddenly rolls up and flies up and away" ("No vnezapno vse dokoratsii vzivaiutsia i uletaiut vverkh," *Sobranie sochinenii*, vol. 3, 19). As Clayton comments, the abrupt removal of scenery and the presence of the author on the stage conspicuously appeal to the *theatrum mundi* tradition, which purports to encompass the whole of life on the stage (*Pierrot in Petrograd* 144). But the rolling up of the scenery also invokes an apocalyptic motif, the passage in the Book of Revelation in which the Lamb of God opens up the sixth seal, whereupon "the sky vanished like a scroll that is rolled up, and every mountain and island was removed from its place" (Revelation 6:14; in Russian, "i nebo skrylos', svivshis', kak svitok"). The quasi-naive artificiality of the play is thus ironically reversed: instead of a playfulness that makes no serious claims on "reality" it makes the ultimate claim by staging the end of, or at least an exit from, reality itself (effectively a synonym for the disruption of history – here, empirical reality – and "intervention" that figures elsewhere in Russian modernism). The puppet theatre here offers itself not as a minor *part* of the urban space it implicitly occupies (assuming the fairground booth is in its traditional setting) but as its totalizing and transforming agent. The quality of *kukol'nost'* that seems most immediately to serve as a sign of artificiality imports another representational mode as well: that of ritual, *obriadovost'*. We are back in the puppet theatre that is the direct descendant of the temple (*khram*, Freidenberg), where eschatological events unfold.[28]

If *The Fairground Booth* shows how modernist interest in the puppet theatre could be deployed in an esoteric allegory about "life," then its successor work *The Twelve* makes a telling shift by anchoring its eschatological drama in the distinctly present historical site of the streets of revolutionary Petrograd in 1918. *The Twelve* thus provides a crucial link between pre-revolutionary modernism and Soviet culture. It is radically different – modernist – in tone and aesthetic manner from the mainstream Soviet literature that followed it; yet it exposes aspirations or intentions that turn out to have been latent in the Soviet experiment from its outset as an inheritance from the modernist avant-garde. In *The Twelve* the Russian modernist logic of "intervention" – the ways in which an aestheticizing attraction to the puppet theatre comes together with its urban identity and eschatological implications – washes up on the shores of the post-revolutionary era. If the poem counts chronologically as the "first significant response in Russian literature to the Great October Revolution," then it is significant that both it and Mayakovsky's *Mystery-Bouffe* – the "first Soviet play" – are oriented toward the mystery genre (Orlov 3).[29] Indeed, in this context Blok's poem emerges as an important predecessor of Bulgakov's *The Master and Margarita*, which offers retrospective ironic commentary on its predecessors' implicit aims.

The spare plot of *The Twelve* reconfigures key elements of the *commedia dell'arte* love triangle involving Pierrot, Columbine, and Harlequin in the more grotesque form of brutish relations among two Red Army soldiers, Van'ka and Petrukha (the latter's name manifestly signalling a link to *commedia dell'arte* via the Russian Petrushka), and a prostitute named Kat'ka (whom the narrator taunts for slumming among the rank-and-file after she had had officers as clients).[30] Van'ka takes up with Kat'ka; Petrukha in a fit of jealousy opens fire on them, killing

Kat'ka. But the poem's true centre of gravity lies in its presentation of an impressionistic portrait of Petrograd in the chaos that followed the October 1917 revolution. For most of the poem the immediacy of its images works to defer any larger, realist framework for understanding what has taken place: it is a pointed immersion in a mere present. It establishes its atmosphere with the repeated, incantory line "chernyi vecher / belyi sneg" (black evening / white snow 233), which looks back to Andrei Bely's experimental novel of 1913, *Petersburg*, in which the hero masquerading in a domino cape flickers in and out of shadows, as well as Gogol's canonical image of the devil lighting the flickering street lamps in "Nevsky Prospect" (which as has been argued is itself an "interventionist" commentary on Peter the Great's new capital).[31] Other fleeting urban images appear – a mangy cur, a bourgeois at an intersection who buries his nose in his fur collar – and the poem incorporates fragments of speech or sound typical of the time (from prayers to soldiers' drunken exultations of "freedom" to revolutionary-military commands: "maintain a revolutionary pace" (*revoliutsionnyi derzhite shag* 236) – even urban noise, with the sound of gunfire resounding in several passages (*trakh-tararakh-takh-takh-takh-takh*, 238). Throughout, emphasis falls on the city's streets at night, which are dominated by a violent and marauding band of Red Army soldiers.

Unlike *The Fairground Booth*, however, whose vague, atemporal quality lends itself to a Symbolist allegory of life in general, *The Twelve* sets its drama in a very specific time and place: the former imperial capital, Petrograd, in the darkness and disarray of January 1918 (the banners proclaiming "All Power to the Constituent Assembly," the winter darkness and ice, and so on, all set the poem's events firmly in early January 1918; Orlov 53).[32] It follows *The Fairground Booth* in sublimating its realia to recognizable aesthetic forms: the *balaganchik*, again, as well as early cinema, folk verse forms such as *chastushki* (a kind of Russian limerick, typically baudy, here a part of the "crudity" of the drama akin to Larionov's imitations of primitive folk woodcuts in his Futurist paintings), and *koliady* or possibly even, self-consciously, Western mystery plays (Gasparov, "Tema sviatochnogo karnavala" 14–15). The poem's first move, therefore, is to take the contemporary moment of historical and social rupture and not so much aestheticize it (Blok's point in giving events over to conventional aesthetic forms is certainly not that civil war Petrograd is beautiful or quaint) as to displace any immediate attempt to find its meaning. If the upheaval of January 1918 might be readable as distorted *commedia dell'arte* or puppet theatre (Kat'ka falling in snow, like the *kartonnaia nevesta* of *The Fairground Booth*), then the effect is grotesque. But the poem's most significant moment involves a tentative rescue of meaning in eschatology (as it happens, a typical conceptual move for Blok, whose essay on "The Intelligentsia and Revolution," for example, urges acceptance of the revolution as a "whirlwind" or "blizzard" whose destructive force will renew Russia): the soldiers – whose number of twelve makes overt if also ironic reference to the Gospels from the start – turn out to be not just a marauding band but also a procession, at whose head suddenly – as if to consummate a mystery procession, in an ultimate episode of "intervention" – appears Jesus Christ, "in a crown of white roses" (*v belom venchike iz roz*, 243).[33]

The Twelve thus reworks the impulses behind *The Fairground Booth* in significant ways: by portraying the urban reality of post-revolutionary Petrograd not as realist contiguity with past experience but as the irruption of otherworldly forces at a moment of profound historical rupture (if not indeed the end of time, since the appearance of Christ at the poem's end could be read as his Second Coming). The aesthetic logic of the poem essentially works to show that the thuggish element of the band of Red Army soldiers ironically resembles a *commedia dell'arte* performance (the precedent taken from *The Fairground Booth*) but that this in turn also ironically resembles – or *is*, since the poem functions as an unveiling of deeper realities – a mystery procession through the city, which is in fact the Second Advent of Christ.[34] The pointed irony is that this rabble should turn out to be led by Christ, and, equally, that this empirically – which is to say, historically – very real city of Petrograd should be *invaded* by Christ.

What *The Twelve* shows is that Blok cannot let his portrait of revolutionary Petrograd rest in realist depiction: the poem registers the impossibility of accommodating the October Revolution in a historical narrative, the premises of which (the scenic details and *dramatis personae* clearly pointing to January 1918) are displaced to make way for an apparition, for the advent of a mystical, transhistorical Christ. The link between the poem and the modernist logic of "intervention" thus runs deeper than its superficial reprise of *commedia dell'arte* themes from *The Fairground Booth*. Lotman argues that the poem epitomizes the confluence of two interests encountered throughout Blok's oeuvre: the city, which for Blok is simultaneously the reality opposed to literary life and a giant theatre; and the folk culture preserved on the city's fringes, with their fairground and tavern entertainments for the lower classes (*Blok i narodnaia kul'tura goroda*, 193). *The Twelve* thus presents a "whole parade of folk theatricality" (*tselyi parad narodnoi prazdnichnoi teatral'nosti*, 195), with particular emphasis on the "fairground puppet theatre" (*kukol'nyi balagan*, 196). The poem borrows its plot from *commedia dell'arte* and Petrushka puppet shows; indeed, its opening cadences imitate the carnival calls of the showbooth barker (*pribaiutochnye zachiny raeshnogo deda*) – its entire structure, in Lotman's view, consciously imitating the physical structure of the western Russian and Ukrainian *vertep* theatre, in which, as discussed in chapter 2, a farce was presented on the lower tier (here represented by the *burzhui* – a German in *vertep* plays and Petrukha – that is, the Petrushka of the *vertep*, here presented as a figure of merry banditry) while a sacred drama on the birth of Christ was presented on the tier above it.[35] For Lotman, what *vertep* gives Blok is a structure in which the solemnity of mystery can coexist with an element of carnival anti-mystery (*kharakternoe sochetanie sakral'nykh i koshchunstvennykh elementov*, 196, 197).[36] In Gasparov's view the very appeal to carnival imports eschatological meaning (in addition to a theme of "joyous self-annihilation" deriving from Wagner and Nietzsche) because carnival itself is associated with "the mediaeval mystery play, with its primitive-woodcut depiction of apocalyptic and elevated themes" ("Tema sviatochnogo karnavala" 21).[37]

A deep irony thus inhabits *The Twelve*: Blok goes out into the Petrograd streets, as it were, only in order to drag the theatre along with him. But in doing so he imagines the revolution as a mystery procession, a ritual bringing about extrahistorical "intervention" in the empirically real streets of Petrograd. Moreover, the poem's playful theatrical element – its puppet-like and fairground-booth quality, the *kukol'nost'* and *balagannost'* that define it – is integral to this conceit: not just an aestheticist way of rendering it playful but the very mechanism (as Lotman suggests) for transforming the everyday into *sacrum* (however ambivalent and ironic that *sacrum* remains). Blok later expressed reservations about the image of Christ at the poem's end. According to Chukovskii, after a lecture by Gumilev about his poetry he remarked, "I don't like the end of 'The Twelve' either. I wanted it to turn out differently. When I got to the ending, I was surprised myself: why Christ? But the closer I looked the more clearly I saw Christ" (Kalb 250n74; see also Pyman, *Life*, vol. 2, 285, 302–3). Blok's startling use of the image, however, arose out of considerable thought about the meaning of Christ as a historical figure and about his advent in an urban setting. Blok's turn toward this theme both resonates with the religious orientation of panoramas of the late nineteenth and early twentieth centuries that projected the events of the Passion onto the modern city and anticipates its related, if more complex, assimilation by planners of early Soviet festivals. Around the time he composed *The Twelve*, Blok asked his mother to send him the Gospels; he was also reading Renan's 1861 *Vie de Jésus* and writing an outline for a play about Christ. The outline itself reveals little thought about history – Jesus figures as a distracted and misunderstood artist-figure – but the essay "Katilina" ("Catiline") that Blok wrote in 1918 suggests that Christ had a very distinct historical meaning for him.

"Catiline" shows Blok to have been thinking about Russian events in terms that linked them explicitly to Rome and the advent of Christianity (Rome and Jerusalem serving as functional equivalents in the context of mystery plays: Jerusalem as the actual site of the Passion, but Rome as metonym for the Roman Empire to which Jerusalem belonged as well as centre of the Western Church and its rituals; recall also the prominence of Rome and Jerusalem in panoramas).[38] The essay suggests that for Blok, revolution, as epochal change, represented a rupture of history so profound that it resembled intervention from another world. The essay is an exercise in "mythologized history" (Kalb 109) but of a very specific sort. Despite an opening disclaimer that declares the drawing of historical parallels to be the province of "bookworms and corpses" (*knizhnikov i mertvetsov*, in *Sobranie sochinenii*, vol. 4, 281) – an undoubted jab at Merezhkovskii – Blok identifies Russia in its revolutionary moment with ancient Rome (an idea originally promoted by Merezhkovskii; Kalb 107). The Roman period "in its historical processes most closely resembles our own time" (*Sobranie sochinenii*, vol. 4, 273). For Blok, however, Rome serves as an analogue for Russia not in its imperial greatness (as it had, for example, for Peter the Great) but in its imperial weakness and decline: "both worlds, ancient and modern, were undergoing transformations of profound significance" (Kalb 109). Blok declares Catiline, a former consul who led an armed uprising against the Roman state in 63 BC after having been denounced before the Roman senate by Cicero, to have been a "Roman bolshevik" (in his revisionist admiration – Roman historians make a monster out of Catiline – Blok was following Ibsen, whose first play, written in 1850 in response to the revolutions of 1848, was about Catiline; *Sobranie sochinenii*, vol. 4, 291–2; Kalb 108). For Blok the figure of Catiline focuses a number of philosophical ideas. Though frightening in his violence, he is an embodiment of the Dionysian spirit of eternal rebellion and thus potentially a force of renewal: "In Catiline's day there blew that wind which swelled into the storm that destroyed the old, pagan world" (*Sobranie sochinenii*, vol. 4, 276; Kalb suggests that Blok's Catiline echoes certain traits of Renan's Christ, who is a revolutionary); but in Blok's historiosophical perspective Catiline is oddly decentred. The real agent of change turns out to be not the "bolshevik" Catiline, but Christ. Catiline was merely caught up in the extrahistorical whirlwind heralding the advent of Christ into the world ("Ego podkhvatil veter, podul pered rozhdeniem Iisusa Khrista, vestnika novogo mira," 276). His conspiracy was "the pale forerunner of the new world" (283). At stake, again, is a notion of extrahistorical judgment: several decades after his trial "a sentence was pronounced irrevocably and forever in a different court [than that which condemned Catiline, TS] – in an unhypocritical court, the court of Jesus Christ" (278). In Blok's conception "Christ," too, is tinged with Nietzschean ideas (he represents the unleashing within history of a Dionysian wind of radical change; 119), but in his role as agent of historical rupture he remains transcendent. Both Catiline and Christ are "revolutionary archetypes ... who renounce themselves and are transformed as they momentarily leave profane, historical time to enter into and relive a sacred, past, and inspirational moment" (107). Russia in Blok's view is like Rome not so much because it is a dying empire serving up ripe conditions for revolutionary wrath as it is the site for experiencing (or at least anxiously awaiting) otherworldly intervention.

Equally interesting in the essay, and symptomatic of the broader modernist concerns outlined here, is Blok's interest in the urban setting of Catiline's rebellion, which in his description distinctly echoes the Petrograd of *The Twelve*:

> Imagine now the dark street of a large city, in which part of the inhabitants give themselves over to debauchery [*razvratnichaiut*], half of them are asleep, a few men of counsel remain awake, faithful to their policing duties, while the majority of the residents, as it true always and everywhere, doesn't in the least suspect that something is going on in the world. Now, against the black backdrop of this city at night (revolution, like all great events, always emphasizes blackness) imagine a band led by a man gone mad from frenzy [*iarost'*], forcing them to carry before them the symbols of consular dignity. (*Sobranie sochinenii*, vol. 4, 289)

This madman, Blok notes, is Catiline, "and he walks with his very same walk – now lazy, now hurrying; but frenzy and fury (*iarost' i neistovstvo*) have given his gait a musical rhythm ... in the step of this man there is – blizzard, uprising, the fury of the people's anger" (289).[39] The parallels between this procession in Rome and that of Christ in Petrograd are strikingly close. In *The Twelve* the band of marauding soldiers at whose head appears the figure bearing transcendent change into the world "marches in the distance with a mighty gait [...] The old world, like a mangy cur, / They've broken through! I'll bash your head in [...] And so they march with mighty tread [...] Ahead of them, with a bloody flag [...] in a white crown of roses, treading delicately above the storm [...] does Jesus Christ."[40] It is the same tread of "intervention," its entry into and suspension of the historical present.

Chapter Four

Rituals of "Intervention" in the Early Soviet Era

The question of how these various currents within Russian modernism – its sense of exhaustion with history and the present, its expectation of some form of apocalypse, its longing for some form "intervention" that would bring about transcendence, its determined revival of archaic forms with cultic significance – transmitted themselves to the Soviet era is one that leads us to some of the essential features of the Soviet culture that developed in the twentieth century. Of obvious consequence was that fact that Soviet culture itself arose out of a moment of historical rupture, the two revolutions of 1917 (February and October) that first overthrew centuries of tsarist rule and then installed a new state intent on reshaping the political, social, and physical world it had inherited from the Russian empire.

Blok had already cast the revolution as an incongruent advent in *The Twelve*, and his trope found an immediate response in the poet Andrei Bely's "Khristos voskrese" ("Christ Is Risen"). The poem appeared on 12 May 1918 in the newspaper *Znamia truda*, where *The Twelve* had been published earlier the same year, then was reprinted in the first issue that year of the journal *Nash put'*, as was *The Twelve* (Belyi, *Sobranie sochinenii* 536). Bely's poem offers a lurid physical description of the Crucifixion – Christ's broken wrists, the dark sockets of his eyes, his broken body – but offers it as a cosmic event. Although the Crucifixion took place "on the Jordan," it resonates everywhere ("V glukhikh / Sud'binakh, / V zemnykh / Glubinakh, / V vekah, / V narodakh, / V sploshnykh / Sinerodakh / nebes," 432). In an evident appeal to the nineteenth-century notion that Christ walked *unnoticed* through Russia (cf. Tiutchev's "Eti bednye seleniia," discussed in chapter 1), Bely's poem charges that the Crucifixion, with its outstretched arms, twisted wrists, and swaddled loins, had been replayed in the nineteenth century while "we" did not realize that "in these very days and hours the worldwide mystery is taking place" (*imenno v eti dni i chasy / Sovershaetsia / Mirovaia / Misteriia* 438). But Bely's Christ is now pierced from head to foot by a ray of light discharged from the heavens to announce "the New Testament age" (433). He has become a Symbolist-mystical "Solar Man" (*solnechnyi chelovek*), whose radiant body is now the body of Earth (439). Russia in turn has become the Bride of Christ, whom Bely urges, in April 1918, to heed "the tidings of spring" (440; cf. Blok's call to the Russian intelligentsia in "Intelligentsiia i revoliutsiia" to "listen to the [music of the] revolution"). Like Blok, Bely invokes the irony of contrast between the chaotic elements of the immediate historic moment – rain, railway lines running off into the fog, a telegraph line signalling the words "Third International" (cf. the banner in Blok's poem), a bespectacled intellectual evading cannon fire (cf. Blok's bourgeois, hiding his face in his fur collar), the shot of a Browning that kills a railway worker, and so on. All this constitutes the "pitiful sallow body" (*zhalkoe, zheltoe telo*) hanging from the cross (443). Like Blok, Bely ends his poem with the advent of Christ into this troubled world of revolutionary Russia. But Bely declares his Russia to be "the Mother of God" (*Bogonositsa*, 444) and prophesies that radiance will descend onto the heads of everyone, that out of the spring heralded by the winter storm (*buria*) will resound the words, "Christ Is Risen!" (445; cf. the blizzard in which Blok's Christ suddenly appears). In a gesture toward Symbolist otherworldliness Bely thus rewrites the ending of Blok's poem, seeking mystical transcendence in the disharmonies and ambivalence of *The Twelve*.[1]

A far more influential (and ironic) response to Blok's poem and its cultural precedents was the Futurist poet Vladimir Mayakovsky's play *Mystery-Bouffe* (1918).[2] That play was a response not to the Bolshevik coup d'état of October 1917 but to the broader atmosphere of the time and the cultural currents pulsing through it. Mayakovsky began work on the first draft of the play before the October Revolution, in August 1917, and finished it in September, at which time it received its first reading, in the presence of Anatoly Lunacharsky (whose own "intervention" play, *Faust and the City*, we encountered in chapter 1; Maiakovskii, *Sobranie sochinenii*, vol. 9, 300). Nonetheless *Mystery-Bouffe* can be considered chronologically the first Soviet play, "the first play written by a Soviet author and staged in a Soviet theatre" (299), as Soviet editions tell us. To that extent at least it is relevant to a nascent Soviet aesthetic. It was quickly embraced by the new Soviet government as useful propaganda. After a reading of the play the Party bureau created to organize celebrations of the first anniversary of the October Revolution agreed to stage it, and the play premiered as a "theatrical-poetic manifesto of October" at celebrations of the first anniversary of the revolution, on 7 November 1918 at the Theatre of Musical Drama in Petrograd, under the direction of Vsevolod Meyerhold, with sets by Kazimir Malevich (302; Mayakovsky evidently wanted the play to be performed at MKhAT, but the play's avant-garde staging was too much for the conventional tastes of that theatre; 310). Blok, whose *The Twelve* had appeared earlier that year, attended the premier and considered the play to be one of the most noteworthy events in the first-anniversary celebrations (302). For the Futurist camp Mayakovsky's play became a *cause célèbre* (whereas the Symbolist Evreinov's 1924 play *Kommuna pravednykh* [*Commune of the Righteous*] was a parody of it; Clark, *Petersburg* 116, 184).

Mystery-Bouffe both perpetuates and parodies the modernist impulse toward "intervention" – a marker of its liminal status, reminiscent perhaps of Cervantes's *Don Quixote* in its relation to the tradition of the chivalrous novel. With sardonic cartoonishness, it miniaturizes the cosmism of Calderón de la Barca's *Great Theater of the World*, in which God appears on stage as director to settle the affairs of allegorically represented members of humanity – an antecedent it self-consciously invokes. The sites of action are listed as nothing less than "I. The Entire Universe. II. The Ark III. Hell, Heaven, the Promised Land." After a prologue that rejects the otherworldly visions of redemption offered in the Gospel and the Koran (together with "bourgeois passions" and, with a nod toward the Faustian preoccupations of the epoch, "the cloak of Mephistopheles" – the prologue itself is a nod to Goethe's drama, with its conversation among God, three archangels, and Mephistopheles), the play opens on a globe supported by two walruses, while an "Eskimo" tries to plug a hole in the earth from which gushes the "red flood" of revolution (the globe may also have been meant to parody the "planetarism" prevalent in the works of proletarian poets active at the time). The action then opens on a parade of figures from the upper classes of various nationalities – a device Meyerhold once identified as a means for signalling the manifestly artificial, ludic nature of the drama to follow[3] – who are collectively referred to as "the pure" (*chistye*), among whom also moves a group of downtrodden workers referred to as the "impure" (*nechistye*). As the flood approaches the characters resolve to build an ark – with the labour delegated to the workers. Once afloat, "the pure" conspire to confine "the impure" below deck and deprive them of food. Above deck the characters indulge in schemes that parody the events of 1917, debating the merits of tsarist autocracy but eventually declaring a democratic republic. While they feast the workers seize the weapons they have laid aside and proclaim a revolution. In a pointedly parodic moment of "intervention" (and jibe at Blok's mystical-revolutionary Christ) a figure referred to as "just a person" (*chelovek prosto*) appears walking on water toward the ark – and turns out to be Mayakovsky himself.[4] He promises them paradise on earth. After a sojourn in hell, during which the demons prepare to roast them but release them because they are just skin and bones, the workers land in heaven, where saints and angels sit around eating clouds. But they leave, declaring "We are our own Christ and saviour!" and eventually make it to the promised land of socialism, an avant-garde dreamland of towering transparent factories filled with machines, where bread grows on trees and the shop windows are full of talking goods that declare they have no "owners" (cf. the similar eschatological plot in Mayakovsky's later play *The Bedbug*, on which more in chapter 5).

The dramatic elements of Mayakovsky's play thus playfully encapsulate much of the semiotic of aspirations toward "intervention" more broadly operative in the Russian fin de siècle. On the one hand, the cosmic scope of its allegory embodies a monumentalizing gesture reminiscent of the modernist vogue for staging dramas in city streets. When the play received a more daring production in Meyerhold's RSFSR Theater No. 1 in 1921 the format of the box stage was broken and the curtain removed. The action spilled into the auditorium, with gangways and staircases replacing conventional scenery. The globe was situated at the feet of the audience in front of the stage, while the centre of the stage was taken up by the deck of a ship (Rudnitsky 62). The effect was a spatial expansiveness that implicated the space outside the theatre: as the critic Emmanuil' Beskin commented in *Vestnik rabotnikov iskusstv*, "there is no stage and no auditorium. There is a feeling that there is not enough space for it within these walls. It calls for a city square, a street. It needs more than these several hundred spectators which the theatre accommodates. It calls for the masses" (quoted in Rudnitsky 63).[5] The play's salvation plot, which simultaneously parodies modernist dreams of advent and appeals to the lingering religious sentiments of its potential working-class audience, also recalls more earnest projects for public monuments in the same era. In 1915–16, for example, the sculptor Ivan Shadr proposed erecting a "Monument to the World's Suffering," which was to include a pyramid representing "humanity's Golgotha," inside of which would be a "Chapel of Resurrection" (Steinberg 247–8; Shadr's monument, which would seem to have been most immediately influenced by such French revolutionary monuments as Boullée's Newton cenotaph and Lequeu's Temple Consecrated to Equality [see Starobinski 78, 93] implicitly preserves memories of panoramas as well). Friche remarked that a socialist version of the pyramid would lead the visitor "through torment and sorrow, in unceasing struggle for liberation from all chains, toward a pyramid of light, perfection, and happiness" (248). As Steinberg comments, "To become socialist art, this monument needed to be cleansed only of its literal religiosity, not of its religious feeling or its essentially religious metaphor" (248).

At the same time, however, the expedient manner in which *Mystery-Bouffe* packs its cosmological drama into four acts (five in the extended 1920 version), and the toy-like representations of large objects in it, such as the globe supported by two walruses and the ark, recall the comically diminutive stagings of the puppet theatre – which, as we have seen, carries its own lingering memory of sacred rites – while the farcical *personae* have a cardboard-cutout quality that both recalls puppets and anticipates the caricatures in the posters Mayakovsky later produced for ROSTA, the state telegraph agency (the two genres may, in fact, be related). The parallel is not coincidental: Mayakovsky had consulted the "ex-entrepreneur of the *balagans*" Alekseev-Iakovlev for the staging of *Mystery-Bouffe* (Kelly 192; Alekseev-Iakovlev 162). What is significant in the history of the culture is that Mayakovsky chose the puppet theatre as the idiom for representing the epochal events of the revolution. The form seems particularly to have appealed to him because of its capacity to place the lofty and the base in close proximity – a linkage foregrounded in the play's very title. As Mayakovsky himself remarked, "the mystery is that which is great in the revolution, the bouffe that which is comical" (*misteriia – velikaia v revoliutsii, buff – smeshnoe v nei*, 300). Or another way of putting it: the burlesque of the mystery genre mounted in Mayakovsky's play was less an original gesture on his part and more a reversion to the semiotics, the meaning-horizons, of the modernist revival of the puppet theatre and the "interventionist" aims it served.

Yet the modernist desire to stage some form of "intervention" and disrupt history found its most imposing realization in the Soviet era not in literary works like Blok's and Bely's imagined advents or even in the performative irony of Mayakovsky's play but in a series of mass spectacles organized after 1917.[6] In the years immediately following the October Revolution, Russian cities, especially Petrograd (after 1924, Leningrad) and Moscow, were appropriated as sites for a variety of festivals and mass performances (Mazaev cites the May Day celebrations in Moscow, Petrograd, Kyiv, Saratov, Voronezh, and other cities as the birth of the whole phenomenon of the Soviet festival; 243). It might be tempting to see these events as a unified, spontaneous response to the revolutionary events of 1917 – as a nation "displaying its soul to itself," in Lunacharsky's hopeful phrase ("O narodnykh prazdnest-vakh" 4; Binns 591); but in fact the spectacles were directed from above by representatives of the Bolshevik government. They arose out of diverse intentions and were directed by a diverse group of organizers. All, however, participated in the same logic of "intervention" outlined here. Or, as one researcher puts it, for all the differences among early Bolshevik festivals and their directors, "behind their worldview stands one and the same 'potential text,' various fragments of which they reproduced," namely, "the voice of Russian culture of the fin-de-siècle which had nurtured and raised them" (*za ikh mirooshchushcheniem stoit odin i tot zhe 'potentsial'nyi tekst', raznye fragmenty kotorogo oni vosproiz-vodiat: golos russkoi kul'tury rubezha vekov, vskormivshei i vospitavshei ikh*; Glebkin 88).

There had been pre-revolutionary precedents for mass spectacle in Russia, such as the 1913 celebration of three hundred years of Romanov rule (Rolf 19), the commemoration of the "Fall of Azov" in 1912, and a staging of Yermak's conquest of Siberia (also in 1912; Clark, *Petersburg* 132). Soviet spectacles, however, had a far more expansive and transformative agenda. The most ambitious were the mass spectacles staged by members of the pre-revolutionary avant-garde, who sud-denly had the resources of the state – albeit a state struggling for sur-vival during the civil war – as well as prominent urban sites at their disposal. As we have seen in chapter 3, Russian modernists in the fin de siècle came to believe, following Nietzsche and Wagner, that the path to the regeneration of culture ran through the theatre. This preoccupation with theatre only intensified after the October Revo-lution of 1917, when the stage came to be viewed by the new Soviet government as a platform for political agitation; there was even some-thing of a "theatre epidemic" during the civil war (Rudnitsky 41, 44; Marx himself, after all, had used theatrical metaphors – such as the claim made in *The Eighteenth Brumaire of Louis Bonaparte* that tragedy repeats itself as farce – to describe history; Clark, *Petersburg* 78). Newly recruited by the Soviet government, iconoclastic directors like Evre-inov and Meyerhold sought to realize their pre-revolutionary dreams of liberating art and theatre by taking them out "onto the streets"; indeed, the streets themselves, the squares, and even the buildings around them were all to be repainted (124).[7] Natan Al'tman's deco-ration of Palace Square in Petrograd with Cubist forms on the first anniversary of the October Revolution famously alienated workers and government officials alike and led to protests against avant-garde participation in the celebrations of 1 May 1919 (103); but as early as a week before the first anniversary of the October Revolution the government set up a Committee for the Organization of October Celebrations (Komitet po organizatsii oktiabrskikh prazdnestv) under Lev Kamenev, chairman of the party's Central Executive Committee, and Vadim Podbel'skii, head of ROSTA, the Post and Telegraph Service (Corney 53). In 1919 a Decree on the Unification of the Theatre crafted by Lunacharsky, by then Commissar for Enlightenment, established a special government department of "mass festivity and pageants"; it included a guarantee of state financial aid (Binns 591). Even the Symbolist high priest of theatre as mass choral rite, Viacheslav Ivanov, long adamantly opposed to the Bolsheviks, served in the theatrical division of Narkompros from 1918 to 1920; he delivered an influential report titled "The Organization of Creative Forces of the People's Collective in the Realm of Artistic Activity" (Berd 175–6; in fact, as Berd suggests, the prospect of organizing mass festivals may have helped entice Ivanov to collaborate with the Soviet government). The enthusiastic participation in staging these spectacles by pre-revolutionary members of the artistic avant-garde may in part have had to do with the fact that they did not yet, in these early years, see them as specifically *Bolshevik* in tenor. Rather, many saw October as the prelude to a larger "revolution of the spirit" that might be coming (Corney 73; the phrase is Michel Aucouturier's). The leading theoretical lights in the early Soviet period were Wagner (still), Romain Rolland's *Théâtre du peuple* of 1903, and Kerzhentsev's *Tvorcheskii teatr* of 1919 (Kleberg, "'People's Theater' and the Revolution" 189).

Meyerhold, who had spent the months between the February and October revolutions of 1917 organizing "masques" – outdoor festivals – in support of war bonds (Clark, *Petersburg* 99), now held out to recalcitrant members of the former Imperial Mariinsky Theatre the prospect of becoming the spearhead of a "theatre of the entire world" (Clark, *Petersburg* 85). His post-revolutionary plans went far beyond the traditional theatre to promote an even more aggressive spatial agenda. In a 1921 report on the destruction of theatre buildings he enthused about the possibilities for spectacle offered by "Crimean mountains and ravines" ("Ob istreblenii teatral'nykh zdanii. Doklad 24 dekabria 1921 g.," *Stat'i. Pis'ma. Rechi. Besedy. Chast' vtoraia*. 1968, 486) and expressed confidence that the theatre of the future would reject buildings in favour of "more rational forms of siting" (*bolee ratsional'nye formy pomeshcheniia*, 486). It was Meyerhold's disciples who ran most of the Soviet mass spectacles of the 1920s (Clark, *Petersburg* 87). One of these, Adrian Piotrovskii, an influential theoretician of early Soviet street theatre, was a translator and scholar of ancient

Greek drama (he was also, as it happens, the illegitimate son of the classicist F.F. Zelinskii) as well as a student of Viacheslav Ivanov, one of the principal modernist promoters of the idea of theatre as unfettered choral ritual (Glebkin 86; see also Berd 181–8 on Piotrovskii's partial adaptation of Ivanov's ideas about mass choral art to early Soviet festivals). The self-awareness with which these early Soviet planners saw their work as a continuation of modernist efforts to replicate such historical precedents for mass theatre as ancient Greek drama, the medieval mystery play, the Italian *commedia dell'arte*, and its Russian counterpart, the *balagan*, was conspicuous (Clark, *Petersburg* 80).[8] In 1920 Piotrovskii suggested that contemporary theatre "bears the clear traits of resemblance to ancient drama as well as school dramas of the middle ages" (quoted in Berd 182). The first mass spectacle of 1920 was explicitly titled *Misteriia osvobozhdennogo truda* (*The Mystery of Liberated Labor*) and portrayed humankind's progression through the ages toward a socialist utopia (Clark, *Petersburg* 126; in his *Mystery-Bouffe* Mayakovsky already parodies this impulse). At the first meeting of the Proletarian Cultural-Educational Organization (Proletarskaia kul'turno-prosvetitel'skaia organizatsiia) in October 1917 a leading figure in the Proletkul't movement and head of ROSTA, the newly formed telegraph agency, Platon Kerzhentsev (real name Lebedev), proposed "mass theatre under the open sky" (*massovyi teatr pod otkrytym nebom*) as the most important form for the revolutionary era (Kerzhentsev had experience of "mass historical chronicle plays, so called pageants, in England and the United States"; Kleberg, "'People's Theater' and the Revolution" 190; Kleberg elsewhere calls Kerzhentsev's *Tvorcheskii teatr* a "proletarization" of the idea of cultic theatre; "Vjačeslav Ivanov and the Idea of Theater" 69). In the second, 1923 edition of *Tvorcheskii teatr* Kerzhentsev continues to enthuse about "spectacles under the open sky" (*zrelishche pod otkrytym nebom*), with a mass proletarian audience as the typical theatrical production of the future (73), and mentions as examples of recent theatrical innovations the "resurrection of ancient mystery plays in Munich" as well as "mystery plays closed to outsiders performed by the dukhobors in the Caucasus" (61).

Both the modernist and the early Soviet endeavours to stage such spectacles involved much more than a mere aestheticization of urban space (as extant scholarship has tended to view it), much more even than the modernist desire to break out of the "box" of the conventional theatre. What stands out equally in these early Soviet festivals is their spatial aggression, their intention to transform urban space in a disruptive and transformative act – as can be sensed already in Kerzhentsev's disparagement of a 1919 Kyiv staging of the French writer Romain Rolland's *The Taking of the Bastille* as nothing more than a play that had been taken outdoors (136). As Clark argues, these early Bolshevik festivals realized the "master narrative" of the avant-garde's "great experiment," its attempt to produce a revolutionary culture in the 1920s, specifically through a "repurification or resacerdotalization of space" (*Petersburg* 3). In particular, the avant-garde sought to destroy time and space as then understood so as to clear the ground for a new spatial order (46). To some extent, that ground had already been cleared. Groys suggests that the devastation wrought by war and revolution had reduced Russian culture to the very "ground zero" on which the pre-revolutionary avant-garde had hoped to realize its dream of creating a new reality (*Total Art of Stalinism* 19–20). A decree of 13 April 1918, for example, had ordered the removal of symbols of tsarist rule (Mazaev 236). The theme of the *interruption* of history, of the destruction of the old order, even of the urban here-and-now, figures recurringly in early Soviet spectacles. One press release from the committee formed to organize celebrations of the first anniversary of the October Revolution proposed evening gatherings on squares in Petrograd, the theme of which was to be the "symbolic destruction of the old order and the birth of the Third International." A figure representing the old order was to be constructed and then burned in the square, the release informs (Bibikova and Levchenko 39). Among the cantatas sung on Red Square in Moscow on the first anniversary of the revolution was one titled "The Transformation of the Old World"; a ceremonial "burning of the old order" was also planned (Galushkina et al. 102, 105). A Moscow city district conducted a "burning of the old world" on Lobnoye mesto on Red Square (Galushkina et al. 106). Equally significant – and, as will be argued, consequential – for the eventual development of Soviet culture was the fact that such intentions carried forward within themselves a more extensive symbolic agenda derived from a deep historical past. To import parts of that cultural memory ineluctably meant importing much of the whole.

The extent to which these actions by the early Soviet government were not casual but in fact represented a conscious and aggressive assault on Russian urban space can be sensed from the conflict they generated with the Orthodox Church. As Francesca Silano has argued in her study of him, Patriarch Tikhon regarded Orthodoxy as the means for human salvation but was also "convinced that the vehicle for Orthodoxy was Holy *Rus'*" (114), an entity he moreover saw as "a unique geographical and temporal space, located in 'time immemorial'" (119).[9] The Soviet and Orthodox views of space collided in May 1918, when the government introduced a new holiday: International

Workers' Day. As Silano remarks, "in Moscow, the Kremlin was designated as a celebratory space. The buildings and territory which Tikhon and the Council had claimed as parts of their narrative of Russia's
past and future were co-opted for a new version of history" (205). In
response, Tikhon issued a proclamation to all Orthodox believers asking them to participate in a Procession of the Cross to the Nikolskii
Gates of the Kremlin" (205) – that is, to the very doorstep of the new
government.

In contrary mode, the type of early Soviet spectacle orchestrated by
the avant-garde is best represented by the five open-air mass pageants
mounted, on an increasingly grand scale, in 1920 in Petrograd (they
decreased significantly in number after 1920, with the end of the civil
war; Binns 591; Clark, *Petersburg* 122). As the Prolekul't activist A.A.
Mgebrov put it, the "narrow, stuffy boxes of the old theatre stage" were
to be destroyed so that the avant-garde spectacle could be enacted in
"huge, free squares" (quoted in Clark, *Petersburg* 146). With titles like
The Liberation of Labour, *Towards the World Commune*, and *The Taking of the
Winter Palace*, they presented dramatic re-enactments of the Bolshevik
view of history (Binns 591). All were characterized by their iconoclasm
(not least, their use of tsarist buildings and monuments in ways sub-
versive of their original meaning), their striving toward monumentalism (even "gigantomania"; Clark, *Petersburg* 146) and epic might, and
their stagings designed to remove the barriers between theatrical performance and real life (Glebkin 80–1). All featured plots tending toward
eschatology, toward a dramatic disruption of history leading to the apotheosis of proletarian rule.

The first mass spectacle of 1920, *The Hymn of Liberated Labor*, was
organized as part of that year's May Day celebrations (*Gimn osvobozhdennogo truda*, or, Kerzhentsev notes, "a mystery play [*misteriia*] as the
Petrograd comrades called it," 136; the spectacle was also known as
The Mystery of Liberated Labor). Held on the steps of the former Stock
Exchange in Petrograd, it involved 2,000 performers, among them
units of the Red Army as well as professional actors. Approximately
35,000 viewers occupied the square in front of the building and adjacent streets. The performance was intended to show the struggle of
slaves for freedom throughout history and culminated in an "apotheosis" in which performers and viewers were to merge in a mass throng.
(Rudnitsky suggests that this allegorical plot involving the conflict
between slaves and rulers, "clean" and "unclean," as well as the combination of pathos, in depictions of the downtrodden, with satire, in
depictions of their rulers, were borrowed directly from Mayakovsky's
Mystery-Bouffe, 44 – the original intention and its ironic reflection

thus engaging in a tango of sorts.) The square directly in front of the exchange symbolized "an occupied country, the R.S.F.S.R." The scenery consisted of two giant gates with an immense castle suspended above them. The allegorical action depicted such things as an off-stage "wondrous world of the new life" signalled by "magical music," from which, however, "slaves" are barred and instead forced to perform hard labour. A procession of "rulers of all ages" led by an "eastern monarch in sumptuous dress" files past. But the music inspires the slaves to rise up, and "before the viewer pass various scenes of the centuries-long struggle of the proletariat" (including Spartacus and Stenka Razin, leader of a Cossack rebellion in the seventeenth century). Eventually a red star rises glowing on the horizon and the Red Army appears. The gates to the "castle of freedom" come crashing down, and the final act of the performance presents an "apotheosis of the free, joyous life into which humanity enters" after the October Revolution. In the closing tableau an enormous chorus representing "workers of all nationalities" sings "The Internationale" against the backdrop of a rising red sun (Kerzhentsev 136–9). Particular emphasis in the staging fell on the blending of theatrical and "real" elements – a way of signalling the "mystery's" pointed intervention in this historical moment: real automobiles and cannons were involved, actual soldiers marched in procession, and even the patently symbolic scenes involving various peoples of the world included representatives of actual trade unions (Bibikova and Levchanko 25–6) – a distant memory, perhaps, of medieval rituals' fusing of liturgical and representational elements.

In Piotrovskii's view, the kind of schematic and conventionalized narrative represented in this spectacle and in *K mirovoi commune* (*Toward a Worldwide Commune*, which used the same setting of the former Stock Exchange in Petrograd) compressed hundreds of years into an hour and a half with the aim of transforming before the assembled chorus the "real" city and "real" history into contiguous action, that is, into life. Like his mentor Ivanov, Piotrovskii saw the mass festival as the direct transformation of social space and the conversion of "time" into "history" (Berd 183–4; save that what was really involved was the disruption of history in the sense of ongoing, everyday events – Piotrovskii's notion of history was its transcendent form). Piotrovskii's assessment of the spectacle, however was not uniformly positive: the steps of the former Stock Exchange were used too much like a traditional stage, he complained (Mazaev 337), and, compared with Ivanov's ideas about visceral "choral" art, it was still a large-scale *actor's* performance – scripted rather than spontaneous (182).

Toward a Worldwide Commune, staged that same year, was a still larger mass pageant featuring this kind of redemptive allegory. Organized by the Petrograd Theatrical Division of the Commissariat of Enlightenment (Brudnyi 64) and staged during the meeting of the Congress of the III International, again in front of the Stock Exchange building (Kerzhentsev 139), the drama again represented the world-historical ascent of the proletariat to freedom, from the 1871 Paris Commune to the civil war still raging in parts of the Soviet Union. Again, a group of "slaves" situated below (at the foot of the entrance) struggled to overthrow the "masters" (situated higher up the steps). Tsar Nicholas II was caricatured in the form of a huge puppet, which was lowered from the top of the pediment (a recourse to the puppet theatre reminiscent, again, of *Mystery-Bouffe*). A group of Red Army soldiers liberated the "slaves" as the cannon at the Peter and Paul Fortress, on the opposite bank of the Neva, were fired. Girls in red dresses with golden trumpets hailed the advent of the "RSFSR" (Rudnitsky 44).

Arguably the most ambitious of the 1920 Petrograd spectacles was the staging of *Vziatie zimnego dvortsa* (*The Storming of the Winter Palace*). Organized for the third anniversary of the Revolution by the political directorate of the Petrograd Military District (Brudnyi 64), directed by Nikolai Evreinov, and performed on Palace Square in Petrograd on 8 November 1920 (Corney 76–82), it shows the extent to which a totalizing effort at transforming urban space – the historical present – defined these endeavours. As Corney remarks, "The organizers intended the ambitious *Storming of the Winter Palace* (*Vziatie Zimnego dvortsa*) on November 8, 1920 to be October's 'total event,' the reduction of the entire revolutionary narrative to an emotive and transparent symbol" (75–6). In a nod to the festivals of the French Revolution, organizers chose the Winter Palace and the theme of "storming" in an effort to invent a Bastille for the October Revolution, despite the fact that the palace had never been a prison and its actual takeover had been anticlimactic (80). The performance took place on Uritskii (formerly Palace) Square in Petrograd (76). Some 6,000 soldiers and sailors (out of an originally planned 10,000; Berd 186) acted out the struggle between the "Reds" (whose actions were directed by Petrov) and the "Whites" (directed by Kugel' and Derzhavin) on two platforms linked by a bridge (designed by Yury Annenkov) on which the two sides engaged in battle before an audience of nearly 100,000 spectators, which occupied the square. The spectacle's narrative arc ran from the July Days, in which workers, soldiers, and sailors rose up in unsuccessful rebellion against the Provisional Government, to the storming of the Winter Palace itself on 25 October. The Red stage portrayed an initially chaotic mass, which by the end of the spectacle came together in concerted mass action. The White stage was dominated by an actor playing Kerensky, head of the Provisional Government, on a raised platform; its performers for their part gradually descended into chaos (Corney 78–9). The massive windows on the second floor of the Winter Palace itself were used for light effects as well as silhouetted battle scenes directed by Evreinov (79, 81). At the climactic moment members of the Petrograd Red Guard entered the square in armoured cars through the Arch of the General Staff, while armed sailors marched in through the Admiralty Passage (79). The apotheosis came in the form of "The Internationale," which was sung by a chorus of 40,000, while red stars were lit up and a huge red banner was raised above the Winter Palace itself (Rudnitsky 44).

Like the *Mystery of Liberated Labor*, the schematizing structure of this mass spectacle, in which the opposed Red and White stages established a "symbolic social polarization" (Corney 80), recalls the reductive allegorical staging of Mayakovsky's *Mystery-Bouffe*, with its stark division between the "clean" and the "unclean," above-deck and below-deck. Both partake of the same performative idiom of totalizing drama, and in a further ramification of that idiom the *Taking of the Winter Palace* may also have served as the prototype for the parallel scene of the storming of the Winter Palace in Sergei Eisenstein's *October* (although Eisenstein disavowed the influence; Berd 185). Similar spectacles were staged in the provinces: a May Day (1921) celebration in Ekatarinodar that portrayed four key moments in the revolutionary struggle; and on the same day, in Astrakhan', one portraying various scenes from the Russian, French, English, and other revolutions (Kerzhentsev 146). On a deeper level, both the spectacles and Mayakovsky's play recall medieval dramas of "intervention," especially the mystery and Corpus Christi plays, in which a transcendent spectacle is staged on the city square similarly parsed between good (the church on one side) and evil (the gates of hell set up across from it) – absorbing both setting and narrative in a ritual enactment.

Particularly notable in these monumentalizing spectacles was their aggressive attitude toward the city *per se*: unlike the mass fêtes of the French Revolution, which may have provided a partial inspiration (Corney notes that some revolutionary artists were influenced by the Russian edition of Julien Tiersot's 1908 *Les fêtes et les chants de la revolution française*, 52) and which were held in the "free and open space" out of town, Soviet spectacles pointedly targeted important urban sites – *loci* of power – such as the Palace Square and Stock Exchange in Petrograd (Clark 128) and Red Square in Moscow. Soviet planners had cities at their disposal in a way that was unprecedented, at least since medieval times (e.g., during Corpus Christi or royal processions). In the perception of Soviet planners, this newfound possession meant more than just spatial convenience. "Our era," Kerzhentsev claimed, "is a time of cities, *cities represent the completion of history (goroda vershat istoriiu)*, ideological celebrations tied to the era of revolution must naturally take place in cities" (169; emphasis added). About a plan A.M. Glan devised for a spectacle devoted to the "history of the three Communist Internationals," Kerzhentsev further enthused, "the general task of this decorative plan is to present the communist city of the future" (152; the plan was ultimately unrealized). All the squares in which the action would take place were to be renamed for various sciences and the arts: Astronomy Square, Political Economy Square, and so on. "Geography Square," for example, would feature a giant globe with continents of the world painted in the red tones of spreading world revolution (152; cf. the similar totalizing symbolism of the globe in the opening scene of Mayakovsky's *Mystery-Bouffe*). Clark suggests that Vladimir Tatlin's celebrated rotating "tower," his proposed Monument to the Third International, whose three huge glass cubes were to be placed in the Neva River in Petrograd, can be seen as a similar project for "sacerdotalizing" space inspired by the early Bolshevik mass spectacles (*Petersburg* 140).

An important motif in these early Soviet spectacles is thus the intention to include, take possession of, or transect as much of the city as possible – in essence, a projection of the monumentalism of medieval mass spectacles onto the horizontal plan of the city (another way in which Petrograd and Moscow were taken over symbolically in the years following 1917, as Corney points out, was through the renaming of streets and buildings; 58).[10] Lefebvre aptly describes the link between these aesthetic and possessive drives:

> Property in the sense of possession is at best a necessary precondition, and most often merely an epiphenomenon, of "appropriative" activity, the highest expression of which is the work of art. An appropriated space *resembles* a work of art, which is not to say that it is in any sense an *imitation* of a work of art. Often such space is a structure – a monument or building – but this is not always the case: a site, a square or a street may also be legitimately described as an appropriated space. (165)

Plans for May Day celebrations in Moscow in 1918 called for the entire city to be transformed into a stage, with the "proletarian masses" of Moscow as its actors; the entire city in its present form was to be transformed symbolically so as to represent the "communist city of the future" (Bibikova and Levchenko 101–2). A similar proposal for the same festival proposed dividing the city into four quadrants, each representing one quarter of the world – a symbolic projection of possession from the city onto the entire globe. Workers dressed as inhabitants from each part of the world were to march through the city to its symbolic heart on Red Square (87). A report V.M. Friche sent to the Moscow Soviet in 1918 similarly notes that plans for the second day of celebrations of the revolution would involve "a mass procession from the districts into the centre where a series of monuments and commemorative plaques will be unveiled" (quoted by Raikhenstein in Galushkina et al. 76).

For celebrations of the fourth anniversary of the revolution in Moscow another plan was to perform a symphony titled "La" (i.e, the musical note) – on the sirens and locomotive horns of the Zamoskvoretsky district's factories and trains (Bibikova and Levchenko 131; not all such efforts were artistically successful: Kerzhentsev notes that "owing to lack of experience with mass staging" acoustic effects were often lost under the open sky; 145). The very movement of theatre out into the streets, seen by some scholars as an effort to aestheticize urban space, should rather be viewed in this aspect as a gesture of appropriation deployed in the service of symbolic transformation: plans put forward by the Narkompros for the 1919 May Day celebrations in Moscow declared that "the whole celebration should be moved from closed spaces out into the open air, to the noisy city streets, to the squares and meadows [...] On this day theaters should stage their performances exclusively in the open air. Stages should be erected on squares, at intersections, and in parks" (Bibikova and Levchenko 92). An article by Lunacharsky, now head of Narkompros, published in *Vestnik teatra*, proposed dividing festivals into two phases. The first would involve "the movement of the masses from the outskirts to some sort of single centre [...] where a theatrical performance in the nature of an elevated symbolic ceremony would be performed." The second would involve smaller performances staged indoors ("O narodnykh prazdnestvakh" 4; Bibikova and Levchenko 107). As late as November 1933, when much in the world of Soviet festivals had changed, an article in *Sovetskoe iskusstvo* enthused about plans for the upcoming celebrations of the revolution by commenting that "the streets and intersections, the boulevards and quays, preparing to receive the many-thousand columns of demonstrators will [themselves] become festive participants of the celebration." The white building of the Moscow City Soviet would serve as "literal and figurative" centre of all Moscow's squares. Planners pored over maquettes of the entire city – a means of possessing the whole reminiscent of the panoramas popular in the nineteenth century or the globe used in

Mayakovsky's *Mystery-Bouffe* (as well as in actual urban festivals, such as one held in Samara in 1920, in which a stage holding an enormous globe was erected in the town square; on the globe was a banner that read "Long live labour!"; Kerzhentsev 148).

This kind of appropriation of urban space as an occasion for "intervention" can be sensed even in the mythologically inflected plans of Valentin Smyshlaev, who worked for the Moscow Section for Mass Performances and Spectacles: the city was to be awakened before dawn by trumpeters riding on horseback through the streets summoning residents to follow them – their call "shattering the sleeping calm of the city" – to the central square, where they would meet "Prometheus, who today will descend to earth with the sun" (playing itself, as it rose over the city; Kerzhentsev, *Tvorcheskii teatr* 151). This spatial logic was in force as late as celebrations for the tenth anniversary of the revolution in 1927, when planners sought to decorate the city of Moscow according to the "'principle of maximum unity of the decorations of the entire city,'" with all "central points of the city decorated according to the 'single general idea of the festival'" (*Pravda*, 8 September 1927, 5, quoted in Corney 176). "The square in front of the former Kseshinskii Palace, for example, had to symbolize the transition from the Russian empire to the Civil War; the Field of the Victims of the Revolution had to be dedicated to the memory of fallen warriors; the Narva Gates, to the Red Guard; the Moscow Gates, to the Red Army. A monument to Lenin in front of the Finland Station was decorated as 'the apotheosis of October'" (Corney 176). Inevitably, plans for the symbolic appropriation of the city moved from staging and decoration to alteration. Kaganovich had the Iberian chapel on Red Square torn down to make way for processions, and leading designs for the never realized Palace of Soviets were intended to accommodate mass festivals: large arches were to let processions through, with vast squares for "demonstrations" situated in front (Rolf 81).

Parallel to the grandiose spectacles organized by members of the pre-revolutionary avant-garde in the early Soviet era ran a second type of festival whose idiom was informed less by exuberant iconoclasm – although that figured in some of the planning – and more by an impulse toward ritual, or rather toward a ritualization of the new order. One could see these two types of spectacle as emanating from two antithetical "cultures," along the lines of Vladimir Paperny's well-known opposition between "Culture One" of the 1920s (iconoclastic, experimental, open-ended, utopian) and "Culture Two" of the subsequent Stalinist 1930s and 1940s (imperious, monumentalizing, classicizing, traditional). Clark notes a "modal binarism" in the mass spectacles dividing those like Meyerhold, who wanted a grotesque theatre, from those who wanted a regenerated theatre to provide "monumental and mystical rites" (131). Stites, too, finds an opposition in Soviet festivals between a "carnivalesque image of freedom and dance," on the one hand, and "a vision of order, solemn monumentality, and mythmaking," on the other (*Revolutionary Dreams* 79). In the context of the present study this dualism recalls the precedent of embedding ritual in the otherwise representational format of religious drama in the Middle Ages (see chapter 2) – as well as the generic and stylistic heterogeneity of a work like Bulgakov's *The Master and Margarita*, with its chiasmus of Moscow–Jerusalem, fantastic–realistic, and satirical–tragic.[11] The two impulses represented different strands within the same broadly modernist tendencies, and both partook of the same modernist aspiration toward "intervention" in the historical present that have been outlined here. But the second type embraced a more solemn form of Huizinga's "play" than the first, and the shift toward it came swiftly. As early as 1921, as the country emerged from the civil war into the era of Lenin's ameliorative New Economic Policy, the need for mass spectacle was already being rethought. A new official policy was promulgated that sought to transfer spectacles from open squares to less prominent sites or even indoors (to factories, or even back to traditional theatres; Clark, *Petersburg* 146). There was also a shift from "internationalist intellectuals" as organizers to less sophisticated Komsomol activists, and to "mass participation activities which the ordinary man could understand" (Binns 593). By 1924, Ivanov and Evreinov had emigrated from the Soviet Union and Piotrovskii had turned his interest from mass open air festivals to a network of more modest theatrical clubs scattered throughout the Russian Republic (Berd 186). Something like this shift is perhaps even anticipated in Lunacharsky's early prescription for a two-phase festival: the first marching through city streets, the second taking place more intimately, indoors ("O narodnykh prazdnestvakh" 4). Perhaps, too, as Corney suggests, Soviet officials realized that revolutionary enthusiasm could not be sustained for long and needed to be replaced by some other form of ritual (92).

The processions and demonstrations that emerged from this second impulse – with which the avant-garde spectacle had briefly appeared allied – had more to do with the regime seeking to impose the symbols of its nascent rule and its interpretation of recent political events and in so doing to allay its own "genealogical insecurity" (Binns 552), than with any kind of spontaneous celebration. An important context here is the fervent religious atmosphere of the time, which ran parallel to modernism's higher-cultural expectation of "advent" – and which is paradoxical only if one takes the atheism of the new regime at face value. As Mark Steinberg points out in his *Proletarian Imagination*, religious sentiment and to some extent even practice persisted among urban workers – yesterday's peasants – even as they fell away from the traditional Orthodox Church (224–46). In the early twentieth century Russian cities witnessed an abundance of religious meetings and discussions, with sects proliferating alongside the mainstream church ("free Christians," "wailers," "sons of the apocalypse," *skoptsy* and *khlysty* [castrating and flagellating sects]) – to the extent that post-1917 anti-religious debates sponsored by the Party often resembled debates held by the Orthodox Church in this period to dissuade sectarians (228). As Steinberg comments, even when aspiring working-class writers "turned away from the church and conventional faith in God – as most did – they typically kept hold of religious imagery, language, and sensibility [...] They typically viewed human existence as a mythic journey through suffering toward deliverance from affliction, evil, and even death. Images of martyrdom, crucifixion, transfiguration, and resurrection remain[ed] part of their creative vocabulary, as did narrative attention to suffering, evil, and salvation" (232; this kind of "journey" shaped the plots of the 1920s mass spectacles, as well as Mayakovsky's *Mystery-Bouffe*, which draws heavily on this sensibility even while parodying it; so do Shadr's plans for a monument to world suffering). Nor did religious sentiment die at the October Revolution. In fact, "the years after 1917 witnessed, contemporaries noted, 'a wider and wider outpouring throughout Russia of the streams and rivers of free-religious, extra-church, and sectarian' movements" (252). In this atmosphere, "the Russian revolution and the struggles and crises that followed it appeared to many at the time as an apocalyptic moment" (273). One particularly relevant component of this eschatological mood – which itself can already be thought of as an expectation of *advent*, "intervention," of an end to history – was the belief that a saviour of some sort would arrive. As we have seen, Tiutchev's 1855 "These Poor Settlements," Blok's *The Twelve*, Mayakovsky's *Mystery-Bouffe*, Bely's *Antichrist* and "Christ Is Risen," and Esenin's "Advent" – to name just a few examples – all exploit this advent mood, as does, in its own way, the ending of Fedor Gladkov's 1925 proto-socialist-realist novel *Cement*, in which the restarting of a cement factory on the fourth anniversary of the revolution is presented in terms reminiscent of the Second Coming (with the very stones on the mountainside singing out). So, too, ultimately, do the ironic "intervention" plots of works like Mayakovsky's *Mystery-Bouffe*, Erenburg's *Julio Jurenito*, Olesha's *Envy*, and Bulgakov's *The Master and Margarita*. These modernist works partake of the same cultural idiom. But speculation on what would happen "were Christ to return to earth" also filtered down to worker-writers, such as E. Nechaev in his 1907 poem "On Freedom" (freedom will come to heal wounds), and F. Shkulev in "Christ" (Christ returns to earth with a message of revolutionary deliverance from suffering; Steinberg 235, 241; this is the sentiment parodied in Mayakovsky's *Mystery-Bouffe*).[12] The quintessential Proletkul't poem *"Zheleznyi messiia"* ("Iron Messiah") by Vladimir Kirillov, which declares that the Messiah has appeared – in humming wires and shining machines rather than in radiant robes, as Bely's "Christ" had done – makes this mood the essence of revolution, as does much Smithy poetry in general (Steinberg also notes the theme popular among worker-writers of "the factory as cathedral," 260, a prominent motif also in Fedor Gladkov's 1925 *Cement*). In this light Blok's *The Twelve*, Bely's "Christ Is Risen," and Esenin's "Advent" can be viewed merely as the intelligentsia's responses to this underlying trend.

In the years immediately following the October Revolution, Soviet authorities were well aware of this atmosphere and sought by turns both to repress it, through anti-religious campaigns, and to exploit it. Plekhanov may earlier have had to defend the 1905 May Day celebrations from other Marxists against charges of pagan associations (Binns 589), and the "Komsomol Christmas" held on 25 December and then again on 6 January 1923 in Moscow may have had an unambiguously mocking tenor, with anti-religious films and lectures leading up to a procession in which puppets (*chuchela*) of Christ, Mohammed, Buddha, and Oziris were paraded through the streets and then burned in a bonfire on Serpukhov Square (Mazaev 358); but after 1917 "[t]he Bolsheviks had deliberately accepted the ambivalence in meaning" (Rolf 35).[13] In fact, there was a "profusion of religious imagery and emotion" in "public revolutionary discourse" in the years after 1917 (Steinberg 254).[14] Unlike much of Western Europe, Russia prior to 1917 had no tradition of proletarian festivals, so when the early Soviet government set about creating one it turned to Russian Orthodox precedents instead (Rolf 25). In so doing, it created a system of non-religious ceremonies unique among modern European societies (Binns 587). The borrowing from Orthodox rituals was intentional: initially in order to draw in the still deeply observant lower classes, then eventually (from First Five-Year Plan on) in an aggressive effort to displace religion. In fact, early Soviet demonstrations and processions (*manifestatsii*) were so steeped in religious symbolism as to be confused often by their intended audience of peasants and workers with traditional religious processions (Rolf 35). One account notes that peasants in one village, unaware that what they were observing was a May Day procession, "took off their hats and devoutly crossed themselves" on seeing the approaching column of people carrying colourful banners and portraits of august bearded figures (in fact, of Lenin, Kalinin, and Lunacharsky; Binns 590; see also Glebkin 95). Such conduct suggested to one contemporary ethnographer (D. Zolotarev) that the customs and atmosphere of the peasant commune assembly (sel'skii skhod) had been revived in only thinly disguised form (Binns 590).

In addition to developing larger public rituals, the Soviet government sought to establish a set of new life rituals to displace those of the church.[15] "Thus the new regime tried to wrest the initiative from Orthodoxy and established a new pattern of 'social time,' a new rhythm of work and leisure" (Binns 589). This effort was abetted by Lenin's decree shifting the Soviet Union to the West's Gregorian calendar on 23 January/5 February 1918, which effectively erased the Orthodox marking of days (Mazaev 235–6). An October 1923 Party circular on anti-religious propaganda "recommended the holding of secular ceremonies for funerals, requiems, marriages, name-givings and 'admission to citizenship,' as well as secular 'Spring Sowing' and 'Harvest' festivals" (Binns 595). As Steinberg comments, "[w]orkers' clubs were treated as civic temples that could nurture a healthy and satisfying godless spiritual life. New ceremonies were invented to mark both personal and communal rites of passage – such as Octobering rituals (Oktiabrina) to replace baptism, Red weddings, and Red funerals" (254). The results, however, were not always satisfactory. Veresaev argued that life rituals were a psychological and propagandistic necessity under the new order ("the human need for ritual is enormous," he observed; potrebnost' v obriade u cheloveka ogromna, 174); he lamented both the lack of interest in life rituals among members of the Komsomol and their overly solemn and dull realization when they were attempted. Moreover, a distinct air of artificiality accompanied the new rites. One telling experience Veresaev reports is that of a nanny in a state hospital – "herself a communist and the wife of a communist" – who, when she wanted to organize "oktiabriny" for her child (the Soviet surrogate for baptism), was told by the local Party organization that she could not, because "oktiabriny are for non-Party members, for propaganda purposes" (174).

The Christ who suddenly appears at the head of the band of ragtag revolutionaries at the end of Blok's The Twelve belongs to this same cultural context, and the ambiguities captured in Blok's poem were echoed in the practices of the new regime: in mimicking Orthodox traditions, Soviet festivals transported into the new era undertones of salvation and a quasi-religious expectation of "intervention" – a lifting out of the historical present. The peasants who took off their caps as a sign of reverence before portraits of Party leaders may have acted in ignorance; even so, their instincts were correct: "One can read the absorbing of religious components by the Soviet system as an attempt to 'transfer sacrality'" (Rolf 77; the term is from Ozouf 262–83). Indeed, Soviet efforts to organize these new rituals re-enacting the revolution and imposing the regime's own view of history can be seen as reflections of the regime's own "genealogical insecurity" (Binns 592; or as Rolf comments, mass festivals brought a genealogical rationale for the October Revolution to the stage; 34). In this light Soviet festivals emerge as essentially a political act, a means to symbolize and thereby realize Bolshevik power – not simply to spread new ideas about the political order but to make them a reality (Rolf 3). Festival productions were more than simply political instruments for masking or "aestheticizing" political reality, they were "symbolic politics" (10). There was an implicit consensus in 1917 that authority expressed itself in festive demonstration marches and highly ceremonious processions through the streets (28).

Thus, early Soviet rituals drew extensively on the past, and they did so with more ambivalence than cynicism. One feature illustrating this reliance, part of a drive to take possession of urban space as well as a reminiscence of earlier forms of mass celebration, was the incorporation of *processions* into the new Soviet festivals. As one historian commented on celebrations arranged for the first anniversary of the revolution and of May Day in Petrograd in 1918, "the festive procession and its culminating point – the decoration of a brotherly grave – recall old traditional patterns for official celebrations" (Raikhenshtein, in Galushkina et al. 69). In this aspect Soviet festivals again drew on deep roots, replicating the projection of signs as a form of power. The origins of that impulse lay *inter alia* in medieval rites like the Corpus Christi procession and the royal processions staged in European cities from the Middle Ages onward (a phenomenon energetically imitated in Russia since the reign of Peter the Great – see Wortman 42–51 on Peter's "triumphal entry"). The installation – of tapestries, fountains, and other symbols of royalty along the streets forming the "idealized path" of the procession's entry into the city – "not only served decorative and allegorical purposes, but, as Konigson observed, also functioned 'to superimpose on the actual city a [sic] idealized path while removing the lived space"; this represented the sovereign's *conquest* of urban space (Carlson 22–3). "The shared insight of research on mediaeval feudal court ceremonies and ceremonies of early modern times is that authority does not simply exist but needs symbolic representation on the public stage in order to be recognized, accepted, legitimized, and stabilized" (Rolf 11).

Again, what these Soviet festivals involved was not just a parading of slogans in order to display them so that they might passively be observed, but an appropriation and transformation of urban space. One set of plans that particularly recalled this aspect of medieval processions outlining arrangements for the tenth anniversary celebration of the October Revolution in 1927, which specified that the "route would take marchers past 'living pictures,' platforms with spectacles and plays that enacted seminal moments: 1905, the 'dress rehearsal for the October Revolution'; 1914, the War; 1917, the October Revolution; and the Civil War that followed it. The final platform in the central square would be occupied by official representatives of government, unions, and party, who would greet the demonstrators" (Corney 178, quoting Podvoiskii and Orlinskii, *Massovoe deistvo*; cf. the medieval pageants described in chapter 2 involving groups of patricians, burghers, and craftsmen, in which "wooden platforms and scaffolds were erected on sites specially staked out, *tableaux vivants* were carried along in procession and went into scenic action at predetermined stations"; Berthold 229). Still more characteristically, in keeping with the regime's ambivalent borrowings from the Russian religious past, Soviet organizers deliberately copied the Orthodox ritual of the Procession of the Cross.[16] As Glebkin observes, early Soviet "meetings and demonstrations" had their roots not in any history of workers' protests, but "in the space of Russian culture" (*v prostranstve russkoi kul'tury*), namely in the Procession of the Cross (*protsess krestnogo khoda*, 88). Processions of the Cross in Russia followed a distinct spatial and temporal protocol: at the head went the clergy (*dukhovenstvo*), whose representatives carried the cross, icons, and banners (*khorugvy*); then came the laity (*miriane*). The procession would make stops at symbolically important places and was symbolically understood to represent "the soldiers of Christ, who under the banner of the cross wage war against the flesh, the world, and the devil" (*khristovo voinstvo, kotoroe voinstvuet s plot'iu, mirom i d'iavolom pod znamenem kresta*, 95; Blok's *The Twelve*, pace Gasparov's claim for specifically Western motifs in the ending, would seem also to look back to this tradition). In Glebkin's view this trait is especially important for understanding Soviet "manifestations" (*manifestatsii*), as staged political demonstrations were called. Early Soviet May Day demonstrations shared a "syntax" with such Processions of the Cross: procession (*shestvie*) behind a red banner as the basic element, sometimes with portraits of Marx, Lenin, and other leaders, and the singing of revolutionary songs. As in the Procession of the Cross, the marchers (*shestvie*) would stop at certain spots where "meetings" were held (*mitingi*, which in Russian usage meant a scripted reading of political speeches). "The symbolism of these manifestations was often described in terms of a battle with the forces of evil, moreover the very terminology used to describe certain aspects reproduced […] the lexicon used to describe the symbolic meaning of processions of the cross" (96). In a festival organized on the fifth anniversary of the revolution to celebrate the renaming of the Putilov factory to The Red Putilov Worker (*Krasnyi Putilovets*), for example, five steps representing the five years of Soviet power were installed in a large wooden shed housing the factory club. After speeches, a banner with the new name of the factory was presented, followed by choral singing and short speeches. "Then the crowd of people filed out of the shed, preceded by the banner, into the night, carrying firebrands"; they "walked around the whole huge area of the Putilov works, stopping at the gates. To the accompaniment of singing and blows on an anvil the old sign was taken down and the new one put up. The procession moved on, stopping at the various workshops and sections" (Piotrovskii, "Khronika Leningradskikh prazdnestv 1919–22 g." 82–3). As Binns comments, all these elements – the symbolic purification by fire, the power of names, the iconic use of banners and portraits, and the procession around the factory perimeter – are reminiscent of the "Way of the Cross" circumambulating the church (594). Moreover, in this regard Soviet processions differed notably from Western European May Day demonstrations, which featured banners with slogans, an element mostly lacking in pre-revolutionary Russian demonstrations. Western demonstrations also featured much larger numbers of banners, which were dispersed among the crowd rather than set out in front, as in the Russian version; and Western demonstrations did not make stops for meetings, as Russian ones did (Glebkin 97). Western demonstrations had a practical aim: the sacral element was present as mere connotation, whereas in Russian processions, the sacral element was central (97).[17]

A noteworthy extension of this idea of *processing* as a means of taking possession of space in order to impose a new symbolic order was the distinctly modern technological touch of using automobiles, steamships, and trains to display propaganda – a form of spectacle distinctly reminiscent of the wagon stage used in medieval dramas (see chapter 2). The Narkompros plans for May Day celebrations in Moscow in 1919 promised that "trucks will bring in mobile stages and vans [*gruzovoi avtomobil'*] can already serve as boards for troupes of actors. Plays and fragments of plays will be performed, verses staged, etc." (Bibikova and Levchenko 92). For the first anniversary of the revolution in Petrograd in 1918 "at 7 in the morning on 7 November trucks loaded with festive agitational literature, jubilee pins, and posters set out from the Central Bureau for district Soviet offices. On each truck there rode a herald-trumpeter, announcing the commencement of the holiday" (Galushkina et al. 42). In her essay on the design of such vehicles, Bibikova notes that the very first was the "mobile-military front train named after Lenin" ("Rospis' agitpoezdov i agitparokhodov," in Galushkina et al. 169). For the propagandists of the new regime, such vehicles provided an opportunity to "display revolutionary ideas in simple and compre-hensible images," such as allegorical scenes in which capitalism was represented as a dragon, and so on. In one case, the right side of the "Red Cossack" agitational train was decorated with grotesque images of generals, the bourgeoisie, kulaks, and priests (putative enemies of the people), while the left side featured Soviet workers and peasants – a syntax clearly intended to suggest transformation (Bibikova, "Rospis' agitpoezdov i agitparokhodov" in Galushkina *et al. Agitatsionno-massovoe iskusstvo* 179). In addition to propaganda, agitational vehicles (both trains and steamships) offered films and theatrical troupes (e.g., in 1921 the *Krasnaia zvezda* steamboat took along a theatre company consisting of twenty members; Argenbright 150).

As Argenbright comments, "from a historical-geographical perspec-tive" early Soviet agitational vehicles "may be considered a form of colonization" (142; Rolf discusses the spatial aspect of Soviet festivals as a "colonization" of space involving the establishing of a centre, together with a display of symbols of power with the city as a backdrop; 36, 38). To colonize space in order to stage "intervention" within it is the unstated aim of these rituals. "The agitational vehicle was a rolling campaign of bureaucratic restructuring. But these trains and vessels were meant to embody and represent not only the new regime, but also an imaginary future world. It was a means of colonization, not by conquistadors from another land but by the vanguard of the world to come. In this sense the agitational vehicle was a time machine, bring-ing missionaries from the future to minister to people who were seen to be living in the past" (149). "The agitational vehicle carried a group of activists who saw themselves as engaged in transforming society. Their understanding of the nature of that transformation, the nature of what was being transformed, and the means to be employed framed how they understood the spaces through which they passed" (144). The regime's enthusiasm for agitational vehicles, however, was short-lived: in November 1920 the party was planning to organize nine agitational boats to cover regular circuits; it also intended to establish fixed regional networks for agitational trains (157). Instead, the Tenth Party Congress shifted the vehicles' institutional home from Vserossiiskii Tsentral'nyi

Ispolnitel'nyi Komitet (VtsIK) to Glavpolitprosvet, the Commissariat of Enlightenment's agitprop arm – whose head then disparaged them as "toys" (157–8).

Another form of past display energetically recycled in the early Soviet era involved processions with life-size puppets, which often consciously appealed to the tradition of *vertep* processions and their sacred – or rather, in this context, occult – connotations, since here the point was more often than not the *demonization* of the regime's opponents. The "Komsomol Christmas" staged in Moscow on 7 January 1923 was one of these: it featured a banner proclaiming: "Up until 1922 Mary used to give birth to Jesus, but in 1923 she delivered a *komsomolets*" (*Do 1922 goda Mariia rozhala Iisus, a v 1923 g. rodila komsomol'tsa*); this was followed by real, live *komsomol'tsy* bearing poles with stars on them meant to represent the wise men (Chudakova, *Zhiznepisanie* 190). In 1918 Les' Kurbos produced a play called *Rozhdestvenskii vertep* (*A Christmas Vertep*) at the Molodoi Teatr, whose experimental staging involved two tiers and actors who moved like puppets.[18] The staging reflex behind these processions goes back very far, arguably to the kinds of practices and beliefs Freidenberg describes in her essay on the *vertep* theatre: the bearing of mystery through the city in a vessel that serves as its incarnation. Or, another way of putting it, the element in the culture that made these processions plausible and comprehensible to their intended audience of illiterate or semi-literate peasants and workers was their folk connotation, the memory they sustained of the bearing of otherworldly presence into the here-and-now as the focus of certain folk rituals in the Russian village, such as Shrovetide (*maslenitsa*) celebrations, which used a horse-drawn "ship" as a stage, or long, horse-drawn trains of "sledges, logs, or sometimes even heavy armchairs" (Warner, *The Russian Folk Theatre* 5, 19). A related precedent one might note is the tradition of "Chaldeans" (*khaldei*): by the seventeenth century, when the German ambassador Adam Olearius observed them, they were troublemakers allowed to run riot through the streets of Moscow at Christmastime.[19] But they originated in a church play called *Peshchnoe deistvo* (*The Fiery Furnace*), which portrayed the casting of Shadrach, Meshach, and Abednego into the fiery furnace as described in the Book of Daniel (5–6) – a drama of angelic "intervention" that the aggressive release of quasi-biblical figures into the streets may have been meant on some level to reproduce. As Warner comments on the tradition of masking during Christmastime mumming festivities, its pagan significance had been lost by the nineteenth century but "a certain lingering awareness of impropriety was certainly felt by villagers" (7). So, too, may the moments of otherworldly "intervention" built into folk ritual drama and intuitively drawn on by Soviet planner – the hauling of a festive "ship" through the village streets, for example – have sustained certain expectations among the Russian populace as to what such public rituals were all about.

A counterpoint to the religiously derived solemnity of most Soviet festivals was the carnival element some strove to attain. Lunacharsky had argued that in the Soviet era public festivals (*narodnye gulian'ia*) had to be purged of undesirable elements and adapted to communist ideology (Kelly 185). After the civil war such vestiges of pre-revolutionary carnivals as puppet theatres became an important part of agitprop in Soviet villages. Glavlitprosvet, the state agency responsible for educational literature, founded puppet groups (Kelly 193), and even the Petrushka text was recycled as agitprop (Kelly 189). May Day carnivals in Petrograd in 1918 and 1919 similarly used circus acts and puppet shows with socialist elements, agit-vans and even agit-trams to instil a carnival atmosphere – which at the least shows how pertinent the puppet theatre remained as a touchstone within the culture (Smirnova 122, 149). Rolling tram platforms carried circus performers through Petrograd for the 1919 May Day celebrations, while May Day celebrations of 1920 featured twelve wagons circling through the city bearing brightly painting *balagan* theatres while gondolas with singers, mandolin players, and guitarists rowed on the Neva, Fontanka, and Moika rivers and the Leb'iazhii Canal (Mazaev 278–80). As Fitzpatrick comments,

> Summer became carnival time under the new dispensation. Still popular, though less prominent than in the mid to late 1920s, were the parades lampooning various enemies of the revolution and Soviet state. For the eighteenth anniversary of the revolution, 3,000 eighteen-year olds from some of Moscow's biggest industrial plants participated in a "carnival of happy youth" parade, with each district taking a separate theme and organizing its own decoration. The Sokolniki Komsomol branch invited the famous caricaturists, the Kukriniksy, to design their display, which ridiculed everything that belonged to the past. Gods, angels, and saints headed the cavalcade, followed by Adam and Eve. Monks, capitalists, and the Romanov court followed in separate trucks, and "walking self-importantly" behind were ostriches, donkeys, and bears representing "generals, counts, and so on." (95)

To some extent these Bolshevik celebrations were meant to sustain (or insinuate) a festive element by transferring pre-revolutionary memories of carnival (*gulian'e*) to the urban space now claimed by the Soviet regime. (Clark even suggests an affinity between Kerzhentsev's idea of the "intermingling of all" in a reborn theatre and Bakhtin's concept of "carnival"; 125 – a link that will be discussed in the next chapter.) But the *state* sponsorship of these festivities is significant and adds a symbolic element previously lacking: these were now not just festivities arranged for, permitted, but otherwise spontaneously managed; these were festivities assimilated to the agenda of the state's other rituals and meant to *display*, as an object for instructive contemplation, "the people making merry" (*veseliashchiisia narod*; 89–90). As Mazaev remarks of the 1920 May Day celebrations in Petrograd, "As eye-witnesses testified, the Summer Gardens appeared on the outside to resemble a dancing and singing magic city. But this effect was first and foremost created through the efforts of professional actors [*Po svidetel'stvam ochevidtsev, Letnii sad vneshne napominal tantsuiushchii i poiushchii gorodok. Odnako etot effekt sozdavalsia prezhde vesgo isiliiami profesional'nykh artistov*]." The masses who came to the Gardens "found themselves as it were in the role of a typical theatrical audience" (*okazyvalis' zdes' kak by v roli obychnykh teatral'nykh zritelei*, 281).

Still more central to the organizers' intentions was the *staging* (in the sense of performing, not only displaying but also bringing about in the here-and-now) of a "mystery" in which history was subsumed and transcended (interrupted, suspended) in an episode of extrahistorical "intervention." These festivals were re-*enactments* rather than retrospective *depictions*, the dramatic equivalent of a performative utterance.[20] This was the Soviet-era legacy of the *ritual* element that had been incorporated into *representational* forms in medieval European rites. They served as an important instrument with which the new regime sought to establish itself; they were an attempt to seize urban space, announce the new authorities' intentions, and transform the populace's understanding of its place in history and the world. Through its festivals the new regime brought itself into *being*, as a symbolic endeavour. Lunacharsky, as noted, called the festivals a means whereby a whole people "demonstrates its soul before itself" (Bibikov 106) – save that it was the regime that did the demonstrating, not the people. Moreover, even in these early festivals the note of judgment sounds (recall Dostoevsky's Ivan Karamozov, who points out that "in Paris during the reign of Louis XI [...] in the didactic play *Le bon jugement de la très sainte et gracieuse Vierge Marie* [...] she herself personally appears and passes her *bon jugement*"). Rudnitsky notes that on the Southern Front during the Civil War, 10,000 Red Army soldiers took part in a mass spectacle presenting a "theatricalized court case" called "Judgment on Wrangel" (44). The spectacle was meant to serve as a new form of political agitation and was performed on an open square before a large audience. Rather than an overtly symbolic contest of the kind staged in *Mystery-Bouffe*, in a chilling anticipation of the show trails of the 1930s this "performance" closely resembled court proceedings. The court was announced as being in session, the secretary of the court read out the charges against Wrangel, and witnesses were questioned (each of them meant to represent a certain relevant social "type"). The spectacle culminated in a reading of the sentence passed by the "court": Wrangel must be destroyed and the sentence should be carried out immediately by the workers of Soviet Russia (Kerzhentsev, *Tvorcheskii teatr* 147–8).

Chapter Five

Stalinist Ritual and the Impulse toward Judgment

It might be tempting to see an element of Bakhtinian carnival in the modernist and Soviet stagings of "intervention" examined here.[1] Through appeals to fairground traditions they potentially sustain a memory of older carnival practice, especially in their concentration on urban space, the town square, *gorodskaia ploshchad'*, so central to Bakhtin's reading of Rabelais and medieval European traditions (as when Bakhtin speaks of "ritual-spectacle forms" as a principal manifestation of "folk culture of laughter"; *Tvorchestvo Fransua Rable* 6). For Bakhtin, during the calendrical ritual of carnival the town square and city streets become the site on which the structure of social consciousness – its plurality of competing ideologies – is exposed and subverted. The Petrushka puppet plays and their modernist adaptations, a work like Mayakovsky's *Mystery-Bouffe*, and the adaptations of folk-satirical rituals in early Soviet festivals would all seem to manifest such a cultural subtext.

What more essentially characterizes the instances I treat here, however, is their countervailing tendency toward solemnity – especially through an invocation of transcendent values, even if in the Soviet era these are nominally atheist and materialist. As Lane comments, "the transcendent principle inspiring ritual behaviour in Soviet society is, of course, constituted by the norms and values embodied in Soviet Marxism-Leninism" (36). These are rituals (or their imaginings in literary works) that appropriate urban space in order to transform it, to interrupt its otherwise merely present, quotidian agglomeration of signifiers (the former Stock Exchange in Petrograd, Red Square in Moscow, an expropriated factory, etc.) in order to install a higher order of meanings. In its pointed ambivalence, Mayakovsky's *Mystery-Bouffe*, whose very title projects both mystery and farce, is thus iconic of this impulse. Bulgakov's novel, which has served as a sensitive mirror throughout this study, extends the ambivalence of Mayakovsky's play.

Solemn strains were evident in Soviet public spectacles even before the Stalin era. As Clark observes, "Soviet public rituals and even ideology were inflected with the structure and rhetoric of the sublime" (*Moscow, the Fourth Rome* 220). Berd notes the "totalitarian" hints apparent even in Ivanov's pre-revolutionary ideas about mass festival. In his plans for a revitalized theatre Ivanov moves from a concern with art as such to the organization of social space, even the physical corralling of festival participants, insisting on the unity of thought in his ideal "chorus" to the exclusion of any who dissent. "From a contemporary perspective […] we already know how 'mass spectacles' were transformed into the theatricalized political 'trials' of the 1930s" (181). As early as the mid-1920s in the Soviet period, Piotrovskii was calling for a shift from "chaotic mass crowds of untrained people" to brigades (*otriady*) of physically and emotionally trained young people (quoted in Berd 188). The literary theoretician Viktor Shklovsky warned about the drift toward militarization in early Soviet experiments with mass spectacle: "The mass folk festival, the review of troops, and the joy of the crowd are affirmations of the present day and its apotheosis. It is justified when no one watches it from a window or a purpose-built tribunal; otherwise it degenerates into a parade, a ballet performed by serfs, and an orchestra with brass horns. And for that very reason it is already not a masquerade and not theatre."[2]

The extent to which this trend toward solemnity and judgment already informed early Soviet culture can also be sensed from its pervasive presence in the literature of the era. Zamiatin's dystopian fable *My* (*We*, 1920), for example, effectively condenses much of this logic of early Soviet thought. "Unity Day" in the tale's "One State" is celebrated in what the narrator in his diary calls a "mystery": "It seems to me that this is something like what 'Easter' was like for the ancients" (200). On this annual holiday the robot-like residents of the One State "elect" the Benefactor who rules over them (with no other choices on the ballot). The moment of "intervention" comes when the newly re-elected Benefactor descends from the heavens to them "like Jehova of the ancients" in a flying vehicle, wearing white robes. In keeping with the latent agenda of the mystery genre as I have outlined it here, the Benefactor's intervention tends ineluctably toward judgment: the narrator D-503 is effectively lobotomized and becomes once again a willing slave to the state, while "I," the woman who had nearly seduced him to rebel, is exterminated within the glass vacuum chamber of "the Bell," the One State's instrument of execution.

Similar punitive notes sound within the play *The Bedbug*, Mayakovsky's ambivalent but ultimately loyal satire on Soviet life, written in 1928–9. The protagonist, a crude worker with petit-bourgeois pretensions named Prisypkin (later renamed "Skripkin": a satirical type for the "new Soviet man" reminiscent of a range of characters in early Soviet literature, from the violent Cossacks in Isaak Babel's *Konarmiia* [*Red Cavalry*] to the "proletarian" created by transplanting human organs into a dog in Bulgakov's *Sobach'e serdtse* [*Heart of a Dog*] and the boorish protagonists of stories by Mikhail Zoshchenko) is accidentally frozen when the fire that breaks out at his wedding party in the provincial town of Tambov is extinguished by firefighters in the winter. The Futurist setting in the Institute for Human Resurrections in which he is revived fifty years later is poised ambivalently between something like Alexander Bogdanov's earnestly Bolshevik science fiction novel *Krasnaia Zvezda* (*The Red Star*), which *inter alia* enthuses about a possible world in which all human labour will be precisely regulated by a central bureau of labour (cf. the statement by the institute's director in *The Bedbug* that "every worker's life should be exploited down to the last second," *Sobranie sochinenii*, vol. 10, 35), and Zamiatin's dystopian *My*, with its near-complete lack of privacy [the citizens of the One State live in glass houses]) and a government-regulated system for arranging everything from labour to sexual liaisons. The announcement of Skripkin's discovery is made in a vast auditorium devoid of people but filled with machines: loudspeakers broadcast voices from all regions of the Russian republic, and "iron hands" are set to jerk upward in a positive vote on whether to defrost him. Skripkin ends up imprisoned and exposed as an exhibit in a cage at the zoo, to be used as a food source for another parasite survivor from 1929, an ordinary bedbug. The theatrical trial atmosphere of the play, reminiscent of the kind of spectacle staged by Party agitators to educate workers about the evils of drink, tardiness, and other retrograde vices in the early 1920s, takes a pronounced dystopian turn when Skripkin in the final scene addresses the crowd at the zoo (the audience at the play, in its actual performance space): "Grazhdane! Brattsy! […] Chego zhe ia odin v kletke?" (62).[3]

Even Fedor Gladkov's 1925 novel *Cement*, which was written with an attentive eye to the Bolshevik Party line (a quality that later earned it status as an exemplar of the Socialist Realist aesthetic, which had not yet been formulated when it was written), pointedly features a purge of Party members (*chistka*) as a ritual essential to the country's progress toward socialism, as well as the death of a worker on a construction project that is treated as a ritual sacrifice to the revolution ("Comrades, listen! A sacrifice to labour […] The great work of building up the Workers' Republic!," the hero Gleb Chumalov declaims, 149). The novel also leaves no doubt about the eschatological solemnity of its final scene, in which the reopening of the cement factory coincides with the fourth anniversary of the October Revolution. Gladkov turns the ceremony into a cosmic event: as he delivers his triumphant speech, Chumalov "did not know what he was saying; it seemed to him that he was talking incoherent, pitiable nonsense" (310; cf. the apostles speaking in tongues at Pentecost in Acts 2), while the earth itself rejoices: "Again the mountains thundered and burst into a roar of voices and the blaring of brass [...] And the mountains echoed with metallic thunder and the air was shaken by a mad whirlpool of sound [...] And [the shrieks of the factory sirens] seemed to come, not from the hooters, but from the mountains, rocks, crowd, factory-buildings and smokestacks" (311). Gladkov here patently borrows motifs from the ending of the first volume of Gogol's *Dead Souls*, when Chichikov's troika departs amidst a similar ecstatic cacophony of sounds: "The little bell peals out with a wondrous sound, the air trembles and is torn by the wind, [the troika] flies past everything there is on earth, while looking askance other nations and states move to the side and make way for it" (356),[4] as well as from the biblical sources on which Gogol himself draws, such as the passage in which the prophet Elijah is taken up to heaven by a whirlwind in a chariot of fire (2 Kings 2:11–12) and the one in Ezekiel 37 in which the dry bones scattered in a valley come to life (motifs of resurrection figure prominently in the novel: when Gleb returns from the civil war at the novel's opening he is described as "risen from the dead," 3; the idle cement factory is an "austere temple," 17, destined to be brought back to life – Gladkov came from an Old Believer family). These moments of elevated meaning in Gladkov are "interventions" *par excellence*, interruptions of the ordinary course of events in order to reveal a higher meaning. Gladkov, moreover, was hardly an original thinker (cf. his extensive reliance in *Cement* on articles in *Pravda*; Clark, *The Soviet Novel* 70–7). His novel reflects the atmosphere of the time.[5]

The Stalinist rituals that succeeded early Soviet festivals imposed a tenor markedly different from their predecessors, in a shift that conclusively aligned them with the regime's agenda. It was now exclusively the state that orchestrated the rituals. From the late 1920s on, public spectacles in the Soviet Union underwent a number of legal and formal changes that eliminated worker-run spontaneity in favour of centralized management and control – and one irony attending this shift is that it essentially refined the eschatological strain latent within the rituals' medieval precedents. In Moscow from 1924 on, mass festivals on key holidays like May Day and 7 November, the anniversary of the revolution, now marched across the central locus of Red Square rather than through city streets (Binns 596–7). As Papernyi remarks, "[m]ass demonstrations in theaters were a tribute to the idea, widespread in Culture One [the revolutionary culture of the 1920s, TS], that art should be dissolved within life, that the barrier between the theatre and street should be removed [...] Culture Two [dominant in the Stalin era, TS] violate[d] this equality. Its mass demonstrations were now to be held in specially demarcated places, for them even the entire block between the Alexandrine Gardens, the Manezh, Mokhovaia Street, and the 'Moskva' Hotel [was] torn down" (101).[6] A 1927 *Pravda* article further announced that the Moscow city government (Mossovet) had banned all independent street performances (Kelly 186; see also Alekseev-Iakovlev, *Russkie narodnye gulian'ia* 220). Beginning with the tenth anniversary of the revolution in 1927 emphasis also shifted to "industrial" spectacles (*industrial'nye zrelishcha*), with those of 1927–29 in particular marking a new stage in the evolution of open-air Soviet rites with a still more aggressive spatial agenda: projectors now illuminated buildings along the Neva, and in one display a huge five-pointed star was mounted on Dynamo Stadium, out of whose centre a model multistory factory arose with chimneys; suddenly enemies appeared, battle ensued – and the enemies *were executed* and their two-dimensional figures were burned (Mazaev 372–3). Mass "physical culture" parades on Red Square, a signature phenomenon of the Stalin era, first appeared in 1931 (Petrone 30). The 1937 celebrations of the twentieth anniversary of October were especially extensive. Collectively, they marked the consolidation of the specifically Stalinist view of Russian and Soviet history, one that inflated Stalin's role in planning the events of October 1917 and that demonized his now exiled, arrested, or executed Bolshevik rivals like Trotsky, Kamenev, and Zinoviev (151).

Soviet festivals of the 1920s were unique among European workers' demonstrations for placing portraits and banners at the head of a procession rather than dispersed among the crowd (a reflex, as noted in chapter 4, derived from Orthodox religious processions). Stalin-era festivals then took this a significant step further by choreographing such displays to pass before the gaze of Party leaders. The life-cycle ceremonies that had typified efforts to create a new, proletarian culture in the 1920s also now died out, yielding their place to the "civil parade past the podium and leaders" (Binns 598). In 1939 Sovnarkom's Committee for Artistic Affairs took this a step further by issuing Decree no. 625 forbidding portrayals of political leaders in theatrical productions: leaders now were to be subjects of display, not depicted objects (Antonov-Ovseenko 144). The 1930s saw a dramatic change in the objects, slogans, and diagrams used in demonstrations; now most banners featured paeans to the Communist Party and portraits of its leaders. Indeed, this new type of mass festival was choreographed for a *sole* observer – Stalin, who stood atop Lenin's mausoleum, posed in a claim to legitimacy above his predecessor's "sacred" remains.

"Moscow parade participants moved through the main square of ancient Muscovy, but it was now dominated by the mausoleum containing the embalmed body of Lenin. Stalin stood atop Lenin's mausoleum to witness the symbolic representation of the entire country parading before him. According to official rhetoric, Lenin's presence was also felt at this sacred place" (Petrone 25). The beginnings of this implicit deification date back to the Lenin worship that had already begun in 1923 (Binns 599) and that, following his death in 1924, turned into a veritable Lenin cult (see Tumarkin); but now it was Stalin who appeared as a living god, his ubiquitous image increasingly displacing those of other leaders. As Glebkin remarks, the centre of the demonstrations was now the figure of Stalin, whose words on banners and whose portrait were carried along the procession's course. What defined Soviet demonstrations in the Stalin era, in pointed contrast to those of the 1920s, was the addition to the processions (*demonstratsii*) of a tribunal past which they marched – an installation of the very object Shklovsky had warned against. The tribunal signalled the addition of a "receiving and evaluating subject" (*prinimaiuishchii i otsenivaiushchii sub"ekt*, Glebkin 100, 104).

As Stalin assumed the role of supreme subject of Soviet utopian aims rather than mere human, his image on festival banners acquired a transcendent gaze; in a certain light he could even seem already dead and gazing down from extrahistorical space:

As I have suggested elsewhere regarding a 1936 portrait of Stalin painted by Pavel Filonov, an artist who otherwise worked in a fragmented and surrealist manner, the painting's "patent flirtation with the genre of the icon manages to render its subject as if he were at once transcendent and (especially in the eerily vacant eyes) dead. The form of a resurrected self is there, but the essence is gone, as if we were in fact looking at a purified corpse" ("*Razgovor vpolgolosa*" 182). That Filonov's portrait resembles an icon painting reminds us, in this context, that Father Pavel Florensky identifies the origins of the icon in the Egyptian death-mask ("Ikonostas" 169–73).[7] This bifurcation of the image of Stalin into two hypostases, the earthly and the transcendent, extended throughout the culture, whose subjects sensed it intuitively. Consider the response of actor Aleksei Dikii, who played Stalin on the screen, to the director Mikhail Romm, who asked him why he would talk without looking other actors in the eye: "I'm not playing a person; I'm playing a granite monument" (quoted in Dobrenko, 75, who also notes how in the 1950 film *The Fall of Berlin* Stalin "flies to the prostrate Berlin,

5.1. Portrait of Stalin featured as part of a living parade in Red Square involving 75,000 athletes and children in celebration of Soviet Constitution Day. The procession took six hours to cross the square and was watched by Stalin. Smith Archive/Alamy Stock Photo.

5.2. Pavel Filonov's 1936 portrait of Stalin. The Picture Art Collection/Alamy Stock Photo.

dressed in a blindingly white tunic, [and] descends like an angel from the heavens to the crowds of people awaiting him," 83 – an episode of "intervention" in its own right that, in addition to its obvious religious allusions, suggests an eerie parallel to the appearance of the Benefactor in Zamyatin's dystopian tale *We*).

This implicit double deification of Stalin atop the mausoleum containing Lenin's mummified remains was also, essentially, the culmination of a drive toward the "manifestation" of deity inherent in the mystery play and other rites; as noted in chapter 2, Freidenberg equated this with *cystai mysticai*, secret holy chambers or baskets serving as repositories of deity from antiquity onward – again, a deep cultural memory mobilized by the Stalinist regime.

Something of the baroque (or more accurately Babylonian) complexity involved in this new form of Soviet ritual can be sensed in an essay

Meyerhold published in the late 1920s. As we have seen, Meyerhold generally rejected the cultic yearnings of other modernist theoreticians of the theatre; yet in "Rekonstruktsiia teatra (1929–1930 gg.)" he outlines a vision of public ritual as a means for theatrical renovation. Writing against the current of virulently "proletarian" rhetoric during the first Five-Year Plan, he speaks with lyrical hopefulness about the idea of mass urban spectacles as apotheoses of aestheticism and antidotes to the heavy-handed indoctrination of RAPP-era culture.[8] Almost as if through metonymic association, the fact that the forms of theatre in which he finds genuine "theatricality" tend to be associated with the street or the public square turns the essay into an appeal to the idea of the *city* itself as the natural platform for theatrical performance. In France, he comments, competition with the traditional theatre comes from the street: on the Place d'Italie or Place Clichy one may meet a poor worker in shabby clothing, but he will be wearing a fashionable tie because he has seen the paintings of Manet and Cezanne. The influence of art on the street is thus palpable in Paris (*Stat'i, Pis'ma, Rechi, Besedy. Chast' vtoraia* [*SPRB*] 1968, 202). Moreover, "the fêtes and carnival booths [*balagany*] that appear now in this, now in that district provide more pleasure to the Parisian than what theatre directors offer him" (203). It is true, Meyerhold concedes, that the modern viewer is "rudderless" (*bez rulia*) and lost among all the fêtes, cinemas, and street theatres (205); but in this essay it is clear that for him, it is the urban street that comes closest to realizing his ideal of genuine theatricality.

Meyerhold makes a concession to the ideology of the Five-Year Plan by claiming that in the Soviet Union the new task facing the theatre is to transform viewers so that over the course of the performance there emerges in them a "firm will to fight" (*krepchaishaia volia k bor'be, SPRB* 209), one that will make them fit for "socialist construction" (209). But he nonetheless holds out for a measure of aestheticism in theatre. Aggressively agitational and anti-aesthetic theatre has recently been unmasked as a harmful phenomenon, he remarks, thus turning the period's overheated political rhetoric against it (193). Instead, to meet the demands of the modern spectator the theatre should emulate the scale of cinema and sporting events. The "box-stage" (*stsena-korobka*, 196) must be destroyed if performances are to become dynamic. In an echo (intentional or not) of the changes in theatrical design that Wagner sought to embody in his Festspielhaus in Bayreuth in the 1870s, he urges Soviet theatres to get rid of loggias and terraced seats because only an "amphitheatrical arrangement of the auditorium" will accomplish the aims of the new theatre (196). Still more remarkably for the late 1920s – that is, well into the "re-cameralization" of Soviet theatre that

Clark speaks of (*nota bene*, it was around this time that Bulgakov began *The Master and Margarita*) – the essay then turns into a paean to street theatre, to the street *as* theatre (at least in Western Europe, especially Paris), in contrast to the traditional theatre, which Meyerhold characterizes as a little box on a side street in which plays are put on for a handful of viewers. He contends that the modern spectator wants stadiums, as evidenced, again, by the popularity of the cinema. But he finds his best evidence of this modern desire for large-scale spectacle not in any theatre or stadium *per se* but in large-scale street performances. In Italy, he remarks, it was the Church that finally gave the people the kind of theatre they wanted. As if explicating the logic of the mystery genre when it is taken up by a dictatorship, he observes that "the Vatican became a laboratory for the art of directing" (199) because "*there is a natural harmony between Catholic religious processions and fascist parades,* both of which are part of a revival of authentic street theatre in Italy [*vosstanovlenie podlinno ulichnogo teatra*] and other countries which have given free rein to the Catholic church" (200, emphasis added; even the Russian Orthodox, he wryly notes, has picked up on this by using modern instrumental music – stooping even to accordions – to attract young people to its services). That "entrepreneur" living in the Vatican has such a talent for theatrical direction, Meyerhold remarks, that when he organizes a grand spectacle even atheists flock to it because the Pope and his minions understand the power of such displays (*grandioznoe zrelishche*, as examples of which Meyerhold names papal excursions, religious processions, illuminations, fireworks, and audiences at which people can kiss the Pope's hand, 200–1). Mussolini, moreover, is shrewd enough to realize that he does not need any theatre as such, he needs only to insinuate his fascist parades into the processions organized by the Catholic Church (201). On the rare occasions when mass spectacles are organized in the Soviet Union, Meyerhold then comments, they rival these papal fests. The parallel between fascist Italy and the Stalinist Soviet Union may not have been at all far-fetched. Shcheglov notes that in 1930 Pope Pius XI called for "anti-Bolshevik" processions of the cross; this set off a virulent anti-papal campaign in the Soviet Union (commentary to Il'f and Petrov, *Zolotoi telenok* 517n8) – while Tucker still more compellingly suggests that an article Bukharin published in *Pravda* on 7 March 1930, "ostensibly a long polemic against the Papacy," was in fact widely read as an Aesopian attack on Stalin (*The Great Purge Trial* xix). Read in this light, Meyerhold's anachronistic appeal to the aims of modernist theatre at the turn of the 1930s emerges as an ambivalent accommodation – shrewdly perceptive in its realization of the bond between spectacle and state power – to Stalinist ritual as a form of open-air urban monumentalism that at least triumphs over the traditional stage.

Paradoxically in this climate of rising solemnity, official appeals to carnival culture actually increased in the Stalin era. Private fairgrounds were closed down in the late 1920s and 1930s, but they were replaced by a network of *parki kul'tury i otdykha* (parks of culture and rest) designed and administered by the state, in which the authorities organized new mass demonstrations (Kelly 186; Alekseev-Iakovlev 220). Petrone notes the proliferation around 1937 of officially organized "Soviet carnivals for adults" (100), from which sadness and despair were banned – jokingly, but still by formal instruction – for example, signs at cloakrooms informed visitors that sadness was forbidden inside (101). Fitzpatrick similarly cites an Australian visitor to Moscow's Gorky Park, who commented that "they take their pleasure sadly […] Among the many thousands there we scarcely saw a smile, though we assumed that they were enjoying themselves" (95). Most of these carnivals were organized in response to Stalinism's official slogan boasting that "life [in the Soviet Union] had become gayer" (*zhit' stalo veselee*, 113). Aleksandr Medvedkin's exuberant cinematic celebration of Stalinist urban planning, the 1938 film *Novaia Moskva* (*The New Moscow*), even features a "carnival night" in which costumed characters cavort on the symbolically central space of Red Square under neon portraits of Lenin and Stalin. At the height of the festivities the heroine urges them on, "а теперь веселиться, веселиться, веселиться и танцевать!" (and now make merry, make merry, make merry – and dance!). In its hints of nocturnal grotesquery the scene parallels Woland's ball in *The Master and Margarita* while also calling to mind Shakespeare's *A Midsummer Night's Dream* – the latter projecting putative magical qualities onto Stalinist urban transformation. Sartori observes that "the mass carnivals staged during the very same period [mid- and late 1930s, TS] were a new feature of holiday culture in the time of Stalin" (43). The "political and industrial carnival" of the NEP period had been different (43) – organized by dramatic circles (*dramkruzhki*) as exercises in amateur creativity (*samodeiatel'nost'*) for workers. In the 1930s central planners began to stage much larger-scale events. Workers' club activities came under criticism for their failure to manifest sufficient political consciousness in the culture of the first Five-Year Plan (59) – at which point the directors of amateur circles were replaced by Party officials (60) – an example, as Sartori sees it, of the perennial Bolshevik fear of the spontaneity of the masses (60). In the Stalin era, official holiday rituals like the mass *karnavaly* held in Moscow's Gorky Park "were staged, according to military command" (67). After 1930 there was much greater centralized co-ordination and standardization of the activities of mass holidays (Lane 178–9). In Mazaev's view the genuine carnival elements (as he would see them) still present in festivals of the 1920s yielded to a qualitatively different "political carnival" (*politkarnaval*) in the 1930s, in which the emphasis now fell on the mocking (*osmeianie*) of internal and external enemies of the USSR (359–62). If the earlier festivals of the 1920s indeed harboured any moment of Bakhtinian carnival, in which the old hierarchy was inverted and swept away in an eruption of folk laughter, then one can see a clear progression from that kind of ostensible merriment to *satire* and *mockery*, and, through those, to *judgment*.[9]

Indeed, when considered in its Stalin-era context, even the Bakhtinian concept of "carnival," otherwise readable as a paean to unfettered freedom and the prerogative of the folk over the elite, may comport unacknowledged traces of authoritarian thought. One view of Bakhtin's work holds that, while appearing to ignore Russian carnival, his major scholarly work of the 1930s, the massive book on Rabelais, is "in fact a monument to it that was constructed at the moment when the fairground tradition was about to vanish" (Kelly 189). Stallybrass and White similarly suggest that the notion of carnival that Bakhtin develops in the *Rabelais* book was "a cryptic anti-Stalinist allegory" (11). Like Freidenberg with her attention to the ways in which the ancient world embodied deity in spatial forms, Bakhtin developed his ideas about medieval carnival within a distinctly Soviet – even Stalinist – world. Another way of understanding the shift represented by Stalinist rituals is to see them not as a divergence from Bakhtin's sense of carnival (though they are that, in the strict sense of his concept as outlined in the *Rabelais* book) but as actually mirroring and exemplifying its deeper, historically embedded meanings. As Ginsburg points out, carnival was historically only part of a calendrical ritual whose next phase was Lent ("Karneval und Fasten" 26). Stallybrass and White, too, remark that "carnival was a specific calendrical ritual: carnival proper, for instance, occurred around February each year, ineluctably followed by Lenten fasting and abstinence bound tightly to laws, structures and institutions which had briefly been denied during its reign" (15; see also Grois, "Totalitarizm karnavala" 78; and Clark, *Petersburg* 286).

Several scholars since Bakhtin have also noted the limits of his theory of "carnival." Terry Eagleton speaks of carnival as "a *licensed* affair in every sense, a permissible rupture of hegemony" (in *Walter Benjamin: Towards a Revolutionary Criticism*, quoted in Stallybrass and White 13). As Georges Balandier comments in *Political Anthropology*, "[t]he supreme ruse of power is to allow itself to be contested *ritually* in order to consolidate itself more effectively" (quoted in Stallybrass and White 14).

Given the examples of Bolshevik state planning in the preceding chapter, one could question whether anything like Bakhtinian (read, Rabelaisian) carnival ever took root in Soviet culture of the 1920s or 1930s. But as noted earlier, the transition to still more centralized planning and even greater control over rituals in the 1930s was pronounced, and can be thought of in terms of an example Stallybrass and White give of the curtailment of carnival in late-medieval Europe: in the 1596 Avignon carnival a procession that included transvestites and people in motley costume representing Italians, Spaniards, and Alsatians was met by a second procession of people dressed as apostles, evangelists, and saints, which walked in an orderly manner around the churches – and yielded to it (55).

Other commentators on Bakhtin further see in his notion of carnival not resistance to the Stalinist world, but its refined (if troubled) reflection. In Ryklin's view, for example, Bakhtin's book on Rabelais was indirectly dedicated to the Stalinist terror – the mass arrests and executions unleashed in the mid-1930s – and dictated by it (140). The true subject of Bakhtin's book on Rabelais, he argues, is the Soviet urban populace, a largely peasant stratum conscripted to perform industrial labour in the city and defined by a folkloric element torn from its village roots but still carried by this "nomadified mass which formed in Soviet cities" (*nomadizovannaia massa obrazovalas' v sovetskikh gorodakh*) in 1935–36, the years in which Bakhtin was writing his book (131; moreover, Rabelais's *Pantagruel*, he points out, was itself written in a time of natural disasters in France in 1532; 133). In a still more extensive commentary Groys argues that Bakhtin's concepts of the polyphonic novel and carnival should be understood as inherently in tune with the totalitarianism of Stalinist society. The two master concepts in Bakhtin's *oeuvre* (carnival and polyphony) are related, in Groys's view, because the polyphonic novel, which overcomes the principle of monologism and individual authorship, has its roots for Bakhtin in a carnivalistic ritual that by its nature subsumes all individualization ("Totalitarizm karnavala" 77). Bakhtinian carnival, whose mass celebrations overwhelm the individual, even the individual body, which carnival forces open to emit "base" material like feces and urine, ultimately works to swamp individual dignity and democracy. "What Bakhtin welcomes in all this is precisely the carnival pathos of the 'final death' of everything individual, the victory of a purely material, bodily principle over everything transcendent, ideal, individual, and immortal. In short, Bakhtinian carnival is horrible – God forbid you should end up in one" (78).[10] Carnival laughter in Groys's view is thus not the irony of the thinker over the tragedy of life but a joyous folk or cosmic laughter; it reflects "corporeal" idiocy over the tormented writhings of the tortured individual (78–9). Moreover, in its enthusiasm for carnival's ritual inversion of social hierarchies the Bakhtinian notion of carnival reproduces Stalinism's constant sudden crownings and uncrownings, its mass arrests and executions that opened the way for rapid promotions of individuals who themselves in turn were often then unmasked and removed (*uvenchaniia–razvenchaniia*, 79, a phenomenon the historian Adam Ulam called Stalinism's "lottery of terror and opportunity," 133). The terror assumed a grotesque carnival quality, attended as it was by Stalin's slogan that "life has become gayer," and it is well-known that his favourite film was the giddily carnivalesque *Volga-Volga* (79). "All these observations point to the fact that Bakhtin's goal was in no way a democratic critique of the Revolution and the Stalinist Terror but their theoretical justification *as a ritual action arising out of archaic tradition*" (79, emphasis added).[11] For Groys, Bakhtin at the end of the day was not a Stalinist – but still less was he an anti-Stalinist (80). He interpreted the Stalin era in the Nietzschean terms handed down to him by the Silver Age (80).[12]

In this light it is perhaps not surprising that to an even greater extent than its superficially more festive predecessor in the Leninist 1920s, this stricter regime of Stalinism drew on cultural practices and mindsets going back to the Middle Ages. It is here that the medieval precedent of mixing representational and ritual modes emerges as most consequential in the Soviet era: taken out of its original sacred space, ritual now places its demands – projects its designs – onto the empirical world. In keeping with the symbolic logic of festivals examined in this study, with their latent or manifest aim to take hold of and transform urban space, the monumentalizing impulse informing Stalinist rituals naturally extended as well to plans for a radical redesign of the city of Moscow. As an aspect of the Soviet rituals with which it shared an organic link in the cultural consciousness, Stalin-era urban planning can be understood as a shift from the kind of aspiration to bring about a *temporary* transformation of urban space in order to stage a transcendent event that is implicit in earlier Soviet rituals (an inheritance from their medieval and modernist precedents) to a more explicit intention to bring about a *permanent* transformation of urban space that would install a new symbolic order. Here we can look back to the comments on the semiotics of space with which this study began. As Eliade observes in *The Sacred and the Profane*, "to organize space is to repeat the paradigmatic work of the gods" (32). In a related vein, Groys has provocatively argued that Stalinist aims to remake the world had a still nearer source:

The obvious "Byzantine" attributes of Stalinist culture and its saturation with Christian symbolism are often traced to Stalin's theological training and traditional Russian piety, which was now frustrated and transferred to a new object. All such superficial sociological explanations, however, are unsatisfactory. The usurpation of God's role and the reconstruction and reinterpretation of the myth of God the Artist who shapes "life" and "overcome[s] the resistance of the material" are all hidden avant-garde mythologemes. (*The Total Art of Stalinism* 69–70).[13]

Or, as Colton comments in a more quotidian vein, "Stalin's Moscow may be read as an object lesson in the power of government to remake the world" (354).[14]

Plans for the transformation of Moscow initially had a modernizing, practical cast that was seemingly far removed from the kinds of archaic rituals discussed here and that would seem to place the Stalinist project as a belated addition to a list of grand projects that included such mid-nineteenth-century projects as Haussmann's renovation of Paris, the building of Vienna's Ringstrasse, and, to take an example from the Russian imperial past, the Russian mayor Sokrat Starynkevich's renovations of Warsaw. Efforts to improve infrastructure and services in Moscow began in 1930 with a Politburo discussion of the topic; this was followed by the promulgation on 15 June 1931 of a Central Committee resolution "On Moscow's Urban Services and the Development of Urban Services in the U.S.S.R." (Colton 252–3). Lazar Kaganovich's *The Socialist Reconstruction of Moscow* (1931) continued to concentrate on topics such as transportation and housing, extolling the improvements made to workers' lives under the Soviet regime (from the early to mid-1930s Kaganovich served as head of the Moscow *oblast'* as well as its city government; it was he who organized most of the reconstruction efforts in this period). In 1929–30 the government announced projects for communal housing that would accommodate 2,500 people (Clark, *Petersburg* 252). In the mid-1930s, however, planning priorities shifted, from the poor on the city's periphery to the political elite in its centre (Colton 325; Colton also notes the "egregious centralization of decision making" in the Moscow city government; 324). This was more than just a reorganization of government. As Papernyi remarks, the hierarchy of individuals was superimposed "on a hierarchy of spaces, so that 'good' … people proved to be closer to the centre of the world – Moscow, and even the centre of Moscow – and 'the bad' occupied the periphery" (Papernyi 88, quoted in Colton 284–5).[15]

As a harbinger of more expansive plans to redefine Moscow's urban space, throughout the 1920s many streets in the capital and other cities were given new, Soviet names (Colton 267). But the decisive move came with the promulgation on 19 June 1935 of Resolution no. 1435 by the Central Committee of the Communist Party titled "On the General Plan for the Reconstruction of the City of Moscow," which called for such a plan to be implemented over the course of a decade. The first phase involved destroying existing buildings to make way for monumental new structures. The Triumphal Gates, erected in 1812–14 to commemorate the victory over Napoleon, were demolished; then the sixteenth-century brick Kitaigorod Walls were torn down to make space for several monumental buildings as well as public processions; then Kaganovich had the Iberian Chapel on Red Square demolished "because it impeded the simultaneous arrival of parades marching in from six districts of Moscow" (Rolf 81); then the seventeenth-century Sukharev Tower was demolished – all of this over protests from preservationists (Colton 264–5, 280). Plans were also made to widen several city streets and construct new thoroughfares, to impose a more fitting sense of grandeur on the city – an impulse that may be linked to the *transection* of the city by processions in the 1920s discussed in the previous chapter. The Stalin plan now sought to make permanent this transection of urban space by symbolic markers. Three principal routes were designed to cross the city: from Izmailovo to the Lenin Hills, from the Leningrad Highway (Leningradskoe shosse) to the Stalin Automobile Factory on the south side; and from Ostankino in the north to the Serpukhovskoye Highway on the south side. The new type of festival now staged on the symbolically central space of Red Square, before leaders assembled atop the Lenin Mausoleum and the walls of the Kremlin housing the Soviet government, derived from this same impulse.[16]

As Clark has noted, when Moscow was redesigned in the 1930s, one widely publicized aspect of the transformation was the cleaning out of the petty stall-owners (*lavochniki*); she links this to the avant-garde's enduring desire for a "Christ" who would drive the moneychangers from the Temple of Communism (*Petersburg* 307) – again, a seemingly incongruous note for the militantly atheist Stalinist regime but one entirely consistent with the legacy of the mystery genre examined here, in which both purification and a desire to displace history as here-and-now and replace it with transcendence played a role. Another element in the city's physical transformation involved constructing newly "proletarian" parks, such as the Gorky Park for Culture and Rest in the centre and the spacious Exhibit of Achievements of the Domestic Economy (known usually by its Russian initials, VDNKh) on the city's north side. Installed on the site of the 1922–23 All-Union Agricultural Exhibit, the exhibit became – in keeping with the general trend of these Stalinist initiatives – a permanent presence (in 1947 Vera Mukhina's monumental 24.5 metre sculpture *The Worker and the Collective Farm Worker*, originally displayed at the 1937 International Exposition in Paris, was installed near its entrance, where it stands to this day). Moscow also took on a (somewhat specious) maritime identity with the construction of a network of canals (starting with work on the Moscow-Volga Canal, begun in 1932) that eventually enabled the slogan, "Moscow – Port of Seven Seas" – a way of insinuating it as the centre of the world – which the present author remembers from his youthful visits to the place.[17] The General Plan further envisioned a system of two canals encircling the city in a ring structure. New bridges were built, and existing ones were replaced with larger ones.[18]

One of the most ambitious projects of the Stalin era, technologically as well as symbolically, was the construction of the Moscow subway system. Work on it began in March 1932 when ground was broken on Rusakovskaia Street. The first line, from Sokol'niki to Gorky Park, was completed on 14 May 1932, and the system was opened to the public on 15 May 1935, with 11.2 kilometres of line and thirteen stations in service (Colton 255, 257). The aesthetic designs for the stations far exceeded the system's practical function of facilitating movement around the capital: this was, again, a modernizing project harnessed to a symbolic agenda that intended to lift this element of public space out of a mere present and place it on another, eschatological plane. In its initial realization (i.e., the stations built in the Stalin era – several more were added in the postwar years) it was nothing less than a lavish incarnation in marble (some of which had been taken from the demolished Cathedral of Christ the Redeemer), bronze, and glass mosaics showing the aims of the Stalin regime – an apotheosis of Stalinist symbols and appropriation of space whose subterranean location only added to the impression that a new (or at least other) world had come into being.

As Mikhail Ryklin argued in a celebrated essay, the sculpted and bronze human figures adorning the subway stations collectively amounted to a reflection of the Stalin-era ideal of *narodnost'* (essentially, folk identity); the multitude of jubilant worker and peasant bodies celebrated a mythical agricultural abundance that served as a mirror in which an otherwise decimated social consciousness could gaze on itself as innocent (138) – in this also inadvertently reflecting the Terror (the *tela terrora*, "bodies of the Terror" of his title) in an organic link with the "carnival" bodies of Bakhtin's book on Rabelais.

The most obvious (or egregious) symbol of the eschatology the General Plan sought to impose in its aspiration to position Moscow as the centre of the cosmos – as Clark comments, "In the 1930s, the city of Moscow functioned as a kind of hyperspace that had transcended time and was hence of a different order of reality from that of familiar parts" (*Petersburg* 302)[19] – was embedded in the competition for designs for

5.3. Sculptures in the Revolution Square subway station in Moscow. Sally
Anderson/Alamy Stock Photo.

a "Palace of Soviets" (*Dvorets sovetov*) that had been announced four
years ahead of the General Plan, in 1931. The building was intended
to provide an apotheosis of Stalinism in permanent and gargantuan
architectural form. The design was to be for "a massively enlarged version of […] the Palace of Labour nearly ten years earlier," an aspiration
revived in 1931 "to celebrate 'our success in the building of socialism,'
with auditoria now to hold six and fifteen thousand people" (Cooke
and Kazus 15). As evidence of the project's descent from earlier Bolshevik (and modernist, and medieval) street festivals, the initial statement
of the building's purpose called for it not only to accommodate mass
assemblies but also to be "accessible for mass processions and festival parades" (one of the proposed designs did this by incorporating a
massive archway through which parades could process, although this
requirement was dropped from the final competition; Cooke and Kazus

5.4. Komsomol (Communist Youth League) subway station in Moscow. Jon Arnold Images Ltd./Alamy Stock Photo.

59; see also Rolf 81). In all, 272 proposals were submitted, including entries from Walter Gropius, LeCorbusier, Auguste Perret, and other Western architects, as well as, among several Soviet contributors, from Ivan Zholtovskii (many of whose designs installed a Stalinist neoclassicist style in the capital) and Boris Iofan. On 10 May 1933 the Construction Council announced that the final project would be based on Iofan's design (Colton 260; Cooke and Kazus 59).

The building was designed to be the tallest in the world, with the statue of Lenin atop it projected to be three times the height of the Statue of Liberty (the latter requirement stipulated by the council when it announced that Iofan's plan had been selected; Cooke and Kazus, 59; Colton 332). In a further reflex of the kind of aspiration toward "intervention" this study has explored, the palace was meant to be more than simply an imposing addition to the Moscow skyline; it was to stand for eternity (Colton 333). As Groys suggests in his essay on the origins of Stalinism in the culture of the avant-garde, both the avant-garde and Socialist Realism – of which the palace could be seen as a consummate

5.5. Artist's rendering of Boris Iofan's entry to the design competition for the
Palace of Soviets. Album/Alamy Stock Photo.

architectural example – "aspired to resurrect by technological means
the wholeness of God's world that had been disrupted by technology; to
halt technological progress and the march of history in general by placing it under complete technological control; to conquer time and enter
into eternity" (*Total Art of Stalinism* 72). In Medvedkin's film *The New
Moscow* the image of the palace taken from Iofan's proposal looms large
over images of the city, a distant, ethereal, and even somewhat chilling
sight (the building was meant, after all, to intimidate with its Babylonian
scale) – with the outsized statue of Lenin on top both instantiating, à la
Freidenberg, the presence of the deity in the city (mirroring in its height
the mausoleum holding his corpse on Red Square below) and pointing,
through the gesture of his arm, toward transhistorical utopia.

Papernyi's comment on Stalinist architecture in general finds its
epitome in the plans for the Palace of Soviets: "the architecture of the
1930s–1950s is a vertical stage set for a state spectacle performed for
those in *power*" (71).[20]

The history of the palace's non-construction – which can be seen
as emblematic of the ultimate failure of Stalinist utopian designs in

5.6. Still from Aleksandr Medvedkin's 1938 film *The New Moscow*.

general – is now familiar. Following the pilfering of the more luxurious ornamentation from the nineteenth-century Cathedral of Christ the Redeemer, some of which found its way into the lavish underground stations, the cathedral was dynamited to make room for construction of the palace. The soil on the site adjacent to the Moscow River, however, turned out to be too unstable to support the massive project, even after aggressive efforts were made to shore it up by injecting bitumen and by dumping on the site confiscated tombstones from cemeteries around Moscow (Colton 333). Construction was suspended in 1941 with the beginning of the war and never resumed (Cooke and Kazus 59). After the war the site was turned into an enormous outdoor swimming pool. All of these events were perhaps anticipated by Andrei Platanov in his 1930 tale *Koltovan* (*The Foundation Pit*), in which engineers overseeing the digging of the foundation pit for a workers' dormitory serially revise their plans to accommodate ever larger, more utopian schemes, until all that is produced is an enormous hole in the ground (in a moment of historical irony, an exact facsimile of the original cathedral was re-erected in the 1990s under then-mayor Iurii Luzhkov).

A further eschatological reflex – part of its intention to lift the project out of mere history and elevate it to the plane of eternity – was the General Plan's appeal to the city of Rome as a model. As Papernyi comments, "the idea of Rome, multiplied by Holy Rus', appears throughout Russian cultural history" (44),[21] beginning notably with Metropolitan Filaret's doctrine of Moscow as the "Third Rome" and underscored by Ivan IV's appropriation of the title "Caesar" – in its corrupted Russian form, tsar (Clark notes that Sergei Eisenstein's 1943 film *Ivan Groznyi* implicitly projects the reign of Ivan onto the Stalin era when Filaret's doctrine is invoked during the coronation scene of 1547; *Moscow, The Fourth Rome* 1). The Roman analogy, which in Russian culture has always signalled an orientation toward "history, tradition, and eternity" (Papernyi 45), was then renewed during transformative building campaigns in the reigns of Peter the Great and Catherine the Great.[22] In the case of the Stalinist General Plan, the appeal manifested itself not only in the ponderous neoclassicism of buildings erected in the capital (which often featured imposing columns, a style often referred to as "Stalinist empire" and jocularly mocked in Russian as *ampir vo vremia chumy*, a pun on "empire [style]" and the expression "a feast [*pir*] in time of plague") but also in such instances as the declaration by the architect Aleksei Shchusev (designer *inter alia* of the Lenin Mausoleum and the columned facade of the Moskva Hotel) that "*we* are the sole inheritors of Rome"; in the Soviet government's conscription of the writer Aleksei Tolstoy to produce a novel to be titled *Rome* (including dispatch of him to Italy to gather material) and that author's statement that "Rome is closest of all to *us*"; and the 1935 vote, after a ten-year absence from international architectural forums, by the Organizing Committee of the Union of Soviet Architects to send a delegation to Rome, in response to an invitation from the National Fascist Union of Architects in Italy (Papernyi 45–6).

One recalls again Meyerhold's appeal to contemporary fascist Roman spectacle as an example of state power on display (even its possible use as a veiled reference to Stalinism rests on an assumed parallel between Moscow and Rome), and, beyond that, the prominence of Roman scenes in the panoramas that embodied nineteenth-century projections of meaning onto the cityscape, as ways of locating the city at the centre of cosmic meaning. Here, too, a literary reflection brings forward latent themes in the culture. Mikhail Kuzmin's 1929 play *Smert' Nerona* (*The Death of Nero*) closely resembles both Blok's "Catiline," with its idea of the parallel between ancient Rome and Soviet Russia, and Bulgakov's *The Master and Margarita*, which was begun at about the same time.[23] Kuzmin had written in 1925 that "there can be no doubt about the analogy between the birth of Christianity and the development of socialism. They are linked through their racial origins, the class nature of their message, the composition of their first audience, their attitude toward the family, the state, the extant culture and art, and their internationalism."[24] *The Death of Nero* combines scenes set in 1919 (in Italy, Soviet Russia, and Switzerland) with scenes set in Rome during Nero's reign – a period after the life of Christ when Christianity was in its infancy, a context Kuzmin invokes in his play by including Nero's mistress Acte (*Akteia*), a representative of the new "sect" who calls Nero the Antichrist when he says that he would crucify anyone who could raise the dead (361). Kuzmin draws obvious parallels between the Roman scenes and Soviet Russia of the first Five-Year Plan: Nero fancies himself an "artist" of world significance and has plans for bringing about universal well-being within four years, while the impoverished Roman populace is subject to rising prices.[25] Nero moreover receives a visit from an architect who explains plans for the redesigning the city of Rome (351–2) that are reminiscent of contemporary plans for redesigning Moscow (Timofeev 414). There are, in addition, some remarkable similarities to devices in Bulgakov's novel, suggesting that both writers are responding to impulses in the culture as a whole. Early in the play, while staying in a Roman hotel, Pavel Lukin reads a play he has written about the death of Nero, so that by implication he is the author of the play's ancient Roman scenes, just as the Master is by implication the author of the Jerusalem scenes in Bulgakov's novel. Like the Master and Ivan Bezdomny in *The Master and Margarita*, Kuzmin's Pavel ends up in an insane asylum, where the other patients try to convince him that he is Nero's reincarnation. The parallels between the Roman and modern scenes of Kuzmin's play – for example, the fire in the hotel in which Pavel is staying and the burning of Rome under Nero – are also reminiscent of scenic parallels between Moscow and Yershalaim in Bulgakov's novel (Kalb 176, 188).

All this may seem familiar enough as examples of exotica deriving from Russia's grotesque episode, in the mid-twentieth century, of what Khrushchev denounced at the Twentieth Party Congress in 1956 as Stalin's criminal "cult of personality," of Stalinism's brutally totalitarian rule and aspiration to instantiate, if for now only in representations, a "new world." Less obvious, but equally essential to our understanding of the culture, may be the organic link (subterranean, perhaps, in the social subconscious) between both modernist and early Soviet stagings of "intervention," and a certain principle of *judgment* embedded in their medieval precedents: if Moscow is the centre of the cosmos and Stalin its deity, then the logic of these forms and rituals that bring "deity" down to earth dictates that what must take place on this site will be some form of Final Judgment.

Like Soviet spectacles themselves, the impulse toward staging scenes of judgment had precedents in the pre-revolutionary era, suggesting that a certain impulse to stage public trials was endemic to Russia's still deeply pious culture in the late nineteenth and early twentieth centuries. Wood notes that the "agitational" trials of the 1920s drew on evident pre-revolutionary sources, despite Bolshevik claims that the format had arisen spontaneously in Soviet society.[26] Among these sources were works like the "Trial of Paradise," the "Trial of the Sinful Soul," and "The Last Judgment" performed in Kyiv's Mohyla Academy (similar "school plays" reinforcing religious and moral values were common in other seminaries as well, 16–18, 34; "That these school plays had a direct influence on the creation of agitation plays can be seen in the number of parallels between the two"; 18). The Cossacks had a folk drama called "The Trial of Ataman Burya," which had taken root well before the twentieth century, in which the Ataman meted out justice to landowners, merchants, and other enemies of the lower classes (Stites, "Trial as Theatre" 8; Cassiday 54). Also, Boele cites a "literary test trial" organized by students of St. Petersburg University in February 1909 at which the "decadent" writers Artsybashev, Kuzmin, and Sologub were tried on charges of "pornography" (103; see also Wood 48–9).

"Judgment" spectacles proliferated in the wake of the October Revolution, when "agitational trials" (*agitsud*, i.e., mock trials staged as a form of "agitational" propaganda) were performed as a way to instil the political and ethical values of the new Soviet regime. In a 1922 letter to Dmitrii Kurskii, People's Commissar for Justice, Lenin called for "exemplary trials" (*obraztsovye protsessy*) to redress the absence of "commotion" (*shum*) directed at the enemies of his New Economic Plan. "The educational significance of trials is enormous," he intoned ("O zadachakh narkomiusta" 397; see also Cassiday 37). As Wood comments, "the agitation trials essentially present conversion stories. Individuals 'see the light.' They 'find the truth.' They recognize Soviet power" (141–2).[27] Kerzhentsev records that one spectacle called "Sud nad Gaponom" ("The Trial of Gapon" – Father Gapon was the Orthodox priest who led the worker procession seeking redress from the tsar on what came to be called Bloody Sunday in 1905) was staged shortly after the revolution in Petrograd and other Russian cities (*Tvorcheskii teatr* 133). Another mock process, "The Trial of Wrangel," was staged in the Kuban region of the northern Caucasus in autumn 1919; this elaborate affair drew an audience of 10,000 Red Army soldiers, Cossacks, and peasants (the professional actor hired to play Wrangel reportedly feared for his life at the hands of this agitated mob; Stites, "Trial as Theatre" 10). Kerzhentsev records a similar "Sud nad ubiitsami Karla Libknekhta" ("Trial of Karl Liebknecht's Murderers," 133; Liebknecht was a founder of the German Communist Party and an ally of Rosa Luxemburg, with whom he was arrested and executed in 1919 by elements of the German government). Mock processes with titles like "Sud na negramotnymi" ("The Trial of the Illiterates"), "Sud nad novoi zhenshchinoi" ("The Trial of the New Woman"), and "Sud nad prostitutkoi" ("The Trial of the Prostitute") carried forward into the Soviet era the format of seminary morality plays (133). Mock trials as theatre were typically put on in the 1920s by *dramkruzhki*, amateur dramatic circles organized within ministries or other government bodies with the aim of excoriating abstract vices such as drunkenness, prostitution, and tardiness at work (Wood 2, 78); or they featured fictitious characters who had done wrong, such as a young communist girl who married a NEPman, workers who misused machinery, or peasants who failed to manage their cows "scientifically" (this is the context so vividly present in Mayakovsky's play *The Bedbug*, which in this light emerges as something of a variation on the agit-trial format).[28] Even the Russian Orthodox and Jewish religions were subjected to this kind of ritual trial (Stites,"Trial as Theatre" 9–10).

These agitational trials were manifestly fictional events staged in theatres or on the street for public display, but already in the 1920s the boundary between theatre and genuine judicial proceedings had begun begin to blur. The mock trials themselves were typically publicized as if they were court proceedings, with the command "All rise!" issued to the audience as the performance began (Wood 4).[29] Real political trials in the 1920s began to resemble theatrical performances and were often held in the same venues (such as Moscow's Polytechnic Museum; 50, 82).[30] In a typical public trial of this era, political circles would write up the basic judicial material, literary circles would write the scenario, and a drama circle would stage it, while an art circle designed posters and decorations (83). A defining moment in the evolution of this kind of hybrid political-theatrical trial arguably came with the regime's efforts to suppress the Orthodox Church. As early as May 1922 Patriarch Tikhon was called as a witness in the "Trial of the 54," a proceeding aimed at clergy and laymen who had been accused of counterrevolutionary activity for refusing – on Tikhon's instruction – to surrender church vessels so that they could be sold for famine relief (Tikhon's indictment was written by Andrei Vyshinskii, who played a key role in the later Moscow show trials; Silano 9, 281). As Silano comments, "in this real-life drama, *the new version of the Orthodox morality play*, the prosecution sought to condemn the Patriarch on moral and legal grounds according to precepts of the new world, while Tikhon would appeal to a different morality, a different law, and a different order" (287). The logic of that different order – a sense that what was involved was a violation of morality and sacrality – had nonetheless been taken up by the new regime.

By the 1920s a series of public political trials of this type had begun to define the political climate of the Soviet Union. Between 8 June and 7 August 1922, members of the Socialist Revolutionary Party – erstwhile radical opponents of the Bolsheviks – were put on trial (Antonov-Ovseenko 55; Cassiday 42–9). The proceedings had genuine legal force but were also "conceived as an educational vehicle from the outset, with meetings and demonstrations organized to condemn the accused" and even street carnivals and puppet shows ridiculing the Socialist Revolutionary leaders – the latter elements seemingly grotesquely incongruous with the solemn proceedings but proceeding out of a genetic link, whether acknowledged or not, between the trial and the modernist spectacles discussed in the preceding chapter (Cassiday suggests that in general the *agitsud* format resembled pre-1917 vaudeville performances and Petrushka puppet shows, 53). During the trial a crowd approaching 300,000 marched across Red Square (*nota bene*, a transection that was consistent with the symbolically strategic use of urban space that characterized Soviet spectacles in general); a workers' demonstration was then permitted to enter the courtroom in order to harangue the accused (Cassiday 47). The prominent director Dziga Vertov shot a film of the trial (Stites, "Trial as Theatre" 11).

From 18 May to 4 July 1928 the so-called Shakhty trial (*shakhtinskoe delo*) of fifty-three engineers from the Donbas region, who stood accused of sabotage in the coal-mining industry, was held in the Nobles' House in Moscow (Antonov-Ocvheenko 57; Cassiday claims that this trial was the first to return fully the theatrical and cinematic model of public trial to the courtroom proper, 110). Little actual evidence was presented – Vaksberg notes that in such trials the emphasis shifted from objective, technical factors to purported moral causes – and the prosecutor Nikolai Krylenko, who had also prosecuted the Socialist Revolutionaries, wore riding breeches, perhaps to invoke memories of the civil war, and Klieg lights were set up so that the trial could be filmed (Vaksberg 66; Stites, "Trial as Theatre" 11).[31] On 30 November the so-called Industrial Party (Prompartiia) trial of alleged "wreckers" of the first Five-Year Plan's drive toward industrialization was held. The same year saw trials of the Labor-Peasant Party and the Union-Bureau and Mensheviks (Antonov-Ovseenko 60).

But the defining moment in the Stalinist drive toward "judgment" – and the culmination of the legacy of "intervention" examined here –

came with the high season of the Moscow Show Trials of 1936–38. The immediate precedent for these trials as well as the opening volley in what was to become the Terror – the wave of mass arrests, trials, and executions orchestrated by the Party and the NKVD in the late 1930s – is generally considered to be the trial for the murder of Leningrad Party Chief Sergei Kirov on 1 December 1934. Stalin and the NKVD used the trial as an occasion to target former supporters of Grigorii Zinoviev, an opponent of Stalin's in the Party, then expanded it into an investigation of a supposed "Zinovievite opposition" (Goldman 32). By February 1936 the NKVD was instructing local organs to eliminate the "entire Trotsykist-Zinovievite underground" and uncover "terrorist groups" (38).

The first of the Moscow show trials was held on 19–24 August 1936. The accused were alleged to be part of a "united Trotskyist-Zinovievite centre" (40). A second trial opened on 23 January 1937 and involved 1,000 industrial managers accused of "wrecking and sabotage" following an explosion at a coal mine in Kemerovo (45). In this increasingly paranoid climate the NKVD, the Party, and the press spread accusations of "masking" by terrorist-wreckers and encouraged a vigilant, nationwide campaign of "unmasking" (55). That same year saw the trial of an alleged "Anti-Soviet Trotskyite Center" involving Piatakov, Sokolnikov, Serebriakov, Muralov, and Radek (70). The grandest spectacle, however, was the show trial that opened in March 1938 in which Bukharin, Rykov, Yagoda, and others were accused of having formed a conspiratorial group named the "Bloc of Rightists and Trotskyites" on the instructions of foreign states hostile to the USSR (People's Commissariat of Justice 5). The trial lasted nine days, with morning and evening sessions on each of the days (the English translation of the court proceedings runs to 800 pages).

A variety of real or imagined political imperatives may have motivated these trials. Controversies among historians have focused on such issues as the degree of personal initiative and responsibility on the part of Stalin and the NKVD, as opposed to broader segments of Soviet society. The trials have also been seen as a brutal but effective way to eliminate first the left opposition to Stalin's policies (figures who had advocated, like Trotsky, for more utopian planning), then the right opposition (figures like Bukharin, who had advocated a more gradual approach). The dissident Marxist historian Zhores Medvedev suggested more generally that the Stalin cult and "God-building" ideas of the era were promoted to cover up the economic disasters of the First Five-Year Plan of 1928–33 (Binns 603), while Kuromiya points to geopolitical anxieties over impending war as an important factor (2–3).

Whatever their pragmatic causes, however, as an aspect of culture the Moscow show trials should also be understood as emanating from

Stalinism's inward preoccupation with the kinds of spectacles, mystery plays, and dramas of "intervention" aimed at disrupting history that informed so much early Soviet culture. It would be an exaggeration to claim that Soviet adaptations of the mystery genre and other medieval rituals, together with their modernist offshoots, caused the show trials. But the pervasive presence of these elements in Soviet culture – in particular their widespread use as instruments of political manipulation – created a fertile soil on which an impulse toward staging episodes of judgment came to appear natural, if not, indeed, inevitable. As Ozouf comments on a parallel phenomenon that characterized the aftermath of the French Revolution, "revolutionary violence – the guillotine – did not pervert the utopian festival but brought it to fulfilment" (12). The show trials of the 1930s fully absorbed the theatrical aspect that in the 1920s had still occupied a somewhat marginal place in Soviet affairs. In the 1930s they moved to the centre of the cultural consciousness to become the principal political and moral ritual of Stalinist society. They were, as a result, manifestly theatrical. Indeed, in an argument consonant with the claims of the present study, Cassiday claims that in Western culture the stage and the courtroom share deep genetic links, both having evolved at the same time within Athenian society and drawing on common procedures, rhetoric, formal qualities, and religious overtones (7–8). Clark has observed that the show trials were largely scripted according to the conventions of melodrama, which aims to reveal an inner reality otherwise obscured by quotidian reality; this points suggestively to an underlying parallel between the trials and the dramatic theories of Stanislavsky (*Moscow, the Fourth Rome* 227–8).[32] In his broad survey of Moscow in 1937 Schlögel argues that the show trials provided a platform, a *Kommunikationsraum*, that served Stalinist society as a "panoptical Ur-stage" (*panoptische Urszene*) on which the principles of discipline and self-discipline could be displayed (115) – a latent appeal, one might add, to the phenomenon of the panorama discussed in chapter 2 and the kind of totalizing view of urban space that it facilitated – space appropriated as the site of ritual.

During the 1928 Shakhty trial the defendants were given skeletal versions of their parts but the trial in its entirety was not yet scripted *per se* (Wood 195); the Moscow show trials of the 1930s *were* written out in advance (Vaksberg claims that Stalin personally edited prosecutor Andrei Vyshinsky's speech for the January 1937 trials of Piatakov, Radek, and others; 79). As Fitzpatrick comments:

> The show trials, which were themselves political theater, spawned imitations in the regular theater, both professional and amateur. Lev Sheinin,

whose cross-over activities between criminal investigation and journalism we have already encountered, was coauthor of one of the most popular theatrical works on the themes of the Great Purges, a play called *The Confrontation*, which played in a number of theaters throughout the Soviet Union in 1937. Since Sheinin was reputed to be the author also of the scenarios of the big Moscow show trials, this switch to "legitimate" theater, using the same theme of spies and their unmasking and interrogation, is intriguing." (203)

But this imitation was not happenstance: the entire culture was swept up in a fervour of judging. In a parallel to his implicit role as sole audience for the mass public spectacles being staged at the same time, Stalin watched the proceedings of the Anti-Soviet Trotskyite trial from behind a curtain on the upper level, his presence given away by smoke from his ever-present pipe (Antonov-Ovseenko 75). It was also rumoured at the time that various of the accused had been replaced by actors – for example, the MKhAT actor Nikita Khmelev playing Bukharin – and even that the prosecutor Vyshinksky was played by an actor-double (83). The rhetoric of Antonov-Ovseenko's denunciatory account of Stalinism itself conveys a sense of how closely theatre and politics (meaning statehood, in the Stalin era) were intertwined in the era: the title of his work, meant as an indictment of Stalinist mendacity, is *Teatr Iosifa Stalina*; and he refers to the show trials, aptly if ironically, as a "mystery play" (*misteriia*; 104).[33]

In keeping with their underlying origins in the ritual of the mystery play and its modern derivatives, the trials also abounded in religious references – again, these were incongruous in light of the Soviet state's aggressively atheist ideology but fully in keeping with the logic of the mystery play, which must disclose its vectors pointing toward the transcendent realm. As Wood comments, "The trial format thus fostered a Manichean outlook in which the world was divided into prosecution and defence" (217). The format also ultimately invokes the precedent of the *theatrum mundi* tradition, as represented in the prologues to Calderon's *The Great Theater of the World*, Goethe's *Faust*, and other works discussed in chapter 2, which open by presenting their events as unfolding on the absolute stage of the entire world, in the presence of God as judge.

The summary of the charges in the 1938 trial of the "Bloc of Rightists and Trotskyites" delivered by the Prosecutor Vyshinsky cites the usual paranoias of the Stalinist state, asserting that not a day of Soviet history has passed without attacks by its enemies, with specific reference to alleged British, German, and Japanese conspiracies against the USSR

(*Report of Court Proceedings* 634, 662–3). But Vyshinsky then goes on to deploy a religious vocabulary that would not have been out of place in the Middle Ages, accusing the defendants of "Judas-like betrayal" (631) and denouncing the "devilish work of foreign intelligence services in our country" (637). He further alleges that "with the hypocritical mien of a Pharisee, and hiding behind a mask of sincerity, Bukharin began at the very outset of the struggle to engage in base intrigues, secret factional machinations against the Party and its leadership" (643). Vyshinsky begins another indictment in this way: "If we want to estimate the degree of falsity, jesuitry and hypocrisy of Bukharin ..." (651), somewhat later declaring that in his supposedly false friendship with Lenin "Bukharin reminds us of Vasily Shuisky and Judas Iskariot, who betrayed with a kiss" (656; implying along the way that Lenin is a Christ figure). Ultimately, Vyshinsky states, the evil deeds of Bukharin and his accomplices will be tried not before the present military tribunal, but "before the tribunal of history which knows of no Statutes of limitation, which knows no mercy" (646) – a statement that could be read as tacit recognition of the totalizing *theatrum mundi* tradition that, as we have seen, informed not only Soviet rituals but modernist experiments and their medieval precedents as well. Fitzpatrick similarly notes that in the 1937 trial of the "Anti-Soviet Trotskyite Center" Vyshinsky described Piatakov as a master wrecker, a "Judas-Trotsky," and accused him of running from the masses "like the devil runs from holy water" (194–5).

The show trials thus sought to lift political score-settling by the Stalinist state (or Party) to the level of a cosmic drama that interrupts the present – even the very course of history. In another reflex of their indebtedness to the logic of modernist and earlier urban spectacles, the show trials seem also almost instinctively to have imposed a ritual aspect extending beyond the courtroom. Schlögel goes so far as to label the section of his survey of Moscow in 1937 dealing with the show trials "Human Sacrifice, Nemesis, and Chorus" (*Menschenopfer, Nemesis, Chor*, 188), suggesting that Vyshinsky's primary responsibility as prosecutor was to place the accused, with their assorted biographies, sentiments, and sufferings, on a *stage (Bühne)* before the public gaze (188). The public – *Das Volk* – moreover entered into the scheme in the role of chorus in a Greek tragedy, articulating lamentations and pain, registering what only thousands of eyes could perceive, and propelling the whole affair toward the final issuing of anathema against the accused (191) – a chillingly literal realization of modernist aspirations to revive ancient theatrical rituals. So it is perhaps not surprising that Evreinov, who alongside Meyerhold and Ivanov had transposed onto the Russian context the theatrical innovations of Wagner and Craig calling for the removal of divisions between the stage and the audience, the theatre and life, wrote in his Parisian exile in 1938 a play called *Shagi Nemezidy* (*The Approaching Steps of Nemesis*), based on the Kamenev–Zinoviev trial of 1936, in which he eerily matched the machinations of Stalin's inner circle that led to that legal spectacle (195).[34] On 30 January a mass demonstration was organized in Red Square intended to represent the voice of the people in favour of the judgment handed down in the trial of Bukharin, Rykov, and others (194) – as striking consummation of the logic of the mystery genre in the world of Stalinist Russia.

Photographs published in the central press of the wakes held for the executed defendants and of Stalin, Voroshilov, Kaganovich, and other leaders transporting the urns bearing their cremated remains to Red Square "made manifest the iconography of a death ritual that had first taken on form in the wakes for Lenin and Kirov" (225).[35] "These events followed the polished choreography and elaborated iconography of a death ritual in which the collected Soviet leadership, the senior officials of the state and the city of Moscow, were gathered in Moscow for display. Gloom and solemnity disseminating a *pompes funèbre* in millions of copies of photographs and on the radio created a collective space of grief, uniting the nation in shock and mourning" (238).[36] But a grotesque carnival element also accompanied the trials, suggesting that the carnival and puppet theatre elements accompanying the 1922 trial of the Socialist Revolutionaries were not isolated qualities but rather were symptomatic of an underlying ritual logic that had embedded itself in the culture; they were also a memory, *inter alia*, of the occult aura attaching to puppets: one could say that a memory of puppet theatre haunted these Stalinist rituals. As Groys comments, "Much testimony exists to the peculiar merriment of the 1930s. It is characteristic in particular that the show trials and, especially, the pronouncement of sentences were often accompanied by public laughter" ("Totalitarizm karnavala" 79).[37]

Here again Bulgakov's *The Master and Margarita* provides insight into the political climate and an apt portrait of its underlying aims. Recall again Gasparov's definition of that novel as a parable – at once playful, wry, and ominous – of the 1920s told from the vantage point of the late 1930s ("Iz nabliudenii nad motivnoi strukturoi" 55). Bulgakov had become aware of the darkening political climate in the Soviet Union as early as 1930, when, on 30 November of that year, the trial of the Industrial Party began (at a time when Bulgakov's plays were banned from Soviet theatres); that very same summer A.V. Chaianov, whose *Venediktov* Bulgakov so admired (and which figures in chapter 1 of this study as an example of its era's preoccupation with narratives of occult intervention), was arrested (Chudakova, *Zhizneopisanie* 346). Adding to

5.7. Front page of the 31 January 1937 issue of *Pravda*. The headline reads, "The Country Welcomes a Just Sentence," while the photo of a procession on Red Square features a banner that reads "Execute the Rabid Fascist Dogs." Image used with permission from East View.

the latent "mystery" connotations of the atmosphere in the spring of 1930 for Bulgakov was the coincidence of the shocking suicide of the poet Mayakovsky with the phone call the startled Bulgakov received from Stalin himself, in response to a letter Bulgakov had sent begging permission to seek medical treatment abroad – on Good Friday no less, that is, the very time of the Passion (340–1; Varlamov 478). Bulgakov in fact wrote much of *The Master and Margarita* as the show trials were being conducted. It is known from diary entries, for example, that he closely followed the progress of the March 1938 "Bukharin-Rykov-Iagoda" trial (Ianovskaia 703–4), while his wife Elena Bulgakova noted in her diary the press reports of the 2 March 1937 trial of Bukharin, Rykov, Yagoda, and others (Schlögel 40).

The most direct reflection in the novel of the show trials *per se* is arguably chapter 15, in which Nikanor Ivanovich, who has been arrested for hiding foreign currency (in reality, a bribe he had taken from Koroviev in Soviet roubles, which had miraculously transformed themselves into foreign notes when hidden in the ventilator flue of his bathroom), dreams of a *theatre* in which members of the audience turn out to be on trial and must reveal where they have hidden foreign currency. Also, the atmosphere of the Stalinist Terror suffuses the novel, as in the characters casually mentioned as having "disappeared" over the past months from the house on Sadovaya street where Woland takes up residence, as well as the fear of the NKVD subtly permeating the Moscow chapters – as when Azzello says to Margarita in the Alexandrine Garden, "What is it with you? the minute we start talking to you, you all think we are trying to arrest you." The Yershalaim chapters, with Yeshua's "interrogation" by Pilate, Afranius who functions like the head of a secret police, and so on, too can be viewed as a displaced representation of the Terror.

The apotheosis of the devilry, of occult "intervention," in Bulgakov's novel comes in the scene of Satan's ball, during which a series of murderers and other criminals from the past pass in review before Woland/ Satan. Woland does not explicitly judge them – that has already been done – but a legal context is suggested when Margarita, at least, is given the opportunity to commute a sentence (that of Frieda, who strangled her infant child).[38] As a representation of the show trials the ball scene is in one sense curiously displaced into a kind of operatic mode. In its review of the assorted heinous crimes committed by all the resurrected corpses the scene of course recalls Dante's *Inferno*; but the crimes are all romantic acts of passion (Florentine poisoning of husbands, etc.), and the scene more immediately suggests something like Gluck's *Orfeo ed Euridice* (1762) or, still more likely, Offenbach's *Orphée aux enfers* (1858), the high point of which is the "Galop infernal" from which the carnivalesque "can-can" comes. But in another sense the scene links *otherworldly intervention, trial, and judgment* in a way that deftly reflects the cultural rather than the superficially juridical nature of the Stalinist Terror. As Gasparov comments, the scene set in the Variety Theatre early after Woland appears in Moscow, in which members of the audience are duped into clutching at money and luxury goods that are then turned into worthless mineral water labels, concentrates the text's pervasive sense of theatricality, combining ominous apocalyptic motifs with the farcical atmosphere of the fairground puppet show, the *balagan* ("Iz nabliudenii nad motivnoi strukturoi" 46). Moscow in Bulgakov's novel thus becomes an expanded version of the Variety scene, and everything that happens there acquires the tone of a *balagan* performance (47) – with the addition of yet another, third plane: that of *prison* (47). "It is as if this mystical world, this world of madness and *balagan*, making merry (not always with good will) and at the same time headed for execution, were an expanded scene of the witches' sabbath taking up the whole of the novel's space, whirling in expectation of the cock's crow signalling its disappearance into non-being" (49).[39]

Epilogue

Another work that taps deeply into the modernist subsoil of the Soviet experience in the manner of Bulgakov's *The Master and Margarita* is the poet Anna Akhmatova's *Poema bez geroia. Triptikh. 1940–1962* (*Poem without a Hero. A Triptych. 1940–1962*). Like Bulgakov's novel it was not published fully in its author's lifetime. A poignantly elegiac survey of Russian modernist culture in the early years of the twentieth century, the poem is saturated with Silver Age motifs, particularly reminiscences of Blok's play *The Fairground Booth*, whose metaphor of life as theatre now takes on a tragic turn. Opening on a New Year's Eve celebration on the eve of 1941, the poem presents Petersburg culture as a carnival of masks, among them of Faust, Mephistopheles, Pierrot, and "Dapertutto" (i.e, Meyerhold), who appear before the poet, even though she is the only one still living. "Since childhood I have been afraid of mummers" (*S detstva riazhenykh ia boialas'*), she remarks, before noting that the cock's crow is only heard in dreams while "Petersburg devilry" (*Peterburgskaia chertovnia*) goes on and on – an echo, most likely unconscious, of the Satanic ball that marks the apogee of demonic intervention in Bulgakov's novel, which is itself the dark shadow of the kind of forced midsummer merriment on display in Medvedkin's film. In the depths of the Stalinist night it states, "No matter what, the time of settling accounts is approaching" (*Vse ravno podkhodit rasplata*). The sound of an orchestra is heard "as if from another world" (*kak s togo sveta*). Its mood of elegiac tragedy is encapsulated toward the end of Part Three in the image of an inhabitant of modernist culture gazing in the mirror:

> As if in the mirror of the frightening night
> A person rages and does not want
> To recognize himself,
> While along the legendary quay

> There approached, not the calendrical
> But the real Twentieth Century.[1]

The figure of advent approaching along the quay looks back to the rose-wreathed Christ whose tread resounds at the end of Blok's *The Twelve* at the opening of the Soviet era. These works share a sense that the "real Twentieth Century" manifests itself precisely in such episodes in which the present experiences a form of rupture that opens it to the absolute.

What, then, does this complex, at times seemingly exotic, and ultimately tragic history tell us about Soviet culture in the first half of the twentieth century, especially in its Stalinist phase? To a significant extent, as this study has argued, the "real Twentieth Century" in Russia was pervaded by deep cultural memories that strove to overwhelm a sense of history, in the sense of immediately lived experience. In her study of the relationship between theatre and trials in the Soviet Union, Cassiday speaks of "the emergence of mythopoetic justice out of the utopian aspirations of Russia's avant-garde theatre and cinema" (189). Groys's *Total Art of Stalinism* advances a similar claim, engagingly and polemically (if ultimately with a reductionist bent), asserting that Stalinist culture emerged from the aspirations of the Russian avant-garde.[2] In a narrow sense, this study could be read as arguing for a similar aetiology of Stalinism, at least as concerns the rituals of "intervention" that it so prolifically staged. But as I have also attempted to show, those rituals were linked to a much broader mindset in the modern era, and had far deeper historical roots, than an avant-garde legacy alone can explain. Soviet rituals, especially in their Stalinist variant, can be viewed as perversions of the forms for embodying deity in the here-and-now that have shaped European cultures for centuries. In that more expansive context this study also essentially validates Ryklin's (admittedly rather gnomic) pronouncement on the Stalinist purges that "history is the death of terror, terror is the death of history" (136) – in the sense that the Terror, together with the ritualized trials that displayed and solemnified it, was intended precisely as an interruption of history in its ordinary course. From a still broader, anthropological perspective the Soviet experience would seem to be simply a more extreme and literal example of the relation between theatre and society described by Victor Turner: "The stage drama […] is a metacommentary, explicit or implicit, witting or unwitting, on the major social dramas of its context […] Not only that, but its message and its rhetoric feed back into the *latent* processual structure of the social drama and partly account for its ready realization. Life itself now becomes a mirror held up to art, and the living now *perform* their lives" (16–17).

The forms the "interventionist" agenda took, abetted by the appara-
tus of a totalitarian state determined to reshape reality, were extreme in
the Stalin era; but the impulse toward staging rituals of "judgment" that
shaped Soviet public displays ultimately belongs to a broader impulse
within European cultures whose roots can be traced at least back the Middle Ages. It arises out of periodic dissatisfaction with positivist world
views and an impatience with history, understood as a merely present
unfolding of events. As in the Middle Ages, the Soviet agenda for symbolic display was also thoroughly conditioned by a distinct perception of
urban space, especially of a capital like Moscow, which had come to be
viewed as a reservoir – a symbolic totality, a cosmos unto itself, a Jerusalem or Rome, within which such transcendence could be brought about.

One way of understanding this attraction to the occult trappings of
public ritual in Russia is in terms of the different historical path its culture followed from the Middle Ages to the modern era. It experienced
neither a secularizing Renaissance nor a reformation that would have
separated its devotional life from routinized rituals administered by a
hierarchized clergy (though as Florovsky's history of Russian religious
practice shows, there were divergent strains within its religious culture,
some of which approximated or even borrowed impulses from Protes-
tantism).[3] It instead preserved elements of the kind of ubiquitous sacred
space extended beneath the omnipresent gaze of icons described in
Oleg Tarasov's *Icon and Devotion*. Following the upheaval of Peter the
Great's efforts to westernize Russia – however superficially – in the early
eighteenth century and the more gradualist modernizing reforms of the
1860s (which *inter alia* included the legal, at least, emancipation of the
serfs), that order of things inherited from medieval Rus' had retreated
from much of Russia's cultural landscape. But vestiges of it lingered on,
like stranded mounds of snow left behind in a city by winter's retreat. At
the same time, if our contemplation of the more lurid aspects of Stalinist
ritual like the Moscow show trials and the Babylonian immensity of the
projected Palace of Soviets tends to exoticize Soviet culture, our reaction
needs to be tempered by an awareness that both the motivations and
the forms for realizing these phenomena can be traced back not only to
a culture of modernism that was not unique to Russia (indeed, as much
scholarship has shown, could be seen as having been imported into Russia) but also to broader practices that arguably defined the culture of the
European Middle Ages. These are shared roots.

If those roots were, as this study has argued, deep, but were transmitted by modernist projects that revived much earlier ways of appropriating urban space as a form of resistance to (intervention in) daily
life (history), then its effects have been correspondingly difficult to

eradicate. As Irina Paperno observes in her *Stories of the Soviet Experience*, "The [Soviet] imagination has been shaped by diverse sources: the Hegelian notion of history as a trial, the memories of Stalinist trials, and the expectation of a higher trial, not only a Russian Nuremberg, but also the Last Judgment […] Indeed, in late twentieth-century Russia the familiar notion of history as a tribunal – a secularized rendition of the notion of the Last Judgment – again acquired a religious apocalyptic ring" (43). Exotic and extreme as the Soviet version of this reflex may now appear, its "grammar" extended well beyond the initiatives of the Soviet state and was shared by other European cultures and ages as well. If most of the rest of Europe has long since departed from this ritual mode of civic life and its accompanying practice of "playing" its culture (in Huizinga's sense), it would appear to have re-emerged stubbornly in the modern Russian era.

Notes

Introduction

1 For an example closer to the field of Slavic studies, the approach I take could also be likened to that outlined by Lorenz M. Lüthi in his magisterial history of the Cold War. Lüthi remarks that the narrative structure of his study, which looks beyond the bipolar US–Soviet framework to incorporate agents and developments in parts of the world that previous histories tended to neglect, occurred to him while he was attending a performance of Wagner's opera *Die Walküre* – ironically, a composer of some relevance in these pages. While watching the opera he was inspired by Wagner's "idea of a network of stories that intersect and influence each other" (1).

2 From "Something's Missing: A Discussion between Ernst Bloch and Theodor W. Adorno," quoted in Todorova 5.

3 The Soviet writer Andrei Platonov, who was significantly influenced by Fedorov, could be seen as having spent most of his troubled career producing narratives of failed disruption or "intervention," in which projects for transcending history (by founding a spontaneous communist utopia in the steppes, as in *Chevengur*, or erecting a utopian "Proletarian Home" intended to shield its inhabitants from death in *Kotlovan* [*The Foundation Pit*]) collapse under the weight of a stubbornly insurmountable existential reality. On Platonov and his complex dialogue with Soviet ideology, see my *Andrei Platonov:Uncertainties of Spirit*.

4 Slezkine notes the paradoxical link in the Russian fin de siècle and early twentieth century between revolutionary socialists and chiliastically-minded Christians in the belief that the Last Judgment would occur in their lifetime (11). He in fact situates his expansive study of the political, social, and cultural phenomenon of the Soviet Union – iconicized for him in the massive "house on the embankment" erected in the 1930s on the bank of the Moskva River to house government officials – in the context

of millenarian forms of thought that had been transmitted via Christianity
to the Middle Ages (90), calling the early Bolshevik state a "would-be
hierocracy" (182). He also sees the millennial desire to interrupt history
as deriving from the ancient Israelites, who abandoned the notion of
"time as a straight plot line" (which he conjectures they derived from
Zoroaster) under the influence of their monotheism and its belief in God as
a transcendental ruler (77–8).

5 Joseph Frank offers a similar observation about modernists like Pound,
Eliot, and Proust: "The objective historical imagination, on which
modern man has prided himself, and which he has cultivated so carefully
since the Renaissance, is transformed in these writers into the mythical
imagination for which historical time does not exist – the imagination
which sees the actions and events of a particular time merely as the
bodying forth of eternal prototypes" (62). This "mythical imagination"
informed much of Soviet culture as well, at least in its public, state-
mandated aspect.

1 Narratives of "Intervention" and the Culture of Space in the Early Twentieth Century

1 Bulgakov's satirical plot is closely related to the contemporaneous novels
of Il'f and Petrov (*The Twelve Chairs*, 1928, and *The Little Golden Calf*,
1931) – for example, the MASSOLIT writers' union occupying a house
reputed to have belonged to an aunt of the poet Griboedov in Bulgakov's
novel (whose denizens mostly concern themselves with the restaurant
and arranging vacations) parallels the Gerkules (Hercules) bureaucratic
offices housed in a former hotel in *The Little Golden Calf* – and both of them
look back to the satires on Russian imperial chancelleries in the works
of the nineteenth-century writers Nikolai Gogol' and Mikhail Saltykov-
Shchedrin, and both of them are destroyed by an ironically apocalyptic
fire.

2 The debate is represented by such works as D.F. Strauss's *Das Leben Jesu*
(1835), Ernest Renan's *La vie de Jésus* (1863), and F.W. Farrar's *The Life of
Jesus Christ* (1874). That set of works is dismissively referred to in Tolstoy's
Anna Karenina – in reference to a painting of Pilate before Christ, a scene
important in Bulgakov's novel – as "that same old Ivanov-Strauss-Renan
attitude toward Christ and religious painting" (*vse to zhe ivanovsko-
shtrausovsko-renanovskoe otnoshenie k Khristu i religioznoi zhivopisi* 41).

3 On the nineteenth-century debates and their relevance to Bulgakov's
novel, see J.A.E. Curtis 150–2.

4 However, as the émigré critics Petr Vail and Alexander Genis point out,
the novel exerted its influence on Soviet literature not when it was written,

but some twenty-five to thirty years later, when it was finally published ("Bulgakovskii perevorot"). The first official but partial publication of the novel was in 1966–7; it was first published in full in 1973. On variants of the novel, see Bulgakov, *"Moi bednyi, bednyi master."*

5 As Eric Naiman remarks in *Sex in Public: The Incarnation of Early Soviet Ideology*, sex – a preoccupation with which intensified in early twentieth-century Russia with the failure of hopes for social and political progress in the wake of the 1905 revolution – was something that in the Soviet era could now "be depicted – by virtue of its role in procreation – as the embodiment of historical and therefore antiutopian forces" (15). It is a kindred desire to disrupt, to abrogate, history that I address here. Naiman also notes that "at every step accompanying the desire for something radically better comes a loathing for the unpleasant details one would like to replace and forget" (16). The opposition between the historical realm and the extrahistorical (whether utopian or not) is at stake in my examples as well. Something similar may be captured in Nietzsche's well-known dictum that "it is only as an *aesthetic phenomenon* that existence and the world are eternally *justified*" (52) – that is, in their mere existence as everyday events, as history in this sense, they are unjustified.

6 Livak further notes that in early twentieth-century Russia, both Marxists and modernists – twin rebellious offspring of the historical intelligentsia – "drew on the same religious sources and exhibited kindred transcendental striving beyond the daily grind – *byt* – which filled them with quasimetaphysical dread" (158). This maximalism was a kind of "evolutionary impatience" (158).

7 As Brandist observes, carnival-inflected street theatre declined in the 1920s in the Soviet Union but by the mid-1920s novels "were thoroughly saturated with the carnival spirit" (94). Bulgakov's novel is thus more than a reflection of the modernist impulse toward staging "intervention"; it is one in a series of reconfigurations (or displacements) of that impulse into narrative art.

8 See Fusso on the theme of transformations in Bulgakov. The romantic ascription is not a casual one. As J.A.E. Curtis shows, attitudes toward "romanticism" underwent a complex transformation in the early Soviet era, from enthusiasm for "revolutionary romanticism" (promoted by Gorky in particular) to outright rejection, as in Fadeev's 1919 speech, "Doloi Shillera!" (Down with Schiller!; 188–202).

9 Posner notes that "Hoffmann symbolized the Russian theatricalist revolt against naturalism" (6). On the Bulgakov–Gogol connection, see J.A.E. Curtis 108–28; as well as Chudakova, "M.A. Bulgakov – chitatel'" and "Bulgakov i Gogol'," in which she points out that Bulgakov explicitly borrows a Gogolian title in his "Pokhozhdeniia Chichikova" ("The

Adventures of Chichikov," the actual title of Gogol's *Dead Souls*, which on the work's title page figures as a subtitle) and that during the writing of *The Master and Margarita* he was also working on a play about Gogol' and the writing of *Dead Souls* as well as on a screen adaptation of Gogol's play *Revizor* (*The Inspector General*) – which had been commissioned by Ukrainfil'm (Chudakova, "Arkhiv M.A.Bulgakova" 115). Bulgakov was especially enthusiastic about Hoffmann as a writer and even kept in his library an annotated copy of I. Mirimskii's article, "Sotstial'naia fantastika Gofmana," which had appeared in the journal *Literaturnaia ucheba* in 1938 (J.A.E. Curtis 199; Chudakova, "Arkhiv M.A. Bulgakova" 130n188).

10   Эти бедные селенья,
                Эта скудная природа -
                Край родной долготерпенья,
                Край ты русского народа!

                Не поймет и не заметит
                Гордый взор иноплеменный
                Что сквозит и тайно светит
                В наготе твоей смиренной.

                Удрученный ношей крестной,
                Всю тебя, земля родная,
                В рабском виде Царь Небесный
                Исходил, благословляя.

11 The Saillens tale appeared in the third edition of his *Récits et allegories*, published in Toulouse in 1907; see Nikiforov's commentary to the story in Tolstoi, *Polnoe sobranie sochinenii i pisem*, vol. 25, 681–5. An inclination toward rupture with historical time and meaning can also be sensed in Tolstoy's narrative manner in general, with its tendency toward apodictic statements. As Morson comments, "It seems clear that Tolstoy was deeply concerned with the possibility of transhistorical truth and with the forms of utterance in which such truth might be expressed [...] In effect, Tolstoy wanted to escape from history and his own biography" (*Hidden in Plain View* 23).

12 In general, Dostoevsky is one of Bulgakov's most important Russian precursors, not only for his novel *Besy*, which serves as an important precedent for the demonic theme in Russian literature (see Weiner, *By Authors Possessed*), but also more generally for his sensitivity to Gospel texts and their derivatives (see Gasparov, "Novyi zavet v proizvedeniiakh M.A. Bulgakova").

13 "[…] как раз было в обычае сводить в поэтических произведениях на землю горные силы. Я уж про Данта не говорю. Во Франции судейские клерки, а тоже по монастырям монахи давали целые представления, в которых выводили на сцену Мадонну, ангелов, святых, Христа и самого бога ... В *Notre dame de Paris* у Виктора Гюго в честь рождения французского дофина, в Париже, при Людовике XI, в зале ратуши дается назидательное и даровое представление народу под названием "Le bon jugement de la très sainte et gracieuse Vierge Marie" где и *является она сама лично и произносит свой bon jugement.* У нас в Москве, в допетровскую старину, такие же почти драматические представления, из Ветхого завета особенно, тоже совершались по временам; но, кроме драматических представлений, по всему миру ходило тогда много повестей и «стихов» в которых действовали по надобности святые, ангелы и вся сила небесная. У нас по монастырям занимались тоже переводами, списыванием и даже сочинением таких поэм, да еще когда – в татарщину. Есть, например, одна монастырская поэмка (конечно, с греческого): «Хождение богородицы по мукам», с картинами и со смелостью не ниже дантовских" (224–5).

14 Early in his "poem" about the Grand Inquisitor, Ivan comments: "И вот столько веков молило человечество с верой и пламенем, «Бо господи явися нам», столько веков взывало к нему, что он, в неизмеримом страдании своем, возжелал снизойти к молящим. Снисходил, посещал он и до этого иных праведников, мучеников и святых отшельников еще на земле, как и записано в их «житиях»" (226)

15 See Zholkovskii on the parallels between the characters' OGPU interrogations and Christ's interrogation by Pilate.

16 "[…] многие характеры разыгрывали комедию старого мира. Занавес закрывается. Персонажи должны сбежаться к авансцене и пропеть последние куплеты. Я хочу быть посредником между ними и зрительным залом. Я буду дирижировать хором и последним уйду со сцены […] в глазные прорези маски мерцающим взлядом следит за нами история" (89).

17 See for example Hetényi.

18 J.A.E. Curtis notes that in the first draft of *The Master and Margarita* the hero was a mediaeval historian with an interest in demonology (130). Chudakova indicates that in the earliest drafts of the novel Bulgakov referred to its hero as "Faust" ("Arkhiv M.A. Bulgakova" 109). For a detailed discussion of Bulgakov's depiction of Christ, see Givens, "'Keep in mind that Jesus did exist': Mikhail Bulgakov's Image of Christ," chapter 7 of his *The Image of Christ in Russian Literature* (149–76).

19 Peter Larson observes that in Bulgakov's deliberate attempt to reintroduce the sacred into Soviet life, "ironically, the best agent for this process is

the devil" (10). Bulgakov's primary sources for information about the devil and demonology were M.A. Orlov's *Istoriia snoshenii s d'iavolom* (St. Petersburg 1904) as well as various entries in Andreevskii et al.'s *Entsiklopedicheskii slovar'* dealing with the devil and demonology (Chudakova, "Arkhiv M.A. Bulgakova" 73). Chudakova also notes that Bulgakov's notebooks for the novel indicate that the plot line involving the Master and Margarita came later than that involving Christ and the devil ("Arkhiv M.A. Bulgakova" 79).

20 http://bulgakov.stormloader.com/mim10.htm.

21 http://lunacharsky.newgod.su/lib/dramaticheskie-proizvedenia/faust -i-gorod.

22 "[…] круглое здание огромной, неслыханной до сих пор величины, стоящее на квадратной лестнице о шестнадцати ступенях. Длина каждой стороны – 6.000 локтей. Здание увенчано куполом, под которым легко уместилась бы самая высокая колокольня этого города. Внутри оно под'емлется как бы на четырех величественных устоях, несущих вверху, на высоте уже головокружительной, группы колонн более грациозных, переходящих непосредственно в четыре взлетающие арки. На них–то и ляжет венчающий все здание купол. Там я помещаю окно в 60 локтей диаметром из сверкающе-разноцветных стекол. Там будет величественное изображение божества в белых ризах, мощным движением длани ниспосылающего свет, движение и порядок. Божеству будут приданы наиболее величавые черты, какие видело на земле человеческое око, – черты вашего достославного высочества, первейшего из государей мира."

23 On the role such monuments played in the French Revolution see Starobinski, *1789: The Emblems of Reason.*

24 See Chudakova, *Zhizneopisanie* 297–300, on the popularity of these diabolic tales in the late 1920s, when Bulgakov began writing *The Master and Margarita*, in particular the "strange similarities" (*strannye sblizheniia*) she sees in Bulgakov's novel and A.V. Chaianov's *Venediktov*: "the atmosphere in which diabolism and mysticism envelope the Moscow streets on which events unfold, the supernatural dependence of some people on the will of others, the picture of the repulsive witches' sabbath, the theatre, where key events take place – all this likely influenced the formulation of Bulgakov's plan for his novel" (*Zhizneopisanie* 300).

25 Mindlin's Faust tale and the other examples of demonic literature from the 1920s are collected in Sokolov, ed., *On poiavilsia…Sovetskaia misticheskaia proza 20–30-x godov*. See also Petrovskii 165 on Kyivan "Mephisthophelean" works. A work whose plot and motifs particularly resemble Bulgakov's novel is Aleksandr Grin's "Fandango" (1927). Like Bulgakov, Grin uses his "intervention" plot to satirize life in NEP-era Soviet Russia as a travesty

of Faustian and gospel motifs. Like Erenburg's Jurenito and Bulgakov's Woland, Grin's devil is a foreigner, this time a tall Spaniard calling himself Bam-Gran and wearing a beret with an ostrich feather. Just as Woland at the Variety theatre magically conjures up scarce consumer goods (the subtext in both cases being Christ's multiplication of bread and fishes) and Bulgakov satirizes the Writers' Union by portraying the lavish dinners held at the Griboedov House, Bam-Gran appears at KUBU (the Committee for Improving Scholars' Living Conditions, an actual 1920s institution) with bundles of goods he claims are a gift from the Cuban people to Soviet Russia. When the narrator, after a fantastic series of adventures, magically enters the sunlit room of a painting hanging on the wall – whose interior space expands dramatically, as does Woland's apartment when Margarita attends the Satanic ball – and finds Bam-Gran again, the latter is sitting regally in an armchair, like Bulgakov's Woland ensconced in his Moscow apartment. A fandango then resounds, played by "the best orchestra in the world," like the one that Strauss conducts at Satan's ball in *The Master and Margarita*. Grin's tale thus anticipates the social dimension of Bulgakov's novel: the devil's appearance convulses the society he enters, causing it to display its most painful traits.

26 Another tale from the Soviet 1920s that makes superficial use of the demonic theme, but whose details may have influenced Bulgakov, is Ovadii Savich's 1923 "Inostranets iz 17 No." ("The Foreigner in Room No. 17"; in 1924 Bulgakov and Savich both attended the literary evenings known as Nikitinskie subbotniki; Chudakova, *Zhizneopisanie* 226). Stranded in a provincial town in the aftermath of the civil war, the narrator, Fomin, feels detached from the life around him. An intriguing foreigner (like Bulgakov's vaguely German Woland) named "James Best" (Sokolov suggests that the surname is meant to suggest the Russian *bes*, "demon," 522), who seems to have preternatural knowledge of unfolding events, then moves into room no. 17 of the former hotel in which Fomin resides. "Best" ends up functioning as a fairly trite, Party-minded *raisonneur* by telling Fomin he should not despair because "here it is great time, which means there are also great people" (*zdes' bol'shoe vremia, znachit, i bol'shie liudi*, 42) and "it is people who will save the world" (*mir spasut liudi*, 44); but the notion of the devil as a foreigner (or a foreigner as a devil) reappears in Bulgakov's Woland, who first enters Moscow in the guise of a "foreign consultant."

27 In a 1935 radio broadcast Mandelshtam himself pointed out the origins of *Faust* in the puppet theatre, a topic that will be taken up in the next chapter: "Не браните кукольный театр. Вспомните, сколько он вам доставил радости. Гете на всю жизнь запомнил прыжки и жесты всех этих мавров и мавританок, пастухов и пастушек, карликов и

карлиц и тяжелую поступь Доктора Фауста, который продал душу дьяволу," ("Iunost' Gete [Peredacha po radio]," 64; see also Kelly 173). As further evidence for how prevalent the Faust legend was in the cultural consciousness of the Stalin era one could cite the nickname applied to Genrikh Iagoda, head of Stalin's NKVD, as "Mephistopheles from the Pale of Settlement" (*Mefistofel' iz cherty osedlosti*) in Evreinov's play about the Moscow Show Trail of Bukharin, Rykov, Kamenev, and Zinoviev, *Shagi Nemezidy* (20).

28 Genette notes that it may seem paradoxical to speak of space with regard to literature since the mode of existence of the literary text is in essence temporal; but in his view language, the medium of literature, tends to treat things in terms of space and to spatialize all things (44); this property then reveals itself in the literary text, where "la spatialité manifeste de l'écriture peut être prise pour symbole de la spatialité profonde du langage" (45). He suggests that the source for this is Saussure, with his "relations purement différentielles" where each element is qualified by the place it occupies in a table. Lotman for his part generally considers the representations of space in a given author's works as a provisionally autonomous "secondary model of reality," important primarily as a key to that author's poetics. On Lotman's interest in individual poetics versus the focus on mythological themes in the works of V.N. Toporov, see Hansen-Löve 40 and Koschmal, "Zur mythischen Modellierung" 193–4; Hansen-Löve terms Lotman's approach "typological."

29 For Descartes "space" was the domain of *res extensa*, the mechanistic bodies having movement and form that were opposed to the domain of *res cogitans*, the thinking subject; for Kant space and time formed the subjective condition of every human experience (*Metzler Philosophie Lexicon*, s.v. "Raum"; *Oxford Dictionary of Philosophy*, s.v. "space"; *Cambridge Dictionary of Philosophy*, s.v. "space").

30 Buczyńska-Garewicz 15–16, 46. In Husserl see especially *Die Krisis der europäischen Wissenschaften und die transzendentale Phänomenologie* (*The Crisis of European Sciences and Transcendental Phenomenology*). Husserl was particularly astute at bringing to light the assumptions about the world that were implicit but largely unacknowledged in the Newtonian view of space. "So familiar to us is the shift between *a priori* theory and empirical inquiry in everyday life," he remarks, "that we usually tend not to separate the space and spatial shapes geometry talks about from the spatial shapes of experiential actuality, as if they were one and the same" (24).

31 Buczyńska-Garewicz 37, 16–17, 26.

32 Buczyńska-Garewicz 251.

33 There may be factors specific to Russia at work here. As Bassin remarks, "[a]cross the centuries Russians have articulated, through a process that

may be called the interpretation or construction of geographical space, a variety of highly contrasting geographical or geopolitical self-images: visions, in effect, of Russia as a particular sort of geographical entity" (2). If Russian literature has produced some especially vivid examples of literary space, perhaps it is because the symbolic manipulation of space has long played a role in the culture's recurring bouts of self-definition and redefinition (see my "Getting Across"): from the duality of a mediaeval world view that regards the West as a land of pagan darkness (see Lotman and Uspenskij, "On the Role of Dual Models in the Dynamics of Russian Culture") to Peter the Great and, later, Stalin's program for building "socialism within one country" and the Stalinist slogan claiming that Moscow is "port of the seven seas," and so on.

34 A similar view can be found in Pavel Florenskii's diatribes against the epistemological shift toward egoism occasioned by the rise in perspectival painting during the renaissance; see, for example, his "Obratnaia perspektiva."

35 A closely related example in this line of commentary is Aleksandar Flaker's "Die Strasse: Ein neuer Mythos de Avantgarde," which examines the new meanings such spatial themes as "the city" and its synecdoche, "the street," acquire in the transition from modernism to the avant-garde (with Mayakovsky as the pre-eminent poet of the street). See also Walter Koschmal's "Semantiserung von Raum und Zeit. Dostoevskijs *Aufzeichnungen aus einen Toten Haus* und Čechovs *Insel Sachalin*," which focuses on modernist expectations of the advent of the apocalyptic "new time and new space" (as the narrator of Bely's *Chetyre simfonii* puts it; 208).

36 Toporov notes that a "peculiar perception of space" (*spetsifika vospriiatiia prostranstva*) as a fairy-tale world that only puts on the mask of reality appears in Gogol's writings as early as his first collection of stories, *Vechera na khutora bliz Dikan'ki (Evenings on a Farm near Dikan'ka)*, and he conjectures that the peculiar tension between realistic and fantastic space that pervades Gogol's works, especially the "ambivalent space" of his novel *Dead Souls*, may well have exerted a subsequent influence on spatial concepts within Russian culture as a whole (440, 445). Lotman in fact suggests a parallel between the Gogolian universe, with its two false worlds – one mechanized, the other demonic – posing a threat to the hero, and the structure of Bulgakov's *The Master and Margarita* (*Problemy* 438n26). He also gives as his first example of spatial themes in a literary work Bulgakov's *A Theatrical Novel*, specifically, the passage in which the narrator invokes a three-dimensional miniature of a room (413). Hansen-Löve extends Lotman's remarks on spatial themes in Gogol's works, suggesting that the point of the opposition between realistic and fantastic space in the Petersburg stories is "the capability of transformation, of

metamorphosis from one type of space to another" (67) – a relevant precedent in this context, given the role magical transformations often play in Bulgakov's works, in an echo of larger designs within Soviet society.

37 Lotman comments re. Gogol that «специфика восприятия пространства» appears as early in his works as *Evenings on a Farm near Dikan'ka* ("*Problemy khudozhestvennogo prostranstva v proze Gogolia*" 420). Larson remarks that "Bulgakov's oeuvre is centred around space and spatial usage ... Qualities and conditions of space are an obsession for Bulgakov equally in his personal life and his writing" (43).

38 Lotman similarly notes the "geographical isolation (*otgorozhennost'*) of the domain of the old-world landowners" as a characteristic of the tales in that collection by Gogol ("*Problema khudozhestvennogo prostranstva v proze Gogolia*" 426). From September 1916 to September 1917 Bulgakov himself, fresh out of medical school, served as a doctor in the village of Nikolskoe in the Sychev region of Smolensk province (Chudakova, "Arkhiv M.A. Bulgakova" 35).

39 On the prominence of the city as a theme among both the Russian Symbolists (who tended to lament what they saw as its inhumanity) and the Futurists (who welcomed what they saw as its fast-paced modernity) see Harte 42–4.

40 Chudakova notes that a significant part of Bulgakov's literary output during his first Moscow years were *feuilletons* and chronicles of Moscow life, which were published in the newspaper *Nakanune* and its literary supplement ("Arkhiv M.A. Bulgakova" 37).

41 For a markedly different aesthetic approach to this theme, which was popular in the early twentieth century, consider the Futurist poet Vasilii Kamenskii's poem "Strannik Vasilii" (Vasilii the Wanderer), in which the poet imagines flying over Moscow, and which ends with the lines, "After the flight / In an auto to the cafE / From there to the Circus / Then the VarietY Theater" (quoted in Harte 53). The Variety Theater is where Bulgakov's Woland holds his séance unmasking black magic in *The Master and Margarita*.

42 J.A.E. Curtis notes that "Bulgakov's affinity with Gogol also finds expression in a specific way through the theme of the city, which is a recurring and unifying feature of Bulgakov's writing" (124).

43 According to Toporov's account of Russian literary history, an important revolution in spatial depiction took place in the shift from nineteenth-century realism to the modernism of the early twentieth century. The depiction of space in Dostoevsky's *Crime and Punishment* accomplished nothing less than a transformation of novelistic space in general, reinventing the *topos* of St. Petersburg as a phantasmagoric space in which "all is possible" (241). For Toporov the modernist successor who most

fully realized the possibilities this transformation opened up was Andrei Bely, in whose novel *Petersburg* the antagonist Apollon Apollonovich seeks to "geometrize" the "chaotic narrowness" of the city's space as it had been experienced by Raskolnikov, disrupting its contiguity by segregating it into cubes, squares, planes, and lines, all of which however turn out to be nothing but mirages lifted from "classical descriptions of the city in the nineteenth century" ("O strukture romana Dostoevskogo v sviazi s arkhaichnymi skhemami mifologicheskogo myshlenia," 290–1). Katharina Hansen-Löve makes a similar claim regarding Chekhov's tale "Step'" (1888), which she sees as marking a turning point in post-realist Russian literature toward a sense of space as playing an autonomous, even disruptive, role (a process she also sees as culminating in Bely's *Petersburg*; *The Evolution of Space in Russian Literature* 109). Although in his prose as well as his dramaturgy Bulgakov was closer to the aesthetic of nineteenth-century realism than to avant-garde experimentation, he developed as a writer in a culture in which the literary representation of space had focused renewed attention even as it abandoned the certitudes of the realist age.

44 This type of ironic humour was characteristic of Bulgakov. In a letter to his friend P.S. Popov in 1934 Bulgakov describes his meeting with a theatre director in a room in the Astoria hotel in Leningrad, during which the director expressed undiluted enthusiasm for staging Bulgakov's play *Blazhenstvo* (*Bliss*) – after which he stepped out for a moment and never returned. "One can only assume," Bulgakov wryly notes, "that he disappeared into the fourth dimension" (quoted in Chudakova, *Zhizneopisanie* 401).

45 The appellation "sorok-sorokov" that Bulgakov appropriates for the title of this sketch literally means "forty forties" and refers to the abundance of churches in pre-Soviet Moscow. But it also implies *totalizing* abundance; see, for example, in biblical numerology the rain of forty days and forty nights that produces the flood (Genesis 7:4), and also the algebraic operation of squaring, as in the description in Revelation 21:15–17 of the New Jerusalem, whose "length is the same as its breadth" and whose wall is "a hundred and forty-four cubits" (i.e., 12x12).

46 Ianovskaia notes that as a young man in his native Kyiv Bulgakov was fond of climbing the city's "vertical paths" and that he had a habit of looking down on the city from atop one of its hills (489–90).

47 Petrovskii goes so far as to claim that all of Bulgakov's novels are "theatrical novels" directed by a Mephistophelean figure (92 – Shpolianskii in *The White Guard*, Woland in *The Master and Margarita*, Rudol'fi in *A Theatrical Novel*, 253); see also his claim that Bulgakov's works are all really theatrical (144).

48 Volkov describes the performance as shifting from a gambling house to "a masquerade where myriad masks swirled before the audience, then to a ball" – motifs reminiscent at once of Bely's *Petersburg* and Bulgakov's *The Master and Margarita* (201). McQuillen comments that for Meyerhold "the dominos and half-masks of the Venetian carnival tradition […] produced an atmosphere appropriate to the end of an Empire" and that Akhmatova conceived the idea for what became her *Poema bez geroia* (*Poem without a Hero*, discussed in the epilogue to this study) after watching the dress rehearsal of *Masquerade* at the Aleksandriiskii Theater in February 1917 (232n39).

49 To some extent this theatrical bent may be understood as a legacy of the nineteenth-century Russian novel. Lotman, for example, notes a distinct tendency toward the theatrical in the works of Gogol, one of Bulgakov's most important precursors, where "reality is first transformed according to the laws of the theatre, and only then is turned into narrative." The Gogolian tale concentrates its action "on a comparatively small scenic platform," as if the world consisted of footlights and a backstage, and the Gogolian text approximates a dramatic one by dividing itself into monologues, dialogues, and polylogues. Characters do not so much move in a Gogolian tale as perform "gestures" ("Problema khudozhestvennogo prostranstva v proze Gogolia," 421–2). Toporov finds a similar theatrical impulse in Dostoevsky's novels, which "abound in what are in essence directorial comments, which omit verbs of speech, introduce masks and marionettes and describe the given action theatrically, as witness the frequent use of words like 'theatre,' 'scene,' 'backstage,' 'scenery,' 'entr'acte,' 'audience,' 'role,' etc." ("O strukture romana Dostoevskogo v sviazi s arkhaichnymi skhemami mifologicheskogo myshleniia [Prestuplenie i nakazanie]," 254). For Bakhtin, the very roots of the novel lay in the medieval European town square, with its bazaars, folk entertainments, and taverns, "a remarkable chronotope in which all the higher entities, from the state to truth, were represented concretely and embodied, became visibly present" ("Formy vremeni i khronotopa v romane" 168–9). In his view it is precisely the novel that re-established the broken link between literature and the folk square (200), appropriating for itself the right to conduct life (*provodit' zhizn'*) through the intermediary chronotope of the stage (*teatral'nykh podmostkov*), to portray life as comedy and people as actors (198). "Petrushka" – the Russian version of Punch and Puncinello – forms, Bakhtin notes, the hidden chronotope in Gogol's story "The Nose" (201), while a revival of the ancient carnival-mystery associated with the town square stands at the heart of Dostoevsky's quintessentially novelistic novels (281). As will be seen, modernism injected a new interest into such theatrical models.

50 This was evidently historically accurate: Petrovskii contends that Russians in Kyiv characterized the hetman's rule as "comic opera" (*operetka*) and that Bulgakov was aware of it (138; see also Petrovskii 143 on theatrical motifs in the novel).

51 "Aleksei Vasil'evich Turbin [...] returned to Ukraine, to the City" ("Aleksei Vasil'evich Turbin [...] vernulsia na Ukrainu v Gorod," 7); "and when, toward the end of that memorable year, many miraculous and strange things took place in the City" ("Kogda zhe k kontsu znamenitogo goda v Gorode proizoshlo uzhe mnogo chudesnykh i strannykh sobytii," 24); "In the winter, as in no other city on earth, peace descended on the streets and alleys of both the upper City, on the hills, and the lower City, spread out along the arc of the frozen Dniepr" ("Zimoiu, kak ni v odnom gorode mira, upadal pokoi na ulitsakh i pereulkakh i verkhnego Goroda, na gorakh, i Goroda nizhnego, raskinuvshegosia izluchine zamershego Dniepra," 46), and so on.

52 On these motifs see also Gasparov, "Novyi zavet v proizvedeniiakh Bulgakova," 102–3. Chudakova suggests that Rome also serves as a prototype for "Gorod" in *Belaia gvardiia*, especially as filtered through the precedent of Gogol's "Rim" (Rome; "Arkhiv M.A. Bulgakova," 129n185).

53 "Many strange and miraculous things had already taken place in the City" ("v Gorode proizoshlo uzhe mnogo chudesnykh i strannykh sobytii," 24); "[in January 1918] miracles began to take place completely obviously" ("v gorogde nachalis' uzhe sovershenno iavstvenno chudesa," 29); "Miracles began in the City and in connection with this the mysterious word [Peliura]" ("V Gorode nachalis' chudesa v sviazi s etim zhe zagadochnym slovom" [*Petliura*], 67); "The little bells started barking [...] as if Satan had climbed up the belfry" ("Malen'kie kolokola tiavkali...tochno satana vlez na kolokol'niu," 206). The Passion enters through references to "Bald Mountain," "Lysaia gora" – i.e., Golgotha (in *The Master and Margarita* Golgotha is called "Bald Mountain") – just outside the city's boundaries ("He came from Bald Mountain beyond the City walls, above the banks of the Dniepr where there were huge stores of shells and gunpowder" ("On iavilsia s Lysoi Gory za Gorodom, nad samym Dneprom, gde pomeshchalis' gigantskie sklady snariadov i porokhu. Na Lysoi gore proizoshel vzryv," 53).

54 Gasparov notes that Bulgakov often projects New Testament themes onto the Faust legend ("Novyi zavet v proizvedeniiakh M.A. Bulgakova" 99). Gasparov also notes that the murder of a Jew is a frequent motif in Bulgakov's works, often with New Testament connotations ("Novyi zavet v proizvedeniiakh M.A. Bulgakova," 88). Petrovskii identifies a hill called "Chertoryia" as Kyiv's Bald Mountain, by legend a meeting place of witches (291).

55 See also Petrovskii 270 on Roman connotations of "Gorod." Chudakova
    suggests Bulgakov's use of the name "Ga-Notsri" may have been
    influenced by a play by S.M. Chevkin performed in Simbirsk in 1922 titled
    "Ieshua Ga-Notsri. Bespristrastnoe otkrhytie istiny" (Yeshua Ga-Notsri. A
    Dispassionate Revelation of the Truth) (*Zizneopisanie* 193).

56 The late, unfinished *A Theatrical Novel*, a *roman à clef* satirizing Bulgakov's
    experiences in the Soviet theatre, is also obviously preoccupied with
    thought about the theatre. Petrovskii suggests that the central idea of the
    novel is that of the entire world as theatre (42), while Chudakova notes
    that the character of Rudol'fi, who is closely related to that of Woland in
    The Master and Margarita, has "Mephistophelian" traits pointing to *Faust*
    ("Arkhiv M.A. Bulgakova" 84).

57 *The Master and Margarita* also borrows key spatial themes from Goethe's
    Faust, from the *Studierzimmer* in which Goethe's drama begins (paralleled
    in Bulgakov's novel by the underground apartment in which the Master
    initially resides in wounded resignation from the world) to the wilderness
    beyond the city walls; in both cases a *Walpurgisnacht*, a witches' sabbath,
    is held and the "eternal refuge" (*vechnyi priut*) granted the Master at the
    end of the novel, whose kitschy German-operatic facade (a Venetian
    window with a grapevine winding around it) recalls the *Gärtchen*, the
    little garden, granted to Baucis and Philemon in Part 2, Act Five of *Faust*
    (Woland even entices the Master to accept the refuge with visions of
    walking under the cherry trees, listening to Schubert, writing with a
    quill and "sitting, like Faust, over a test tube in the hopes of producing a
    homunculus," 529).

58 E. Sheremet'eva, an acquaintance of Bulgakov's in the 1920s, recalls
    Bulgakov on a walk through an older part of Moscow pointing out to
    her various buildings and noting who the architect had been; "Bulgakov
    undoubtedly loved Moscow's past [*moskovskuiu starinu*] and knew it well,"
    was her remark (Chudakova, *Zhizneopisanie* 345). Ianovskaia notes that
    Bulgakov worked with maps when he wrote, especially when writing *Beg*
    (*Flight*) and *The Master and Margarita*, using maps of Jerusalem (427–8).

2 *Faust* and the Medieval Roots of "Intervention"

1 One could view Bulgakov's orientation toward the idea of supernatural
    "intervention" as the reason for his persistent attraction to three master
    myths or texts: the Gospels, the Apocalypse, and Goethe's *Faust* (Gasparov,
    "Novyi zavet v proizvedeniiakh M.A. Bulgakova").

2 On the various versions of *Faust* relevant to the novel, Gasparov comments
    that the initial parallel with Goethe's seems everywhere undermined: the
    characters are nothing like Goethe's and the operatic version seems pointedly

referred to everywhere. But it is precisely against the background of these disappointed allusions to Goethe that his "canonic" version turns out not only to have inhered at every turn of the narrative, but even to be the key to its meanings ("Iz nabliudenii nad motivnoi strukturoi" 68). Gasparov further notes that Bulgakov's novel combines a serious metaphysical version of the Passion (Golgotha, the crucifixion) with its theatricalized, operatic realization: in the Jerusalem chapters Golgotha is actually called Bald Mountain, with allusions to Mussorgsky as well as the Walpurgis night in Goethe's and Gonoud's versions of *Faust* ("Iz nabliudenii nad motivnoi strukturoi" 40). Petrovskii notes that allusions to Gounod's opera appear in several works by Bulgakov, among them *The White Guard*, "Adam i Eva" ("Adam and Eve"), "Tainomu drugu" ("To a Secret Friend"), and *Zapiski iunogo vracha* (*Notes of a Young Doctor*; 85). According to Chudakova, in the winter of 1912–13 Bulgakov saw "at least ten" performances of the opera in Kyiv (*Zhizneopisanie* 46).

3 Chudakova suggests that the poodle sent outside by the nurse in the psychiatric hospital is an allusion to *Faust* (*Zhizneopisanie* 305). The old couple, Philemon and Baucis, in their seaside cottage with its little garden in Part 2 of *Faust*, might even arguably be the subtext for Master and Margarita in their final idyll in Bulgakov's novel.

4 Milne notes that "the dramatic tradition of the mediaeval mystery play" illumines "the purpose and form" of Bulgakov's *The Master and Margarita* (2); also that in the drafts for the novel that Bulgakov wrote in 1933–4 the hero is named "Faust" (30).

5 There are some suggestive parallels between Marlowe's play and Bulgakov's novel. In the former Faust is at one point ambushed and beheaded by a rival, Benvolio, to whom he had had Mephistopheles give horns for mocking scholars; but Frederick, a gentleman of the court, pleads with Mephistopheles to "give him his head, for God's sake," and Faust arises again (Bates, 68). Bengalski, the master of ceremonies during Woland's performance at the Variety Theater in *The Master and Margarita*, has his head first torn off by Behemoth and then restored to him when he begs for mercy; Berlioz also loses his head in fulfilment of Woland's prediction at the opening of the novel.

6 http://dic.academic.ru/dic.nsf/enc_literature/4702/Фауст.

7 On Bulgakov as a Romantic writer see J.A.E. Curtis, 188–208.

8 Shakespeare's well-known passage defines "all the world" as "a stage":

> All the world's a stage,
> And all the men and women merely players;
> They have their exits and their entrances;
> And one man in his time plays many parts,
> His acts being seven ages. At first the infant,

Mewling and puking in the nurse's arms;
And then the whining school-boy, with his satchel
And shining morning face, creeping like snail
Unwillingly to school. And then the lover,
Sighing like furnace, with a woeful ballad
Made to his mistress' eyebrow. Then a soldier,
Full of strange oaths, and bearded like the pard,
Jealous in honour, sudden and quick in quarrel,
Seeking the bubble reputation
Even in the cannon's mouth. And then the justice,
In fair round belly with good capon lin'd,
With eyes severe and beard of formal cut,
Full of wise saws and modern instances;
And so he plays his part. The sixth age shifts
Into the lean and slipper'd pantaloon,
With spectacles on nose and pouch on side;
His youthful hose, well sav'd, a world too wide
For his shrunk shank; and his big manly voice,
Turning again toward childish treble, pipes
And whistles in his sound. Last scene of all,
That ends this strange eventful history,
Is second childishness and mere oblivion;
Sans teeth, sans eyes, sans taste, sans everything.

9 In this regard Gounod's operatic version is, perforce, simpler:
Mephistopheles "suddenly appears" (*vnezapno poiavliatesia*, in the Russian
translation), "summoned from hell [...] where the golden calf is, there
Satan holds his ball." In its fanciful tale of Satan's intervention in Moscow
Bulgakov's novel resurrects more of the richer spatial logic of Goethe's
drama than does Gounod's opera (http://libretto-oper.ru/gounod/faust).

10 Consider, for example, 2 Timothy 4:1–2: "I charge you in the presence of
God and of Christ Jesus who is to judge the living and the dead, and by
his appearing and his kingdom: preach the word, be urgent in season and
out of season, convince, rebuke, and exhort, be unfailing in patience and in
teaching." The Greek term that appears is "appearing" (επιφανεια, with
accent on the φαν, from which our word "epiphany" is borrowed directly).
This usage is characteristic of the Pastoral Epistles alone, which differ
from the early Pauline letters (which have instead παρουσια, "presence"
or "coming, arrival"; 2 Thessalonians 3:8 has both). In 2 Timothy 1:10, the
same word, επιφανεια, is used in what seems to be a clear reference to the
incarnation. Admittedly, it has been argued, but not persuasively, that we are
to read even this usage as a reference to the final appearing as is the case with

the other four uses of the term in the Pastoral Epistles: see also 1
Timothy 6:14 and Titus 2:13 as well as 2 Timothy 4:8). But 2 Timothy 4:1a
speaks of "Christ Jesus, who is about to judge the living and the dead," and 2
Timothy 4:8 speaks a future hope for those "who have loved his επιφανεια."
The usage in 4:1 therefore refers to the final appearing of Christ (Mark Seifrid,
Professor of Exegetical Theology, Concordia Seminary; private conversation).

11 Bakhtin claims that carnival was from the outset organically linked to
the mystery play, that "a carnival atmosphere reigned on days when
mystery plays and *soties* were being performed" ("karnaval'naia atmosfera
gospodstvovala v dni postanovok misterii i soti"; *Tvorchestvo Fransua Rable*
7), that there even existed a special form of "paschal laughter" associated
with Easter (7), and that forms of folk laughter in general are related to
Christian liturgy genetically ("otdalennym geneticheskim rodstvom," 9).

12 See, however, Hardison's questioning of the "neat theory of drama that
moves from the church to the church portal, from the church portal to the
plaza in front of the church, and from there to moveable pageant cars,
changing its language from Latin to the vernacular in the process" (ix).

13 Ozouf notes that the procession in the French Revolutionary Festival of the
Federation "was itself interminable": "it took two more hours, after it first
passed under the triumphal arch, to take up position in the Champ-de-
Mars" (49).

14 To the extent that Bakhtin is correct in seeing a genetic link between
mediaeval carnival and the mystery play, his comment on carnival is apt
here: "carnival bears the aspect of the universe, it is a peculiar condition of
the entire world" (*karnaval nosit vselenskii kharakter, eto osoboe sostoianie vsego
mira; Tvorchestvo Fransua Rable* 10).

15 "Преисподняя – это своеобразный образ итога, образ конца и
завершения индивидуальных жизней и судеб и одновременно
это – окончательный суд над отдельной человеческой жизнью в ее
целом, суд, в основу которого были положены высшие критерии
официального христианского мировозрения (религиозно-
метафизические, этические, социальные и политические)."
(*Tvorchestvo Fransua Rable* 429).

16 Occasionally such mimus performances could be taken to realistic
extremes: "under the Flavian Emperor Domitian, who was the first to
cause Christian blood to be spilled in the Colosseum, the following
incident happened. The emperor thought the customary mime
representation of the robber chief Laureolus, who is crucified at the end,
was rather feeble. He gave orders that the title role should be given to a
convicted criminal. The play ended in dreadful earnest. Domitian let the
crucified man be torn to pieces by wild beasts" (Berthold 208). Bakhtin
suggests that Rabelais was aware that the Gospel account of the Passion

was informed by a tradition of mock coronation and decrowning of a "carnival king" (*Tvorchestvo Fransua Rable* 215).

17 On the replication of this kind of procession in Petrine and post-Petrine Russia, see Wortman.

18 Krupnianskaia, however, notes that a fresco in Kyiv's Cathedral of St. Sophia dating from the eleventh century depicts the opening of the curtain on a puppet play (393). As for Polish religious theatre, its own history may have been more complex than a simple derivation from the liturgy; see, for example, Kadulska's argument for the influence of Italian *commedia dell'arte* on Jesuit religious drama in Poland – a reverse cycle of sorts that would tend to underscore the close intermingling of farcical and ritual elements in late- and post-medieval theatre ("L'Influence de la 'Commedia dell'Arte' sur le Théâtre des Collèges de la Compagnie de Jésus en Pologne").

19 See also Bogatyrev 396. Marionette theaters *per se* represented a second wave of puppet theatre importation into Russia associated with the westernizing initiatives of Peter the Great. The western- (especially German-) influenced theatres of St. Petersburg nonetheless leaned toward religious and moral works (*O tselomudrennom Iosife ot Seresy zelo liubimom, Raspiatie Khristovo, Zhitie i mucheniia sv. Dorotei*), while the most popular plays in Moscow were *Iudif –* and *Komediia o doktore Fauste* (*The Comedy of Dr. Faust; Entsiklopedicheskii slovar'*, s.v. "*marionetki*").

20 Petrovskii also notes that in the Kyiv *gymnasium* Bulgakov attended the same hall served as both chapel, complete with altar, and theatre (181). Milne also notes Bulgakov's likely familiarity with the *vertep* theatre (3) as well as the mingling of sacred and farcical themes in mystery plays (2).

21 Recall Nelson's claim that puppet theatre originates in the relegation of the Platonic underworld to the grotto. In Russian the original, now archaic, meaning of "vertep" was "peshchera" (cave).

22 The original idea for the play was evidently suggested to the Grand Duke by Piotr Tchaikovsky. Because of its overt religious topic, it was controversial despite receiving the tsar's approval, and it met with resistance from the *tsaritsa* and Rasputin. It was initially read in private groups rather than performed. When eventually approved for performance in the small Hermitage Theatre, its planning proved difficult because it called for grandiose staging with huge crowds in mass scenes and monumental scenery – almost as if in anticipation of early Soviet spectacles (Gievskii 282–4, 286). Even Martin Buber pairs Moscow and Jerusalem: "So long as Russia has not undergone an essential inner change ... we must designate one of the two poles of Socialism between which our choice lies, by the formidable name of 'Moscow.' The other, I would make bold to call 'Jerusalem'; *Paths in Utopia*, trans. R.F.C. Hull (London:

Routledge, 1949), quoted in Todorova's *The Lost World of Socialists at Europe's Margins: Imagining Utopia, 1870s–1920s* (18).

23 Petrovskii goes so far as to suggest that the Grand Duke's play influenced the entire "mystery" orientation of Bulgakov's oeuvre (196).

24 Chudakova notes that the Kyiv professor of theology Vasilii Il'ich Ekzempliarskii maintained a large collection of photographs of images of Christ, among them photos of the frescoes in Kyiv churches as well as of the panorama on Vladimirskaia gorka. Bulgakov's sister Tatiana helped catalogue the collection, and Bulgakov likely saw many of the photographs (*Zhizneopisanie* 36). Adding to the Jerusalem/Rome – that is, early Christian – allusions at the time, there was a Kyivan circus adaptation of Sienkiewicz's *Quo Vadis* presented as a "Roman spectacle" (*rimskie zrelishcha*)" and "historical pantomime of ancient Rome" (*istoricheskaia pantomima drevnego Rima*)." The Italian film adaptation of *Quo Vadis?* by Enrico Guazzoni was also showing in Kyiv in the spring of 1913, when Bulgakov was there, as was Jean Noguès's operatic version in the city theatre (Petrovskii 242; see also 297–9 on evident borrowings from *Quo Vadis* in *The Master and Margarita*).

25 Gasparov suggests that the fires which break out in Moscow in the novel allude to the burning of Moscow during the Napoleonic war but also to the burning of Rome ("Iz nabliudenii nad motivnoi strukturoi" 51). One notes that a similar conflagration, of the "Voronnaia sloboda" communal apartment, marks the plot climax of Il'f and Petrov's *The Little Golden Calf.* Chudakova links the panoramic view of Moscow at the end of *The Master and Margarita* to Bulgakov's reading of Gogol's "Rome" while he was simultaneously writing his novel and working on a screenplay about the writing of that author's *Dead Souls*. The initial version of the screenplay opened with scenes of Gogol' in Rome – the city in which he actually wrote the first part of the novel – but censors forced Bulgakov to cut them and situate the action in St. Petersburg, leading Bulgakov to lament in a 10 June 1934 letter to P.S. Popov, "But – dear God! – how much I regret having to cut Rome!" ("Bulgakov i Gogol'" 43–4). Kalb argues that Bulgakov's *The Master and Margarita* belongs to the hitherto unacknowledged context of "Russia's 'Rome text' of the early twentieth century" (186).

26 The Ardis edition of the novel offers the following commentary in reference to "Forty Times Forty": "The panoramic views of Moscow anticipate here the analogical passages in the author's last novel," that is, in *The Master and Margarita* (Bulgakov, *Sobranie sochinenii*, vol. 8, 424). Chudakova notes a parallel in point of view between Bulgakov's rooftop perspective in "Sorok Sorokov" and the view from "the roof of the Nierensee House" in Valentin Kataev's 1923 tale "Strashnyi perelet g-na Matzal'ia" ("Arkhiv M.A. Bulgakova" 47). Also, Bulgakov first published

his tale "Rokovye iaitsa" ("The Fateful Eggs") under the title "Krasnyi luch" ("The Red Ray") in the journal *Krasnaia panorama* (*Red Panorama*); Chudakova *Zhizneopisanie* 245.

27 Another possible source with a Ukrainian, if not directly Kyivan, connection is Gogol's story "Rim" (Rome), the fragment of an unfinished novel about a young Italian prince titled *Annunziata*. After recounting the hero's sojourn in Paris, with whose charms he eventually becomes disenchanted, the story shows him rediscovering the majesty hidden beneath the tarnished surface of present-day Rome. It ends with the prince standing awestruck before a panoramic view of the city whose effect is as epiphanic as the appearance of the mysterious troika at the end of *Dead Souls* – an episode of "intervention" with decidedly eschatological implications: "But here the Prince paused and gazed at Rome: before him arose the eternal city in a wondrous glowing panorama [...] Not in words or with a brush could one convey the wondrous harmony and accord of all the planes of this picture [...] God, what a view! Possessed by it, the Prince forgot himself, Annunziata's beauty, and the mysterious fate of his nation, and everything on the earth. "Но здесь князь взглянул на Рим и остановился: пред ним в чудной сияющей панораме предстал вечный город [...] Ни словом, ни кистью нельзя было передать чудного согласия и сочетанья всех планов этой картины [...] Боже, какой вид! Князь, объятый им, позабыл и себя, и красоту Аннунциаты, и таинственную судьбу своего народа, и всё, что ни есть на свете" (321–2).

28 Hot-air balloons figured in the design of the festivals of the French Revolution, where they also served a totalizing function. As Ozouf comments, "the heart of the Revolutionary festival was [...] often the ascent of an aerostat into the heavens [...] The aerostatic festival was the utopian festival endowed at last with its own incarnation, for the aerostat drew all eyes at once toward the sky, where the only transcendence of the festival resided [...] It accomplished that simultaneity denied by processions" (132).

29 Cf. Ryklin's claim that the statuary in the Moscow subway system reflected a rural population that had been brought to the city as industrial labour and now found itself oppressed by the Terror.

3 Modernist Dreams of "Intervention"

1 Regarding the general influence of modernist reformers of the theatre like Wagner, Fuchs, Craig, and Ivanov on later Soviet show trials, see Cassiday 11, as well as chapter 5 of this study.

2 As Brandist comments, "The mystery play was adopted as the modern form of tragedy, polarizing the social world into pre- and post-salvation time and the present as the threshold on which the struggle is played out" (38).

3 The ideal of Romain Rolland, another important influence on Russian theatre in the early twentieth century, was the popular "fêtes" arranged after the French Revolution – and he was decidedly opposed to Wagnerian religiosity: "Quel profit le people pourrait-il tirer des complications maladives de cette sensibilité, de la métaphysique du Walhalla, du Désir de Tristan qui souffle la mort, et des tourments mystico-charnels des chevaliers du Graal? Cela est sorti d-une élite infectée de subtilités néo-chrétiennes, ou néo-bouddhiques, de songes peut-être fascinants, mais mortels pour l'action, et qui ont poussé, comme de superbes mousses sur des arbres pourris. Au nom du ciel, ne donnons point au peuple nos maladies, – quelque complaisance que nous trouvions à les cultivers en nous. Tâchons de faire une race plus saine, et qui vaille mieux que nous" (*Le Théatre du Peuple* 47).

4 Shevelenko notes that in the world of ballet, too, the Russian intention was to complete Wagner (227). See also Shevelenko 260–1 on the somewhat more distantly related Russian interest in reviving a "folk" past in modernist art and music. Sergei Durylin, in a work titled *Vagner i Rossiia*, argued that Wagner had failed to outline plans for a genuinely Christian form of mystery, a task that he believed now fell to Russia (Mitchell 53).

5 Nietzsche's essay, which is dedicated to Wagner, had appeared in Russia in 1903, and in Bely's words had the effect of a "bomb" in Symbolist circles (Kleberg, "'People's Theater' and the Revolution" 183).

6 Nietzsche's comment on this in "The Birth of Tragedy" is that "a public of spectators as we know it was unknown to the Greeks: in their theaters the terraced structure of concentric arcs made it possible for everybody actually to *overlook* the whole world of culture around him and to imagine, in absorbed contemplation, that he himself was a chorist" (62–3).

7 On the related efforts in the Soviet era of Velemir Khlebnikov and Ia. Lintsbakh to invent a new language, see my *The Word Made Self* 67–70.

8 Wagner's *Gesamtkunstwerk* itself can be thought of as a form of "intervention" in the sense discussed here, expressing impatience with the separate forms of art left stranded on their own in a mere historical present.

9 See Karshan 4–15 for an overview of the concept of "play" in Russian modernist culture.

10 On this play Kot notes, "In this pseudoritual, the gods come down from Olympus to take part in human affairs" (117).

11 In "Balagan" Meyerhold comments, "Пока Ремизов и Скрябин будут искать свои места на готовящихся для новых театров площадях, пока мистерии их будут ждать собрания посвященных, Театр, отдавшийся жонглеру, будет вести ожесточенную борьбу с драмами бытоописательными, диалектическими, с пьесами à

these и настроений, новый Театр масок будет учиться у испанцев и итальянцев XVII в. строить свой репертуар на законах Балагана, где «забавлять» всегда стоит раньше, чем поучать, и где движения ценятся дороже слова. Недаром у базошских клерков пантомима была излюбленной драматической формой" (*Stat'i. Pis'ma. Rechi. Besedy. Chast' pervaia* 215).

12 The seemingly quaint use of a fairy-tale dragon to embody evil was still active in minds of the Soviet era; cf. the playwright Evgeny Shvarts's 1941 satirical allegory on Stalinism, *Drakon* (*The Dragon*).

13 Two other works by Sologub that could be considered mysteries are "Tomlenie k inym bytiiam. Misteriia" ("A Longing for Other Forms of Being: A Mystery," 1908), a curious metaliterary masochist fantasy in which seven youths (*otroki* again) prepare to subject the narrator to physical torment – a sentence they read off a scroll whose author turns out to be the narrator himself; and "Dar mudrykh pchel. Tragediia" ("The Wise Bees' Gift: A Tragedy," 1908), in which a queen laments the death of her husband the king in battle, and journeys to the underworld and brings him back, only to die herself. The "gift" in question is the beeswax, used in fortune telling.

14 Remizov's *Tragediia o Iude Printse Iskariotskom* (*The Tragedy of Judas Prince Iskariot*, 1908) would seem a more distant echo of these themes, but it is not irrelevant. Remizov based his drama on Russian folk legends of Judas-the-traitor (*Iuda-Predatel'*) rather than the Gospel accounts (270) and interweaves topical allusion to Russia's political turmoil (there are rumours that the "tsar" of Jerusalem is going to be dethroned; he disowns "prince Judas" and designates his brother Stratim successor instead; affairs on the "island" of Iskariot are in disarray) with fairy-tale elements of the kind favoured by Silver Age nostalgia (a tree with golden apples suddenly appears on the day of Judas's birth) and voguish hints at an Oedipal situation (Judas's real mother may also be his wife; Freud's *The Interpretation of Dreams* had appeared in 1899). Yet the play's centre of gravity lies soundly in a mapping of the situation in Jerusalem (which the play pointedly refers to as *tsarstvo* and calls "nachal'noe tsarstvo" and "pupok zemli," 145) during the time of the Passion (however loosely represented) onto contemporary Russia. At one point Judas warns Pilate (whom Remizov depicts as a distracted sybarite rather than the tormented ruler of Bulgakov's novel) that the real threat to the *tsarstvo* will come from from a certain "unusual person" who has recently appeared, who raises the dead and gives the blind their sight (163). When Pilate retorts that his teachings make no sense, Judas tells him he is "more powerful than a prophet" (167–8) – and while they talk a thunderstorm approaches, a motif repeated during Pilate's interrogation of Yeshua in *The Master and Margarita*.

15 Evreinov's earlier *Chetvertaia stena* (*The Fourth Wall*, 1915) had inversely
   acknowledged the centrality of *Faust* as a mystical spectacle to theatrical
   renewal. In this play a theatrical troupe rehearses the opera *Faust*, all the
   while trying to perfect its assimilation to the most natural representation
   possible. The actor who plays Faust spends nights sleeping on the stage
   itself, in the midst of painstakingly exact mediaeval props, including a
   chalice of real poison made of strychnine and prussic acid. As the rehearsal
   progresses, the aesthetic properties of the opera are serially stripped in an
   effort to achieve still greater realism: the separate role of Mephistopheles
   is dropped because he is in fact an aspect of Faust, a vision of Marguerite
   at her spinning wheel is replaced by Marguerite passing by the window
   carrying a spinning wheel, the music is dropped because in real life people
   speak rather than sing, it is decided that the actors will speak Middle High
   German – and so on, with the director at one point remonstrating that "this
   is no puppet show!" (79). The eponymous fourth wall is erected in a final,
   absurd tribute to naturalism, and when the "opera" is actually performed
   in the play's brief second act the actor playing Faust drinks the poison in
   disgust.
16 Posner notes that E.T.A. Hoffmann published a play in 1818 titled *The
   Strange Sorrows of a Theater Manager*, in which a group of ideal actors
   is revealed to consist of marionettes; the play was translated into
   Russian in 1894 and embraced as a proposal for theatrical reform by the
   Alexandrinsky theatre actor Modest Pisarev (18–9).
17 In Bakhtin's view, marionettes in Romantic culture represented an alien
   force that took control of human lives. The dominant aura surrounding
   puppets in Romanticism was therefore that of "the distinct grotesque motif
   of *the tragedy of the puppet*" ("svoeobraznyi grotesknyi motif *tragedii kukly*";
   Tvorchestvo Fransua Rable 47).
18 Maeterlinck could also be included in this account of "intervention" texts
   for his *The Miracle of St. Anthony* (which was staged at the Vakhtangov
   Theatre in 1921; Rudnitsky 54). The play reads like a parody of the kind
   of pious tale of incognito intervention represented by Tolstoy's "Where
   God Is, There Also is Love," or like the kind of satire of self-satisfied
   bourgeois materialism Tolstoy might have written, had Tolstoy written
   parody. St. Anthony shows up on the doorstep of a wealthy home in a
   Flemish provincial town where the mistress has recently died. He reveals
   that he is St. Anthony of Padua and that he has come to raise the woman
   from the dead. The chattering old servant-woman who admits him tells
   him to wipe his muddy feet, then expresses regret that she will lose the
   money her mistress (Mlle Hortense) left her in her will – but thinks better
   and agrees that Mlle Hortense should be brought back to life. The dead
   woman's family, however, is sceptical, believes St. Anthony to be drunk,

and asks a visiting doctor to examine him. St. Anthony nonetheless raises Mlle Hortense from the dead – at which point she asks why a dirty beggar has been let in the house. She is then struck dumb for revealing mysteries that should not be revealed ("mysteries of the dead"). The police are summoned and decide that St. Anthony is either a madman or a drunk, moreover one without any papers. He is led away, barefoot, into a snowstorm, and the Mlle Hortense dies once more. Panova suggests that Maeterlinck's *Bluebird*, with its "basis in mystery" (*misterial'naia osnova*), in particular its scenes of travel to the underworld in search of the blue bird, influenced Daniil Kharms's *Lapa* as well as Mayakovsky's *Mystery-Bouffe* (402).

19 "особенность куклы связана с тем, что, переходя в мир взрослых, она несет с собою воспоминания о детском, фольклорном, мифологическом и игровом мире […] Возможность сопоставления с живым существом увеличивает мертвенность куклы…Мифологические представления об оживании мертвого подобия и превращении живого существа в неподвижный образ универсальный…кукла оказалась на скрещении древнего мифа об оживающей статуе и новой мифологии мертвой машинной жизни […] Таким образом, в нашем культурном сознании сложилось как бы два лица куклы: одно манит в уютный мир детства, другое ассоциируется с псевдожизнью, мертвым движением, смертью, притворяющейся жизнью. Первое глядится в мир фольклора, сказки, примитива, второе напоминает о машинной цивилизации, отчуждении, двойничестве" ("Kukly v sisteme kul'tury" 378–9).

20 A kindred sense of trauma would seem to inhabit the scene in Nabokov's *Lolita* in which Humbert Humbert observes a man vacuuming a shop window in which female mannequins are displayed: "On the floor, at the feet of these damsels, where the man crawled about laboriously with his cleaner, there lay a cluster of three slender arms, and a blond wig. Two of the arms happened to be twisted and seemed to suggest a clasping gesture of horror and supplication" (226).

21 See Kelly; also Partan.

22 Kuzmin has a play, *Vtornik Meri. Predstavlenie i trekh chastiakh dlia kukol zhivykh ili dereviannykh* (*Mary's Tuesday. A Performance in Three Parts for Living or Wooden Puppets*), though there is nothing specifically puppet-like about the characters or stage directions.

23 "Таким образом, неофициальная народная культура имела в средние века и еще в эпоху Ренессанса свою особую территорию – площаль, и свое свободное время – праздничные и ярморочные дни. Эта праздничная площадь […] особый мир внутри средневекового официального мира."

24 A further modernist extension of the demonic connotations of the
    Petrushka figure and the *balagan* can be found in the farcically puppet-
    like character of the executioner, Monsieur Pierre, in Vladimir Nabokov's
    Priglashenie na kazn' (Senderovich and Shvarts, "Verbnaia shtuchka […]
    Stat'ia pervaia" and "Verbnaia shtuchka […] Stat'ia vtoraia").

25 As Senderovich and Shvarts point out, in Nabokov's *Priglashenie na kazn'*
    M. Pierre plays Mephistopheles to a reluctant Cincinnatus-Faust, who
    refuses to succumb to the temptation of the joys M. Pierre describes to him
    ("Verbnaia shtuchka […] Stat'ia pervaia" 101, 104).

26 Warner notes that Petrushka plays and the secular puppet plays in the
    vertep repertoire coexisted in Russia and Ukraine and influenced each
    other (*The Russian Folk Theatre* 118). Kelly, though, suggests that the
    remote ritual origins of *Petrushka* were less important than its capacity to
    entertain (89).

27 Brandist notes that the punning ambivalence between *kosa* as "braid"
    and as "scythe" (mundane physical attribute versus allegorical symbol of
    death) represents the clash of two codes, the realist and the Symbolist, the
    latter being a parodic target for Blok in this play (40).

28 As Senderovich and Shvarts suggest, it was the very *temporary* character
    of the fairground booth that in the eyes of Russian modernists lent it
    eschatological implications: the *balaganchik* stages a world that easily
    passes away ("Verbnaia shtuchka […] Stat'ia pervaia" 106–7). It was this
    uncannily insubstantial quality of Russian fairground entertainments in
    general (shrovetide, catkin week – *gorodskie prazdnichnye guliania*) that later
    so fascinated Nabokov (94). At the end of *Zashchita Luzhina* (*The Defense*),
    the hero jumps like Harlequin out of a window into a depth that resembles
    a chessboard (i.e., a stage decoration), while the novel's final comment
    that in the room now "there was no Aleksandr Ivanovich" leaves his own
    reality in question. The motley and flimsy world in which Cincinnatus
    finds himself imprisoned in *Priglashenie na kazn'*, and which puts him
    to death, also transposes the fairground booth (*balaganchik* in general as
    well as Blok's play *The Fairground Booth*). At the moment of his execution,
    the world Cincinnatus had been inhabiting collapses like cheap stage
    scenery around him, as he rises and walks off in a direction where "судя
    по голосам, стояли существа, подобные ему." Moreover, Cincinnatus's
    trial is not incidental but is essential to the puppet-like world he inhabits.
    The ultimate implication of the *balagan* farce invoked in Nabokov's novel
    is *judgment and death* (and, as Senderovich and Shvarts note, the association
    of fairground entertainment and death is not just Nabokov's conceit: as
    late as the nineteenth century public executions in Rome were scheduled
    to coincide with the start of carnival; "Verbnaia shtuchka […] Stat'ia
    pervaia" 107): "Весь мир, в котором протекает история осуждения

и казни Цинцинната, может быть охарактеризован как балаганный мир, поскольку балаган был центральным институтом праздничного народного гуляния. Уже с самого начала романа обстановка суда над Цинциннатом читается в предлагаемой системе – как комедия в балагане" (106).

29 A.A. Sanin proposed a "mystery-like" idea for a film script to Blok (Petrovskii 195–6).

30 Shleyter-Lavine notes that many commentators on *The Twelve* treat it as a dramatic poem and that Meyerhold once attempted to stage it (570).

31 Gasparov suggests that the flickering black-and-white images are meant to connote the experience of early cinema ("Tema sviatochnogo karnavala" 8).

32 Shleyter-Lavine comments that in *The Twelve* Blok moves away from lyric intimacy toward "epic" engagement with contemporary reality and that the poem's "emphasis of real space and a concrete historical background" is markedly different from the "pointedly artificial, ahistorical setting" of *The Fairground Booth* (573, 586).

33 Shleyter-Lavine notes the precedent for this procession in the torch procession led by Harlequin in *The Fairground Booth* (584). In a broader sense, the advent in Blok's poem also looks back to the divine *troika* whose appearance punctuates the end of Gogol's *Dead Souls* and *its* search for Russia's way out of "history." Regarding the striking image of the white roses, Kalb suggests that although they perhaps "feminize" Christ, they may also refer to the "rose-wreath crown of laughter" in Nietzsche's *Thus Spake Zarathustra* (118–19). For Gasparov, they point to the image's derivation from pointedly Western mystery rituals ("Tema sviatochnogo karnavala" 20). See also the closely related image in Ivanov's "Predchuvstviia i predvestiia" – an essay of 1906, *nota bene*, the same year *The Fairground Booth* was written, subtitled "The New Organic Era and the Theater of the Future": "Сикстинская Мадонна идет. Складки ее одежд выдают ритм ее шагов. Мы сопутствуем ей в облаках. Сфера, ее окружающая, – скопление действующих жизней: весь воздух переполнен ангельскими обличиями. Все живет и несет ее; пред нами – гармония небесных сил, и в ней, как движущаяся мелодия, – она сама; а на руках ее – Младенец, с устремленным в мир взором, исполненным воли и гениальной решимости, – Младенец, которого она отдает миру, или, скорее, который сам влечет в мир ее, свою плоть, и с нею стремит за собою всю сферу, где она блуждает" (*Sobranie sochinenii*, vol. 2, 92).

34 Masing-Delic reads Blok's Christ in a consistent Symbolist vein, arguing that he arrives in order to "lead mankind from this shore of poor reality across the abyss of time into the enchanted distances of *realiora* realms" (196).

35 Blok knew of Ukrainian puppet theatre from P.O. Morozov's study
and possibly also from A.N. Veselovskii's 1870 *Starinnyi teatr v Evrope*
(Lotman, "Blok i narodnaia kul'tura goroda" 196); cf. Petrovskii's
analogous argument about the structure of Bulgakov's *The Master and
Margarita*, a parallel that suggests intertextual borrowing or shared
awareness of the tradition, or both. Gasparov sees the procession of
soldiers in Blok's poem as emerging from the same element: it is not just
a projection of revolutionary violence onto the Gospels, but a specific
imitation of the religious processions that were a part of Western-
Russian and Ukrainian Christmastime carnivals – *koliady* – during which
an icon of the baby Jesus was carried at the head of the procession
(*sviatochnyi karnaval*, 195, 198; see also Gasparov and Lotman, "Igrovye
motivy").

36 Gasparov notes the poem's indebtedness to *vertep* and *koliady*, which
mobilize a "folk-religious consciousness" (*narodno-religioznoe soznanie*)
within the poem, but also argues for an explicitly *Western* Christian aura to
the procession (via the white roses), a connotation that would strengthen
the poem's appeal to the mystery genre. He also suggests that the hungry
cur in the poem may be "Mephistopheles, auguring renewal" ("Tema
sviatochnogo karnavala" 14, 19).

37 Even the circus, for Gasparov, preserves this eschatological orientation:
"All those gymnast-angels flying beneath the cupola and walking on
tightropes (like Christ on the water); all the marvellous transformations,
disappearances into the underworld and equally miraculous resurrections;
a man in a cage with lions and tigers, reminiscent of the first Christians"
("Tema sviatochnogo karnavala" 22).

38 For an extensive discussion of the parallels between "Catiline" and *The
Twelve* see Kalb, "A 'Roman Bolshevik': Aleksandr Blok's 'Catiline' and the
Russian Revolution," chapter 3 in her *Russia's Rome*, 106–28.

39 "[…] идет он все той же своей – «то ленивой, то торопливой»
походкой; но ярость и неистовство сообщили его походке
музыкальный ритм; как будто это уже не тот – корыстный и
развратный Катилина; в поступи этого человека – мятеж, восстание,
фурии народного гнева."

40   …вдаль идут державным шагом …
                    […] Старый мир, как пес паршивый,
                    Провались – поколочу! […]
                    …Так идут державным шагом
                    […] Впереди – с кровавым флагом […]
                    Нежной поступью надвьюжной […]
                    Впереди – Исус Христос.

4 Rituals of "Intervention" in the Early Soviet Era

1 Continuing this series of figurations of the revolution as Christian Advent was the poet Sergei Esenin's "Prishestvie" ("The Advent"). Published in 1918 but dated October 1917, the poem is dedicated to Bely. Opening with the line, "O Lord, I believe!," it recycles images from both Tiutchev and Bely of Christ appearing in the depths of the Russian countryside, among peasants. Like Bely, and anticipating Bulgakov's novel, it then projects onto Russia's current disarray the scene of the Passion, focusing in particular on the apostle Peter's triple denial that he is a disciple of Christ – although he beseeches God to appear in Russia all the same.

2 On the parallels between *The Twelve* and *Mystery-Bouffe* see Rudnitsky 42: both celebrate the Revolution by turning to folkloric primitivism and street poetry.

3 Meyerhold explains the significance of the parade in his 1912 essay, "Balagan": "Пролог и следующий за ним парад, а также столь излюбленное итальянцами и испанцами XVII в. и французскими водевилистами заключительное обращение к публике, все эти элементы Старого театра обязывают зрителя смотреть на представление актеров не иначе, как на игру" (The Prologue and subsequent parade, as well as the closing address to the public so beloved of the Italians and the Spanish in the seventeenth century as well as French vaudevillians, compels the spectator to view the actors' performance as nothing other than play") (*Stat'i. Pis'ma. Rechi. Besedy. Chast' pervaia* 215).

4 Mayakovsky's Christ-pretensions, which appear in several of his works – for example, the 1919–20 *Oblako v shtanakh* (*A Cloud in Trousers*), in which he laments that in the lecture halls of Petrograd, Moscow, Odessa, and Kyiv where he read his poetry there was no one in the audience who did not cry, "crucify him!," declares himself the thirteenth apostle, taunts God for being nothing but a little god (*bozhek*), and suggests that Jesus Christ "sniffs the forget-me-nots" of his soul (*Sobranie sochinenii*, vol. 1, 238, 243, 248) – could be read as an egomaniacal response to works like Bely's "Christ Is Risen" or Vladimir Kirillov's "Iron Messiah," which project the advent of a "Christ" (be it biblical or metaphorical) onto Russia's current historical moment. The Mayakovskian moment here is the flagrantly egoistical identification with Christ. What belongs to the culture at large is the expectation of advent and corresponding focus on the Christian precedent.

5 The art historian Nikolai Punin recorded a similar reaction to Vladimir Tatlin's staging of the Futurist poet Velemir Khlebnikov's poem *Zangezi* a couple of years later, in 1923: "*Zangezi* is not an experiment in plot-construction, not a laboratory for new forms of speech or a rationalist

consruction according to the laws of fate. It is one of the most synthetic plotless mystery plays of our time. It is some kind of exquisite huge poster or tapestry hung above our century" (11).

6 Brandist sees in these early Soviet festivals elements of a carnival "uncrowning" of previous authority (61), though he also notes that as early as 1918 "carnival" existed side-by-side with a principle of "monument" in Soviet festivals, in an uneasy relation of complementarity (66).

7 The efforts by the avant-garde to theatricalize urban space in the early Soviet era are well-documented (especially by Clark, van Geldern, Rolf, Binns, Glebkin, Kerzhentsev, and Speranskaia). Clark suggests an affinity between Kerzhentsev's notion of the "intermingling of all" in Soviet festivals and Bakhtin's concept of carnival (*Petersburg* 125).

8 Clark suggests that in general the mass spectacles of the 1920s can be viewed as examples of Wagnerism (225).

9 Time itself became a contentious issue when in February 1918 the Soviet government shifted the country from the Julian calendar used in the Russian empire and by the Church to the Gregorian, widely used by then in Europe and the rest of the world. As Silano observes, "Liturgical time not only determined the peasants' work life; it also affirmed that time itself was sacred, belonging to an order established by God, and not by the worker-peasant power" (338).

10 Recall from chapter 1 Toporov's notion that modern city streets, which "define the network of links between parts of the whole while underscoring a hierarchy of relations (delineation of a main street and the placement on it, or on a square to which it leads, of sacred symbols of the highest order, or of desacralized secular power)," form a "degenerate" (*vyrozhdennyi*) successor to mythological pathways ("Prostranstvo i tekst" 267).

11 This kind of tension or binarism may indeed have ancient roots. Mazaev notes a difference between ancient Greek festivals (*prazdniki*), which served "as an arena for the spiritual and physical perfection of the human being," and subsequent Roman ones, "which divided participants into those who actively performed and those who merely observed" (97). The one form he calls "festival" (*prazdnik*), the other "official" or "ceremonial" festival (*ofitsial'nyi prazdnik, torzhestvo*; 104).

12 On the broader popularity of such "Christ" poems, see Glaser on Yiddish and black American versions as well as poems on the civil war in Spain (120, 158).

13 Chudakova notes that Bulgakov saw, and was shocked by, the crudely anti-religious sentiment of the "Komsomol Christmas" procession in Moscow (*Zhizneopisanie* 190). Petrone notes the "tension between the rejection of the content of pre-revolutionary religious rituals and

the adoption of their forms" (12). She also comments on early Soviet controversy over whether a secularized *elka* (fir-tree) celebration to replace the pre-revolutionary Christmas was appropriate (85).

14 Sartori notes that the "Komsomol Christmas" processions were staged in 184 cities of Russia between 25 December 1922 and 6 January 1923 and were intended as didactic anti-religious propaganda (51). She also notes that the use of effigies and dummies may have been borrowed from traditional Russian mummeries and masquerades – in an appeal to traditions of satirical folk theatre (57).

15 For a detailed discussion of these, see Lane, *The Rites of Rulers*.

16 This co-optation of traditional sacrality was by no means unique to Soviet experience. Ozouf similarly notes the "abundant analogies" between Catholic rituals and the newly devised festivals of the French Revolution, which sprang from "a wish to replace Catholic worship with a new cult capable of offering its spectators similar satisfactions" (26).

17 A distant satirical echo of this early Soviet mixing of religious and political processions can even be seen in Il'f and Petrov's novel *The Little Golden Calf* when Ostap Bender and his entourage encounter festive greetings in a series of villages as they usurp the lead in a cross-country automobile race: "Villagers often stage festivals of this kind, the leader of the 'Antelope' crew remarked"; and when Bender and his companions get out of the car, Il'f and Petrov even comment, "the weary Antelopians came down to earth" ("*ustalye antilopovtsy soshli na zemliu*" – *soiti na zemliu* being the biblical locution for Christ's appearance on earth; *Zolotoi telenok* 57–8).

18 As Petrovskii conjectures, this spatial configuration may have inspired the structure of Bulgakov's *The Master and Margarita*: "Ибо двухэтажность романного дома Булгакова последовательно осмысляет и изображает как бы два этажа вертепа – украинского кукольного театра, народного мистериально-сатирического действа" (141, 143). Petrovskii notes that *vertep* performances were common in the Kyiv of Bulgakov's youth and that his godfather N.I. Petrov had written articles about them for the journal *Kievskaia starina* (142). There also, apparently, exists a childhood photo of Bulgakov and his sister with professional puppets (361n32, citing A. Konchakovskii and D. Makalov, *Kiev Mikhaila Bulgakova*). Petrovskii also sees a precedent for the mixture of tonalities in Bulgakov's novel and in Mayakovsky's *Mystery-Bouffe* (174). The point may be, rather, that both authors are responding to the pronounced ambivalence in the quasi-religious culture of the era; see also my remarks in chapter 2 on the similarly ambivalent atmosphere in which Goethe wrote his *Faust*.

19 This mediaeval Muscovite practice may have derived from a broader tradition. As Bakhtin observes, during medieval carnivals "легализованные были дьяблерии, причем «чертям» иногда особо

представлялось право «свободно бегать» по улицам и окрестностям уже за несколько дней до постановок и создавать вокруг себя атмосферу чертовщины и необузданности" (*Tvorchestvo Fransua Rable* 101). In 1500 in Amiens, for example, clerics and citizens made a special application for permission during a mystery of the Passion to "faire courir les personnages des diables" (289). The whole premise of Woland and his entourage running around Moscow in Bulgakov's *The Master and Margarita* may derive from this tradition – however unknowingly.

20 On performative utterances, see Austin, *How to Do Things with Words.*

5 Stalinist Ritual and the Impulse toward Judgment

1 Brandist's chs. 1 and 2, 27–80, are largely devoted to this idea.

2 "Народное массовое празднество, смотр сил, радость толпы есть утверждение сегодняшнего дня и его апофеоз. Оно законно тогда, когда на него никто не смотрит из окна или из особой трибуны, иначе оно вырождается в парад, в крепостной балет и в оркестр роговой музыки. И уже поэтому оно не маскарад и не театр" (Shklovskii, "Drama i massovye predstavleniia" 86).

3 The apostrophic reach beyond the dramatic frame at the end of Mayakovsky's play also recalls the famous "mute scene" at the end of Nikolai Gogol's *Revizor* (*The Government Inspector*) in which the inhabitants of the town are shocked at the news that the real government inspector has now arrived (rather than Khlestakov, who had fooled them by posing as him): Gogol's stage directions specifically instruct various of the actors to turn toward the audience with their expressions of dumbfoundedness.

4 "Чудным звоном заливается колокольчик; гремит и становится ветром разорванный в куски воздух; летит мимо все, что ни есть на земли, и, косясь, посторониваются и дают ей дорогу другие народы и государства."

5 The notes of solemnity and judgment in these early works of Soviet literature may not have been all that distant from the mystery genre. Zholkovskii notes that in Iurii Olesha's 1927 *Envy* Ivan Babichev speaks of his private "Golgotha" and of the "conversation" held with him in the GPU – the secret police, forerunners of the NKVD and KGB – resembling Pilate's interrogation of Christ. He further notes that the passage alludes to Julio Jurenito's similarly ominous visit to the GPU and conversation with Lenin in Ehrenburg's 1922 *Julio Jurenito* (105) as well as to the "epidemic of arrests" in Bulgakov's *The Master and Margarita* (109), although that later novel was written in a time when arrests and public trials had become far more visible in Soviet life.

6 "Массовые демонстрации в театре – это дань распространенной в культуре 1 идее растворения искусства в жизни, устранения барьеров между театром и улицей…Культура 2 эту равномерность нарушает, массовые демонстрации должны происходить на специально отведенных местах, для них сносится квартал между Александровским садом, Манежем, Моховой улицей и гостиницей 'Москва'."

7 Recall, too, Nelson's claim that in their immobility dolls and mummies were felt to be close to the divine body "because their static and unchanging nature imitates the permanence of the immortal" (38).

8 By 1937 Meyerhold's type of theatre would be declared "alien" ("*chuzhoi*"; Clark, *Petersburg* 291). He was arrested on 21 June 1939, subjected to torture, then executed on 2 February 1940 (Antonov-Ovseenko 207).

9 Note that in Christian theology the initial advent of Christ is linked to salvation, not final judgment (e.g., "For God sent the son into the world not to condemn the world, but that the world might be saved through him"; John 3:17). It is the prophesied second coming that is to bring final judgment of the world.

10 "Бахтин приветствует при этом именно карнавальный пафос «окончательной смерти» всего индивидуального, победу чисто материального, телесного принципа над всем трансцендентным, идеальным, индивидуально бессмертным. Короче, бахтинский карнавал ужасен – не дай Бог попасть в него."

11 "Все эти соображения указывают на то, что целью Бахтина была вовсе не демократическая критика Революции и сталинского террора, а их теоретическое оправдание в качестве восходящего к архаической традиции ритуального действа."

12 For a cogent summary of the "severe polemics about Bakhtin's work in the 1930s – was he a Stalinist or an anti-Stalinist, for or surreptitiously against the Soviet regime?" – see Tihanov 124–5. On the influence of Nietzsche on Soviet thought, see Rosenthal.

13 See, however, the more nuanced account in Livak of the Nietzschean aspect of "Bolshevik leaders as artist demiurges" (159).

14 Or as he puts it elsewhere more acerbically, "Stalin looked on his adopted hometown as a Brobdingnagian sandbox in which he could sift, heap, and bore at will" (Colton 324).

15 "Постепенно возникающая иерархия людей накладывалась на постепенно возникающую иерархию пространств, в результате чего «хорошие», с точки зрения культуры 2, люди оказывались ближе к центру мира – Москва (и даже к центру Москвы) – а «плохие» занимали периферию."

16 On the darker side of Stalinist use of Moscow urban space, cemeteries at the Donskoi and Novospasskii monasteries and elsewhere in the city

began to fill up with corpses from the mass executions then taking place (Colton 286).

17 The same logic informs the slogan, prominent during the Cold War era, "Moskva –stolitsa mira," a pun that, given the homonymy between two meanings of the Russian word *mir*, meant either "Moscow is the capital of peace" (its ostensibly intended meaning) or "Moscow is the capital of the world" (more honestly revealing of Soviet intentions).

18 https://ru.wikiedia.org/wiki/Генеральный_план_реконструкции _Москвы.

19 "Выделенность Москвы, представление о Москве как о центре Космоса, своеобразной модели Космоса […] достигли апофеоза в 1947 г. во время празднования 800-летия Москвы, когда Сталин в своей речи назвал Москву 'образцом для всех столиц мира'" (Papernyi 87).

20 "Архитектура 30–50-х годов – это вертикальная декорация к государственному спектаклю, разыгрываемую для власти."

21 "Идея Рима, помноженная на Святую Русь, возникает в русской культуре неоднократно."

22 On the persistence of the legacy of Ivan the Terrible and Peter the Great in the Stalin era see Platt. On Peter's appeal to the Rome/Jerusalem analogy in the founding of St. Petersburg, see Lotman and Uspenskij, "Echoes of the Notion 'Moscow as the Third Rome' in Peter the Great's Ideology."

23 Kalb remarks that Kuzmin's play demonstrates "the staying power of Rome as a mythmaking tool in discussing Russian national identity" (163). She also points out thematic and structural similarities between Kuzmin's play and Bulgakov's novel, both of which juxtapose imperial Rome (or Roman-ruled Jerusalem, in Bulgakov's case) with modern Russia, or Russia in Italy, in the case of Kuzmin's play (188).

24 "Аналогия между рождением христианства и развитием социализма не подлежит сомнению. Расовое происхождение, классовый характер проповеди, состав первоначальной аудитории, отношение к семье, государству, существующей культуре и искусству, интернационализм – все общит их между собой" ("Struzhki," *Rossiia*, 1925, no. 5, 164; quoted in Timofeev, "Teatr 'nezdeshnykh vecherov,'" 412). On the parallels Kuzmin drew between the two eras see also Kalb 169.

25 "Если методически и точно проводить все мероприятия, через 4 года мы изживем все общественные бедствия: голод, повальные болезни, пожары, нищету, сами стихии будут нам обузданы. Сам этот план есть уже победа и достижение" (353).

26 See also Cassiday, chapter 1, on imperial precedents for Soviet show trials.

27 Clark comments, "It is a cliché in talking about Stalinist ritual that it was religious in nature. Essentially, what we find in these rituals

of the late 1920s is the structure of a conversion experience. The past evaporates as the 'born again' subject experiences a totally new reality (e.g., "Industrialization Day" of August 1929) – which intentionally replaced the religious festival of the Transfiguration of the Lord" (*Petersburg* 248).

28 See Cassiday 149–53 on parallels between *The Bedbug* and the mock-trial format.

29 Cassiday notes the survival of at least 130 published scripts from these mock trials (59).

30 The 1922 "Trial of the 54" was also held in the Polytechnical Museum, which Silano notes was one of the largest lecture halls in Moscow, with seating for 1,000 (286).

31 The *New York Times* correspondent who reported on the trial, Eugene Lyons, saw the rider's breeches as hunter's attire, with the prosecutor therefore dressed for his role as "man-hunter" (Cassiday 114).

32 See also more broadly her discussion throughout the chapter in which these remarks appear – chapter Six: "Face and Mask: Theatricality and Identity in the Era of the Show Trials (1936–1938)," 210–41.

33 In his biography of Andrei Vyshinsky, Vaksberg also calls the Zinoviev trial a "mystery play" (73).

34 "Jewreinow war noch vor 1917 und unmittelbar danach als Theoretiker des „bedingten Theaters" her vorgetreten, ein brillianter und hochkultivierter Theatermann, in seiner Zeit so strahlend wie Wsewolod Majerhold. Ganz in der Tradition des revolutionären Theaters von Richard Wagner und Edward Gordon Craig zielte er auf die Aufhebung der Distanz von Bühne und Zuschauerraum, der Kluft zwischen Schauspielern und Zauschauern, zwischen Theater und Leben."

35 "Photos von den Totenwachen, von der Überführung der Urne zum Roten Plaz, getragen von Molotow, Stalin, Woroschilow, Kaganowitsch, Andrejew, Postyschew, Shdanow. Es kristallisiert sich eine Ikonographie des Totenrituals heraus, die schon mit Lenins und Kirows Aufbahrung erste Umrisse angenommen hatte."

36 "Die Ereignisse folgten einer ausgefeilten Choreographie und elaborierten Ikonographie eines Totenrituals, in das die gesamte sowjetische Führung, die Belegschaften der großen Betriebe und die Stadt Moskau als Schauplatz einbezogen waren. Düsterkeit und Festlichkeit in über millionenfache Bilder und das Radio verbreiteten *pompes funèbre* schufen einen kollektiven Trauerraum, in dem die Nation in Schock und Trauer vereinigt war."

37 "О специфической веселости 30-х годов сохранилось множество свидетельств. Характерно, в частности, что показательные процессы и, особенно, вынесение приговоров часто сопровождались тогда смехом

публики." Vaksberg also notes that during the show trials the courtrooms were filled with laughing people who had come to be entertained (122).

38 Ianovskaia suggests that the 2–13 March 1938 show trial of Bukharin is the subtext for these passages (703–4).

39 "Этот мистический мир, мир безумия и балагана, веселящийся (не всегда по доброй воле) и в то же время идущий на казнь, как бы являет собой разросшуюся и заполнившую все пространство романа сцену шабаша, кружащегося в ожидании крика петуха, чтобы исчезнуть, уйти в небытие."

Epilogue

1

Словно в зеркале страшной ночи
И беснуется и не хочет
Узнавать себя человек,
А по набережной легендарной
Приближался не календарный –
Настоящий Двадцатый Век.

2 For controversy surrounding Groys's view of Bakhtin, discussed in chapter 5 of this study, see Emerson.

3 For a vigorous modern rejection of the culture that emerged in Western Europe from the Renaissance and Reformation, consider Florenskii's *"Ikonostas,"* which rails against a range of aesthetic forms, from oil painting to organ music.

Bibliography

Note: in Ardis edition of Bulgakov, *Zapuiski iunogo vracha* and Feueilletons are in vol. 1. *Belaia gvardiia* is vol.8; *M&M* is vol. 8.

Akhmatova, Anna. *Poema bez geroia. Triptikh. 1940–1962*. In her *Stikhotvoreniia i poemy, 352–78*. Leningrad: Sovetskii pisatel', 1976.

Alekseev-Iakovlev, Aleksei Iakovlevich. *Russkie narodnye gul'an'ia*. Moscow: Iskusstvo, 1948.

Andreevskii, I.E., et al. *Entsiklopedicheskii slovar'*. St. Petersburg: Brokgauz i Efron, 1890–4.

Antonov-Ovseenko, A. *Teatr Iosifa Stalina*. Moscow: „Gregori-Peidzh," 1995.

Argenbright, Robert. "Soviet Agitational Vehicles: Bolsheviks in Strange Places." In *Space, Place, and Power in Modern Russia: Essays in the New Spatial History*, edited by Mark Bassin, Christopher Ely, and Melissa K. Stockdale, 142–63. DeKalb: Northern Illinois University Press, 2010.

Aucouturier, Michel. "Theatricality as a Category of Early Twentieth-Century Russian Culture." In *Theater and Literature in Russia 1900–1930*, edited by Lars Kleberg and Nils Åke Nilsson, 9–21. Stockholm: Almqvist & Wiksell International, 1984.

Audi, Robert, ed. *The Cambridge Dictionary of Philosophy*. Cambridge: Cambridge University Press, 1995.

Austin, J.L. *How to Do Things with Words*. Oxford: Oxford University Press, 1962.

Bachelard, Gaston. *The Poetics of Space*. Translated by Maria Jolas. Boston: Beacon Press, 1994.

Bakhtin, M.M. "Formy vremeni i khronotopa v romane. Ocherki po istoricheskoi poetike." In his *Literaturno-kriticheskie stat'I*, 121–290. Moscow: Khudozhestvennaia literatura, 1986.

– *Tvorchestvo Fransua Rable i narodnaia kul'tura srednevekov'ia i renessansa*. Orange: Antiquary, 1966.

Bartlett, Rosamund. *Wagner and Russia*. Cambridge: Cambridge University Press, 1995.

Bassin, Mark. "Russia between Europe and Asia: The Ideological Construction of Geography." *Slavic Review* 50, no. 1 (Spring 1991): 1–17.

Bates, Paul A. *Faust: Sources, Works, Criticism*. New York: Harcourt, Brace and World, 1969.

Belyi, Andrei. "Khristos voskrese." In his *Sobranie sochinenii. Stikhotvorenia i poemy*, 431–45. Moscow: Respublika, 1994.

– "Past' nochi. Otryvok misterii." *Zolotoe runo* 3 (1906): 62–71.

Belyj, Andrej [=Andrei Belyi]. *Antichrist. Abbozzo di un mistero incompiuto*. Edizione e commento di Daniela Rizzi. Testi e richerche n.3. Dipartimento di Storia della Civiltà Europea. Trento: Università di Trento, 1990.

Benjamin, Walter. *The Arcades Project*. Translated by Howard Eiland and Kevin McLaughlin. Cambridge, MA: Harvard University Press, 1999.

Berd, R. [R. Bird]. "Viach. Ivanov i massovye prazdnestva rannei sovetskoi epokhi." *Russkaia literatura* no. 2 (2006): 174–97.

Berthold, Margot. *The History of World Theater: From the Beginnings to the Baroque*. Translated by Edith Simmons. New York: Continuum, 1999.

Bibikova, I.M., and N.I. Levchenko, eds. *Agitatsionno-masovoe iskusstvo: oformlenie prazdnestv*. Moscow: Iskusstvo, 1984.

Binns, Christopher A.P. "The Changing Face of Power: Revolution and Accommodation in the Development of the Soviet Ceremonial System: Part I." *Man*. New Series. 14, no. 4 (December 1979): 585–606.

Blok, Aleksandr. *Sobranie sochinenii v shesti tomakh*. Leningrad: Khudozhestvennia literatura, 1980–83.

Boele, Otto. *Erotic Nihilism in Late Imperial Russia: The Case of Mikhail Artsybashev's Sanin*. Madison: University of Wisconsin Press, 2009.

Bogatyrev, P.G. *Cheshskii kukol'nyi i russkii narodnyi teatr*. Berlin-Petersburg: Opoiaz, 1923.

Brandist, Craig. *Carnival Culture and the Soviet Modernist Novel*. New York: St. Martin's Press, 1996.

Briusov, V.Ia. "Nenuzhnaia pravda." *Mir iskusstva* 1902, no. 4. http://dugward.ru/library/brusov/brusov_nenujnaya_pravda.html.

Brown, Jane K. *Goethe's "Faust": The German Tragedy*. Ithaca: Cornell University Press, 1986.

Brown, Peter. *Society and the Holy in Late Antiquity*. Berkeley: University of California Press, 1982.

Brudnyi, V.I. *Obriady vchera i segodnia*. Moscow: Nauka, 1968.

Buczyńska-Garewicz, Hanna. *Miejsca, strony, okolice. Przyczynek do fenomenologii przestrzeni*. Kraków: Universitas, 2006.

Bulgakov, Mikhail Afanas'evich. *"Moi bednyi, bednyi master ..." Polnoe sobranie redaktsii i variantov romana* Master i Margarita. Moscow: Vagrius, 2006.

– *Sobranie sochinenii*. Ann Arbor: Ardis, 1982–8.

– *Sobranie sochinenii v piati tomakh*. Moscow: Khudozhestvennaia literatura, 1990.

– *Neizvestnyi Bulgakov*. Moscow: Knizhnaia palata, 1993.
– *Sobranie sochinenii v vos'mi tomakh*. St. Petersburg: Azbuka-Klassika, 2004.
– *Velikii kantsler*. Moscow: Novosti, 1992.
– *Zapiski pokoinika. Teatral'nyi roman*. In his *Sobranie sochinenii v vos'mi tomakh*, vol. 1: *Zapiski pokoinika. Avtobiograficheskaia proza*. St. Petersburg: Azbuka-klassika, 2004.
Calderón de la Barca, Pedro. *The Great Theatre of the World*. Adapted by Adrian Mitchell. Woodstock: Dramatic, 1990.
Carlson, Marvin. *Places of Performance: The Semiotics of Theatre Architecture*. Ithaca: Cornell University Press, 1989.
Cassiday, Julie A. *The Enemy on Trial: Early Soviet Courts on Stage and Screen*. De Kalb: Northern Illinois University Press, 2000.
Chadaga, Julia Beckman. *Optical Play: Glass, Vision, and Spectacle in Russian Culture*. Evanston: Northwestern University Press, 2014.
Chaianov, Aleksandr. *Venediktov, ili Dostopamiatnye sobytiia zhizni moei*. In *On poiavilsia … Sovetskaia misticheskaia proza 20–30-kh godov*, edited by Boris Sokolov, 14–35. Moscow: PROZAiK, 2009.
Chudakova, M.O. "Arkhiv M.A. Bulgakova. Materialy dlia tvorcheskoi biografii pisatelia." *Zapiski otdela rukopisei* 37, 25–151. Moscow: Kniga, 1976.
– "Bulgakov i Gogol'." *Russkaia rech'* 2 (1979): 38–48. *Russkaia rech'* 3 (1979): 55–9.
– "M.A. Bulgakov – chitatel'." *Kniga. Issledovaniia i materialy* 40 (1980): 164–85.
– *Zhizneopisanie Mikhaila Bulgakova*. Moscow: Kniga, 1988.
Clark, Katerina. *Moscow, The Fourth Rome: Stalinism, Cosmopolitanism, and the Evolution of Soviet Culture, 1931–1941*. Cambridge, MA: Harvard University Press, 2011.
– *Petersburg: Crucible of Cultural Revolution*. Cambridge, MA: Harvard University Press, 1995.
– *The Soviet Novel: History as Ritual*. Chicago: University of Chicago Press, 1981.
Clayton, J. Douglas. *Pierrot in Petrograd: The Commedia dell'Arte/Balagan in Twentieth-Century Russian Theatre and Drama*. Montreal and Kingston: McGill–Queen's University Press, 1993.
– "The Play-within-the-Play as Metaphor and Metatheater in Modernist Russian Drama." In *Theater and Literature in Russia 1900–1930*, edited by Lars Kleberg and Nils Åke Nilsson, 71–82. Stockholm: Almqvist & Wiksell International, 1984.
Colton, Timothy J. *Moscow: Governing the Socialist Metropolis*. Cambridge, MA: Harvard University Press, 1995.
Cooke, Catherine, and Igor Kazus. *Soviet Architectural Competitions 1920s–1930s*. London: Phaidon Press, 1992.
Corney, Frederick C. *Telling October: Memory and the Making of the Bolshevik Revolution*. Ithaca: Cornell University Press, 2004.

Craig, Edward Gordon. *On the Art of the Theatre.* London: Heinemann, 1980.

Curtis, J.A.E. *Bulgakov's Last Decade: The Writer as Hero.* Cambridge: Cambridge University Press, 1987.

Deleuze, Gilles, and Félix Guattari. *A Thousand Plateaus: Capitalism and Schizophrenia.* Translated and Foreword by Brian Massumi. Minneapolis: University of Minnesota Press, 1987.

De Schloezer, Boris. *Scriabin: Artist and Mystic.* Translated by Nicolas Slonimsky. Berkeley: University of California Press, 1987.

Dobrenko, Evgeny. *Late Stalinism: The Aesthetics of Politics.* Translated by Jesse M. Savage. New Haven: Yale University Press, 2020.

Dostoevskii, F.M. *Brat'ia Karamazovy. Knigi I-X.* In his *Polnoe sobranie sochinenii v tridtsati tomakh,* vol. 14. Leningrad: Nauka, 1976.

Durrain, Oswald. "The Character and Qualities of Mephistopheles." In *A Companion to Goethe's Faust: Parts I and II,* edited by Paul Bishop, 76–94. Rochester: Camden House, 2001.

Eliade, Mircea. *The Sacred and the Profane: The Nature of Religion.* San Diego: Harcourt Brace Jovanovich, 1987.

Emerson, Caryl. "The Bakhtin of Boris Groys: Pro and Contra." *Dialogic Pedagogy* 5 (2017): 6–10.

Erenburg, Il'ia. *Khulio Khurenito.* In his *Sobranie sochinenii v deviati tomakh,* vol. 1, 11–232. Moscow: Khudozhestvennaia literatura, 1962.

Evreinov, N. "The Fourth Wall: A Buffoonery in Two Parts (1915)." In *Russian Satiric Comedy: Six Plays,* edited and translated by Laurence Senelick, 75–99. New York: Performing Arts Journal Publication, 1983.

– *Istoriia russkogo teatra. S drevneishikh vremen do 1917 goda.* New York: Izdatel'stvo imeni Chekhova, 1955.

– *Samoe glavnoe.* St. Petersburg: Gosudarstvennoe izdatel'stvo, 1921. Reprint: Ardis, 1980.

– *Shagi Nemezidy. Dramaticheskaia khronika v 6-i kartinakh iz partiinoi zhizni v SSSR (1936–1938).* Paris: Société des Auteurs et Compositeurs Dramatiques, 1956.

Fitzpatrick, Sheila. *Everyday Stalinism: Ordinary Life in Extraordinary Times: Soviet Russia in the 1930s.* Oxford: Oxford University Press, 1999.

Flaker, Aleksandar. "Die Strasse: Ein neuer Mythos de Avantgarde." *Mythos in der slawischen Moderne. Wiener Slawistischer Almanach.* Sonderband 20 (1987). 139–55.

Florenskii, Pavel. "Ikonostas." In his *Ikonostas. Izbrannye Trudy po iskusstvu,* 1–174. St. Petersburg: Mirfil/Russkaia kniga, 1993.

– "Obratnaia perspektiva." In his *Ikonostas. Izbrannye Trudy po iskusstvu,* 175–281. St. Petersburg: Mirfil/Russkaia kniga, 1993.

Florovskii, Prot. Georgii. *Puti russkogo bogosloviia.* Paris, 1927. Reprint Vilnius: Vil'niusskoe pravoslavnoe eparkhial'noe upravlenie, 1991.

Frank, Joseph. "Spatial Form in Modern Literature." In his *The Widening Gyre: Crisis and Mastery in Modern Literature*, 3–62. New Brunswick: Rutgers University Press, 1963.

Freidenberg, O.M. "Semantika arkhitektury vertepnogo teatra." *Dekorativnoe Iskusstvo SSSR* 2 (243) 1978: 41–4.

Fuchs, Georg. *Die Revolution des Theaters. Ergebnisse aus dem Münchener Künstler-Theater*. München: Georg Müller, 1909.

Furmanov, D. *Chapaev*. In *D. Furmanov. Chapaev. A. Serafimovich. Zheleznyi potok. N. Ostrovskii. Kak zakalialas' stal'*, 23–271. Moscow: Khudozhestvennaia literatura, 1967.

Fusso, Susanne. "Failures of Transformation in *Sobač'e serdce*." *Slavic and East European Journal* (3): 387–99.

Galushkina, A.S., E. Speranskaia, et al. *Agitatsionno-massovoe iskusstvo pervykh let Oktiabria*. Moscow: Iskusstvo, 1971.

Gasparov, B.M. "Iz nabliudenii nad motivnoi strukturoi romana M.A. Bulgakova 'Master i Margarita.'" In his *Literaturnye leitmotivy*, 28–82. Moscow: Nauka, 1994.

– "Novyi zavet v proizvedeniiakh M.A. Bulgakova." In his *Literaturnye leitmotivy*, 83–123. Moscow: Nauka, 1994.

– "Tema sviatchnogo karnavala v poeme A. Bloka 'Dvenadtsat.'" In his *Literaturnye leitmotivy*, 4–27. Moscow: Nauka, 1994.

Gasparov, B.M., and Iu.M. Lotman. "Igrovye motivy v poeme 'Dvenadtsat'.'" In *Tezisy I vsesoiuznoi (III) konferentsii "Tvorchestvo A.A. Bloka i russkaia kul'tura XX veka,"* edited by Z. Mints, 53–63. Tartu: Tartuskii gosudarstvennyi universitet, 1975.

Genette, Gérard. "La Littérature et L'Espace." In his *Figures II*, 43–8. Paris: Éditions du Seuil, 1969.

Gievskii, N. "Iz teatral'nykh vospominanii." *Novyi zhurnal* 10 (1945): 276–96.

Ginsburg, Ruth. "Karneval und Fasten. Exzeß und Mangel in der Sprache des Körpers." *Poetica* 21, nos. 1–2 (1989): 26–42.

Givens, John. *The Image of Christ in Russian Literature: Dostoevsky, Tolstoy, Bulgakov, Pasternak*. DeKalb: Northern Illinois University Press, 2018.

Gladkov, Fyodor Vasilievich. *Cement*, translated by A.S. Arthur and C. Ashleigh. Evanston: Northwestern University Press, 1994.

Glaser, Amelia M. *Songs in Dark Times: Yiddish Poetry of Struggle from Scottsboro to Palestine*. Cambridge, MA: Harvard University Press, 2020.

Glebkin, V.V. *Ritual v sovetskoi kul'ture*. Moscow: "Ianus-K," 1998.

Gogol', N.V. *Mertvye dushi*. In his *Sobranie khodozhestvennykh proizvedenii v piati tomakh*, vol. 5. Moscow: Akademiia Nauk SSSR, 1960.

– "Rim." In his *Sobranie khodozhestvennykh proizvedenii v piati tomakh*, vol. 3: *Povesti*, 265–322. Moscow: Akademiia Nauk SSSR, 1960.

Goldman, Wendy Z. *Inventing the Enemy: Denunciation and Terror in Stalin's Russia*. Cambridge: Cambridge University Press, 2011.

Groys, Boris. *The Total Art of Stalinism: Avant-Garde, Aesthetic Dictatorship, and Beyond*. Translated by Charles Rougle. Princeton: Princeton University Press, 1992.

– [Grois, B.] "Totalitarizm karnavala." *Bakhtinskii sbornik III*, 76–80. Moscow: Labirint, 1997.

Hansen Löve, Katharina. *The Evolution of Space in Russian Literature: A Spatial Reading of 19th and 20th Century Narrative Literature*. Studies in Slavic Literature and Poetics, vol. 22. Amsterdam: Rodopi, 1994.

Hardison, O.B., Jr. *Christian Rite and Christian Drama in the Middle Ages: Essays in the Origin and Early History of Modern Drama*. Baltimore: Johns Hopkins University Press, 1965.

Harte, Tim. *Fast Forward: The Aesthetics and Ideology of Speed in Russian Avant-Garde Culture, 1910–1930*. Madison: University of Wisconsin Press, 2009.

Heller, Erich. "Faust's Damnation: The Morality of Knowledge." In his *The Artist's Journey into the Interior. And Other Essays*, 3–44. New York: Random House, 1959.

Hetényi, Zsuzsa. "Enciklopedija otricanija: 'Hulio Hurenito' Ilji Erjenburga." *Studia Slavica Academiae Scientiarum Hungaricae*. 45, nos. 1–4 (19 January 2001): 317–23.

Huizinga, Johan. *Homo Ludens: A Study of the Play Element in Culture*. London: Routledge, 1998.

Husserl, Edmund. *The Crisis of European Sciences and Transcendental Phenomenology*. Translated and introduction by David Carr. Evanston: Northwestern University Press, 1970.

Ianovskaia, Lidiia. *Posledniaia kniga, ili treugol'nik Volanda. S otstupleniiami, sokrashcheniiami i dopolneniiami*. Moscow: PROZAiK, 2013.

Il'f, I. and E. Petrov, *Zolotoi telenok*. With commentary by Iu.K. Shcheglov. Moscow: Panorama, 1995.

Ivanov, Viacheslav. "Esteticheskaia norma teatra. In his *Borozdy i mezhy*, 259–78. Moscow: Musaget, 1916.

– "Predchuvstviia i predvestiia. Novaia organicheskaia epokha i teatr budushchego." In his *Sobranie sochinenii v cheterykh tomakh*, vol. 2, edited by D.V. Ivanov and O. Deshart, 86–104. Brussels: Foyer Oriental Chrétien, 1974.

– *Sobranie sochinenii v cheterykh tomakh*, vol. 2, edited by D.V. Ivanov and O. Deshart. Brussels: Foyer Oriental Chrétien, 1974.

Kadulska, Irène. "L'Influence de la 'Commedia dell'Arte' sur le Théâtre des Collèges de la Compagnie de Jésus en Pologne." In *Les Innovations théâtrales et muscales italiennes en Europe aux XVIIIe et XIXe siècles*, edited by Vittore Branca, Irène Mamczarz, et al., 733–89. Paris: Presses Universitaires de France, 1991.

Kalb, Judith. *Russia's Rome: Imperial Visions, Messianic Dreams, 1890–1940*. Madison: University of Wisconsin Press, 2008.

Kamiński, Antoni A. *Michał Bakunin. Życie i myśl*, vol. 2: *Podpalacz Europy (1848–1864)*. Wrocław: Wydawnictwo Uniwersytetu Ekonomicznego we Wrocławiu, 2013.

Kapinos, Elena. "'Formy vremeni' i kontseptsiia istorii (ot S.L. Franka k B.M. Eikhenbaumu i Iu.N. Tynianovu)." In *Epokha 'ostraneniia'. Russkii formalizm i sovremennoe gumanitarnoe znanie*, edited by Ia. Levchenko and I. Pil'shchikov., 471–9. Moscow: Novoe literaturnoe obozrenie, 2017.

Karshan, Thomas. *Vladimir Nabokov and the Art of Play*. Oxford: Oxford University Press, 2011.

Kelly, Catriona. *Petrushka: The Russian Carnival Puppet Theatre*. Cambridge: Cambridge University Press, 1990.

Kennedy, Janet. "Shrovetide Revelry: Alexandre Benois's Contribution to *Petrushka*." In *Petrushka: Sources and Contexts*, edited by Andrew Wachtel, 51–65. Evanston: Northwestern University Press, 1998.

Kerzhentsev, P.M. *Tvorcheskii teatr*. Moscow and Petrograd: Gosudarstvennoe izdatel'stvo, 1923.

Kleberg, Lars. "'People's Theater' and the Revolution: On the History of a Concept before and after 1917." In *Art, Society, Revolution. Russia 1917–1921*, edited by Nils Åke Nilsson, 179–97. Stockholm: Almqvist and Wiksell International, 1979.

– "Vjačeslav Ivanov and the Idea of Theater." In *Theater and Literature in Russia 1900–1930*, edited by Lars Kleberg and Nils Åke Nilsson, 57–70. Stockholm: Almqvist and Wiksell International, 1984.

Kolve, V.A. *The Play Called Corpus Christi*. Stanford: Stanford University Press, 1966.

Koschmal, Walter. "Semantisierung von Raum und Zeit. Dostoevskijs *Aufzeichnungen aus einen Toten Haus* and Čechovs *Insel Sachalin*." *Poetica* 12, vols. 3–4 (1980): 397–420.

Koss, Juliet. *Modernism after Wagner*. Minneapolis: University of Minnesota Press, 2009.

Kot, Joanna. *Distance Manipulation: The Russian Modernist Search for a New Drama*. Evanston: Northwestern University Press, 1999.

Krupnianskaia, V.Iu. "Narodnyi teatr." In *Russkoe narodnoe poeticheskoe tvorchestvo*, edited by P.G. Bogatyrev, 382–441. Moscow: Gosudarstvennoe uchebno-pedagogicheskoe izdatel'stvo, 1954.

Kuromiya, Hiraoki. *The Voices of the Dead: Stalin's Great Terror in the 1930s*. New Haven: Yale University Press, 2007.

Kuzmin, M. *Teatr v cheterekh tomakh (v dvukh knigakh)*, vols. 1–3. Modern Russian Literature and Culture. Studies and Texts, vol. 30. Oakland: Berkeley Slavic Specialties, 1994.

Lane, Christel. *The Rites of Rulers: Ritual in Industrial Society – the Soviet Case.* Cambridge: Cambridge University Press, 1981.

Larson, Peter G. *Space as Means of Resistance: Bulgakov and Dostoevsky.* PhD diss., University of Alberta, 2009.

Lefebvre, Henri. *The Production of Space.* Translated by Donald Nicholson-Smith. Oxford: Blackwell, 1991.

Le Goff, Jaques. *My Quest for the Middle Ages.* In collaboration with Jean-Maurice de Montremy. Translated by Richard Veasey. New York: Palgrave Macmillan, 2005.

Lenin, V.I. "O zadachakh narkomiusta v usloviiakh Novoi Ekonomicheskoi Politiki. Pis'mo D.I. Kurskomu." *Polnoe sobranie sochinennii*, 5th ed., vol. 44, 396–400. Moscow: Politicheskaia literatura, 1970.

Livak, Leonid. *In Search of Russian Modernism.* Baltimore: Johns Hopkins University Press, 2018.

Lotman, Iu.M. "Blok i narodnaia kul'tura goroda." In his *Izbrannye stat'i v trekh tomakh*, vol. 3, 185–200. Tallinn: Aleksandra, 1993.

– "Kukly v sisteme kul'tury." In his *Izbrannye stat'i v trekh tomakh*, vol. 1, 377–80. I. Tallinn: Aleksandra, 1992.

– "Problema khudozhestvennogo prostranstva v proze Gogolia." In his *Izbrannye stat'i v trekh tomakh*, vol. 1, 413–47. Tallinn: Aleksandra, 1992.

Lotman, Ju.M., and B.A. Uspenskij. "Echoes of the Notion 'Moscow as the Third Rome' in Peter the Great's Ideology." In Lotman and Uspenskij, *The Semiotics of Russian Culture*, 53–67. Ann Arbor: Department of Slavic Languages and Literatures, 1984.

– "The Role of Dual Models in the Dynamics of Russian Culture (Up to the End of the Eighteenth Century)." In Lotman and Uspenskij, *The Semiotics of Russian Culture*, 3–35. Ann Arbor: Department of Slavic Languages and Literatures, 1984.

Lukács, Georg. *Goethe and His Age.* Translated by Robert Anchor. New York: Howard Fertig, 1978.

Lunacharskii, A., et al. "O narodnykh prazdnestvakh." *Vestnik teatra*, 27 April–2 May 1920, 4.

– *Teatr. Kniga o novom teatre. Sbornik statei.* St. Petersburg: Shipovnik, 1908. Reprint Moscow 2008.

Lüthi, Lorenz M. *Cold Wars. Asia. The Middle East. Europe.* Cambridge: Cambridge University Press, 2020.

Maeterlinck, Maurice. *A Maeterlinck Reader: Plays, Poems, Short Fiction, Aphorisms, and Essays,* edited and translated by David Willinger and Daniel Gerould. New York: Peter Lang, 2011.

– *The Miracle of Saint Anthony.* Translated by Alexander Teixeira de Mattos. New York: Dodd, Mead, and Co., 1913. https://archive.org/stream/miraclesaintant00unkngoog#page/n8/mode/2up.

Maiakovskii, Vladimir. *Sobranie sochinenii v dvenadtsati tomakh*. Moscow: Pravda, 1978.

Mandelshtam, Osip. "Iunost' Gete {Peredacha po radio]." In his *Sobranie sochinenii v trekh tomakh*, vol. 3: *Ocherki, pis'ma*, edited by G.P. Struve and B.A. Filippov, 61–80. New York: Inter-Language Literary Associates, 1969.

Marx, Karl, and Friedrich Engels. "The Communist Manifesto." In *The Marx–Engels Reader*, 2nd ed., edited by Robert C. Tucker, 469–500. New York: W.W. Norton 1978.

Masing-Delic, Irene. *Abolishing Death: A Salvation Myth of Russian Twentieth-Century Literature*. Stanford: Stanford University Press, 1992.

Mason, Eudo C. *Goethe's Faust: Its Genesis and Purport*. Berkeley: University of California Press, 1967.

Mazaev, A.I. *Prazdnik kak sotsial'no-khudozhestvennoe iavlenie. Opyt istoriko-teoreticheskogo issledovaniia*. Moscow: Nauka, 1978.

McQuillen, Colleen. *The Modernist Masquerade: Stylizing Life, Literature, and Costumes in Russia*. Madison: University of Wisconsin Press, 2013.

Meierkhol'd, V.E. *Stat'i. Pis'ma. Rechi. Besedy. Chast' pervaia. 1891–1917*. Moscow: Iskusstvo, 1968.

– *Stat'i. Pis'ma. Rechi. Besedy. Chast' vtoraia. 1917–1939*. Moscow: Iskusstvo, 1968.

Meletinsky, Eleazar M. *The Poetics of Myth*. Translated by Guy Lanoue and Alexandre Sadetsky. New York: Garland, 1998.

Milne, Lesley. *The Master and Margarita: A Comedy of Victory*. Birmingham Slavonic Monographs no. 3. Birmingham: University of Birmingham, 1977.

Mitchell, Rebecca. *Nietzche's Orphans: Music, Metaphysics, and the Twilight of the Russian Empire*. New Haven: Yale University Press, 2015.

Montefiore, Simon Sebag. *Jerusalem: The Biography*. London: Weidenfeld and Nicolson, 2011.

Morson, Gary Saul. *Hidden in Plain View: Narrative and Creative Potentials in "War and Peace."* Stanford: Stanford University Press, 1987.

Nabokov, Vladimir. *The Annotated Lolita*, edited, with preface, introduction, and notes, by Alfred Appel, Jr. Revised and updated edition. New York: Vintage Books, 1991.

– *Zashchita Luzhina*. In his *Sobranie sochinenii russkogo perioda v piati tomakh*. vol. 2, 306–465. St. Petersburg: Simpozium, 2009.

Naiman, Eric. *Sex in Public: The Incarnation of Early Soviet Ideology*. Princeton: Princeton University Press, 1997.

Nelson, Victoria. *The Secret Life of Puppets*. Cambridge, MA: Harvard University Press, 2001.

Nietzsche, Friedrich. "The Birth of Tragedy." In his *Basic Writings of Nietzsche*. Translated and edited by Walter Kaufmann, 28–144. New York: Modern Library, 1992.

Nikiforov, A.I. Commentary to Tolstoi, "Gde liubov', tam i bog." In L.N.
    Tolstoi, *Polnoe sobranie sochienenii*, vol. 25: *Proizvedeniia 1880-kh godov*, 681–5.
    Moscow: Gosudarstvennoe izdatel'stvo Khudozhestvennaia literatura, 1937.
Nikolesku, Tat'iana. *Andrei Belyi i teatr*. Moscow: Radiks, 1995.
Oetterman, Stephan. *The Panorama: History of a Mass Medium*. Translated by
    Deborah Lucas Schneider. New York: Zone Books, 1997.
Orlov, V. *Poema Aleksandra Bloka "Dvenadtsat'."* Moscow: Khudozhestvennaia
    literatura, 1967.
Ozouf, Mona. *Festivals and the French Revolution*. Translated by Alan Sheridan.
    Cambridge, MA: Harvard University Press, 1988.
Palmer, Philip Mason, and Robert Pattison More. *The Sources of the Faust
    Tradition: From Simon Magus to Lessing*. New York: Oxford University Press,
    1936.
Panova, Lada. *Mnimoe sirotstvo. Khlebnikov i Kharms v kontekste russkogo i
    evropeiskogo modernizma*. Moscow: Vysshaia shkola ekonomiki, 2017.
Paperno, Irina. *Stories of the Soviet Experience: Memories, Diaries, Dreams*. Ithaca:
    Cornell University Press, 2009.
Papernyi, Vladimir. *Kul'tura 'dva'*. Ann Arbor: Ardis, 1985.
Partan, Olga. *"Shinel' – Polichinelle – Pulcinella*: The Italian Ancestry of Akaky
    Bashmachkin," *Slavic and East European Journal* 49, no. 4 (2005): 549–69.
People's Commissariat of Justice of the U.S.S.R. *Report of Court Proceedings
    in the Case of the Anti-Soviet "Bloc of Rights and Trotskyites" Heard before the
    Military Collegium of the Supreme Court of the U.S.S.R. Moscow, March 2–13,
    1938*. Moscow: People's Commissariat of Justice of the U.S.S.R, 1938.
    [trans. of *Sudebnyi otchet po delu Antisovetskogo "Pravo-trotskistskogo bloka"
    rassmotrennomu Voennoi kollegiei verkhovnogo suda SSSR 2–13 marta 1938 goda*]
Perloff, Marjorie. *The Futurist Moment: Avant-Garde, Avant Guerre, and the
    Language of Rupture*. Chicago: University of Chicago Press, 1986.
Petrone, Karen. *Life Has Become More Joyous, Comrades: Celebrations in the Time
    of Stalin*. Bloomington: Indiana University Press, 2000.
Petrovskii, Miron. *Master i gorod. Kievskie konteksty Mikhaila Bulgakova*. Kyiv:
    Izdatel'stvo Dukh i Litera, 2001.
Phelan, Anthony. "The Classical and the Medieval in *Faust II*." In *A Companion
    to Goethe's Faust: Parts I and II*, edited by Paul Bishop, 144–68. Rochester:
    Camden House, 2001.
Piotrovskii, A., ed. "Khronika Leningradskikh prazdnestv 1919–22 g." In
    Massovye prazdnestva. Sbornik komiteta sotsiologicheskogo izucheniia iskusstv,
    edited by N. Izvekov, 55–83. Leningrad: Akademiia, 1926.
Platt, Kevin M.F. *Terror and Greatness. Ivan and Peter as Russian Myths*. Ithaca:
    Cornell University Press, 2011.
Posner, Dassia N. *The Director's Prism: E.T.A. Hoffmann and the Russian
    Theatrical Avant-Garde*. Evanston: Northwestern University Press, 2016.

Prechtl, Peter, and Franz-Peter Burkard, eds. *Metzler Philosophie Lexicon*, vol. 2: *Erweiterte Auflage*. Stuttgart: Verlag J.B. Metzler, 1999.

Punin, N. "Zangezi." *Zhizn' iskusstva* 20 (23 May 1923), 10–12.

Pyman, Avril. *A History of Russian Symbolism*. Cambridge: Cambridge University Press, 1994.

– *The Life of Aleksandr Blok*. Oxford: Oxford University Press, 1978–80.

Rampton, Vanessa. *Liberal Ideas in Tsarist Russia: From Catherine the Great to the Russian Revolution*. Cambridge: Cambridge University Press, 2020.

Remizov, A.M. *Sochineniia. Rusal'nye deistva*, vol. 8. St. Petersburg: Shipovnik, n.d.

Rilke, Rainer Maria. "Some Reflections on Dolls" ["Puppen. Zu den Wachs-Puppen von Lotte Pritzel"] In his *Where Silence Reigns: Selected Prose*. Translated by G. Craig Houston., 43–50. New York: New Directions, 1978.

Rolf, Malte. *Soviet Mass Festivals, 1917–1991*. Translated by Cynthia Klohr. Pittsburgh: University of Pittsburgh Press, 2013.

Rolland, Romain. *Le Théatre du Peuple. Essai d'Esthétique d'un Théatre Nouveau*. Paris: Librairie Hachette at Cie, 1913.

Rosenthal, Bernice Glatzer. *Nietzsche and Soviet Culture: Ally and Adversary*. New York: Cambridge University Press, 1994.

Rudnitsky, Konstantin. *Russian and Soviet Theatre: Tradition and the Avant-Garde*. Translated by Roxane Permar. London: Thames and Hudson, 1988.

Ryklin, Mikhail. "Tela terror (Tezisy k logike nasiliia)." *Voprosy literatury* 1 (1992): 130–47.

Sartori, Rosalinde. "Stalinism and Carnival: Organisation and Aesthetics of Political Holidays." In *The Culture of the Stalin Period*, edited by Hans Günther, 41–77. New York: St. Martin's Press, 1990.

Schanze, Helmut. *Goethes Dramatik. Theater der Erinnerung*. Theatron. Studien zur Geschichte und Theorie der dramatischen Künste, vol. 4. Tübingen: Max Niemeyer Verlag, 1989.

Scheithauer, Th. Friedrich L.J. *Kommentar zu Goethes Faust*. Stuttgart: Philipp Reclam Jun., 1959.

Schlögel, Karl. *Terror und Traum. Moskau 1937*. Munich: Carl Hanser Verlag, 2008.

Segel, Harold B. *Pinocchio's Progeny: Puppets, Marionettes, Automatons, and Robots in Modernist and Avant-Garde Drama*. Baltimore: Johns Hopkins University Press, 1995.

– *Turn-of-the-Century Cabaret: Paris, Barcelona, Berlin, Munich, Vienna, Cracow, Moscow, St. Petersburg, Zurich*. New York: Columbia University Press, 1987.

Seifrid, Thomas. *Andrei Platonov: Uncertainties of Spirit*. Cambridge: Cambridge University Press, 1992.

– "'Getting Across': Border-Consciousness in Soviet and Emigré Literature," *Slavic and East European Journal* 38, no.2 (Summer 1994): 245–60.

– *"Razgovor vpolgolosa*: Pasternak's Novel, Its Discourse, and Its Times." In *The Life of Pasternak's* Doctor Zhivago, edited by Lazar Fleishman, 173–84. Stanford Slavic Studies, vol. 37. Berkeley Slavic Specialties, 2009.

– *The Word Made Self: Russian Writings on Language, 1860–1930*. Ithaca: Cornell University Press, 2005.

Senderovich, S.Ia., and Elena Shvarts. "Kukol'naia teatral'nost' mira: K kharakteristike peterburgskogo serebrianogo veka (Opyt fenomenografii odnoi kul'turnoi epokhi)." In *Sushchestvuet li peterburgskii tekst?*, edited by V.M. Markovich and V. Shmid, 235–75. *Peterburgskii sbornik* no. 4. St. Petersburg: Izdatel'stvo S-Peterburgskogo universiteta, 2005.

– "'Verbnaia shtuchka'. Nabokov i populiarnaia kul'tura. Stat'ia pervaia." *Novoe literaturnoe obozrenie* 24 (1997). 93–110.

– "'Verbnaia shtuchka'. Nabokov i populiarnaia kul'tura. Stat'ia vtoraia." *Novoe literaturnoe obozrenie* 26 (1997). 201–22.

Senderovich, Savelii, and Elena Shvarts. "Starichok iz evreev (kommentarii k *Priglasheniu na kazn'* Vladimira Nabokova)." *Russian Literature* 43 (1998). 297–327.

Shcherbenok, Andrey. "'Killing Realism': Insight and Meaning in Anton Chekhov." *Slavic and East European Journal* 54, no. 2 (Summer 2010). 297–316.

Shevelenko, Irina. *Modernizm kak arkhaizm. Natsionalizm i poiski modernistskoi estetiki v Rossii*. Moscow: Novoe literaturnoe obozrenie, 2017.

Shklovskii, Viktor. „Drama i massovye predstavleniia." In his *Gamburgskii schet. Stat'i—vospominaniia – esse (1914–1933)*. Moscow: Sovetskii pisatel', 1990.

Shleyter-Lavine, Ludmila. "Aleksandr Blok's *The Twelve*: The Transformation of *commedia dell'arte* into an Epic." *Slavic and East European Review* 49, no. 4 (2005): 570–90.

Silano, Francesca. "'In the Language of the Patriarch': Patriarch Tikhon, the Russian Orthodox Church, and the Soviet State (1865–1925)." PhD diss., University of Toronto, 2017.

Slezkine, Yuri. *The House of Government: A Saga of the Russian Revolution*. Princeton: Princeton University Press, 2017.

Smirnov, Igor' P. "Ne-iskusstvo v esteticheskoi teorii formalistov." In *Epokha 'ostraneniia'. Russkii formalizm i sovremennoe gumanitarnoe znanie*, edited by Ia. Levchenko and I. Pil'shchikov, 41–53. Novoe literaturnoe obozrenie, 2017.

Smirnova, Nataliia Il'inichna. *Sovetskii teatr kukol*. Moscow: Izd. Akademii Nauk SSSR, 1963.

Smitten, Jeffrey R. "Introduction: Spatial Form and Narrative Theory." In *Spatial Form in Narrative*, edited by Jeffrey R. Smitten and Ann Daghistany, 15–34. Ithaca: Cornell University Press, 1981. 15–34.

Sokolov, Boris, ed. *On poiavilsia … Sovetskaia misticheskaia proza 20–30-kh godov*. Moscow: PROZAiK, 2009.

Sologub, Fedor. *Liturgiia mne. Misteriia*. In his *Sobranie sochinenii v shesti tomakh*, vol. 5, 7–30. Moscow: NPK "Intelvak", 2002.

Solov'ev, Vl. "Tri razgovora o voine, progresse i kontse mirovoi istorii." In his *Sochineniia v dvukh tomakh*, vol. 2, 635–762. Moscow: Mysl', 1988.

Stallybrass, Peter, and Allon White. *The Politics and Poetics of Transgression*. Ithaca: Cornell University Press, 1986.

Starobinski, Jean. *1789: The Emblems of Reason*. Translated by Barbara Bray. Charlottesville: University of Virginia Press, 1982.

Steinberg, Mark D. *Proletarian Imagination: Self, Modernity, and the Sacred in Russia, 1910–1925*. Ithaca: Cornell University Press. 2002.

Steiner, Peter. *Russian Formalism: A Metapoetics*. Ithaca: Cornell University Press, 1984.

Stites, Richard. *Revolutionary Dreams: Utopian Vision and Experimental Life in the Russian Revolution*. Oxford: Oxford University Press, 1988.

– "Trial as Theatre in the Russian Revolution." *Theatre Research International* 23, no. 1 (Spring 1998). 7–13.

Swales, Martin. "The Character and Characterization of Faust." In *A Companion to Goethe's Faust: Parts I and II*, edited by Paul Bishop, 28–55. Rochester: Camden House, 2001.

Taylor, Charles. *Hegel*. Cambridge: Cambridge University Press, 1975.

Tihanov, Galin. *The Birth and Death of Literary Theory: Regimes of Relevance in Russia and Beyond*. Stanford: Stanford University Press, 2019.

Timofeev, A.G. "Teatr 'nezdeshnykh vecherov.'" In M. Kuzmin, *Teatr v cheterekh tomakh (v dvukh knigakh)*, vols. 1–3. Modern Russian Literature and Culture. Studies and Texts. Vol.30. Oakland: Berkeley Slavic Specialties, 1994. 383–421.

Todorova, Maria. *The Lost World of Socialists at Europe's Margins: Imagining Utopia, 1870s–1920s*. London: Bloomsbury Academic, 2020.

Tolstoi, L.N. "Gde liubov', tam i bog." In his *Sobranie sochinenii v dvadtsati tomakh*, vol. 10, 281–92. Moscow: Gosudarstvennoe izdatel'stvo Khudozhestvennaia literatura, 1963.

Toporov, V.N. "O strukture romana Dostoevskogo v sviazi s arkhaichnymi skhemami mifologicheskogo myshleniia (*Prestuplenie i nakazanie*)." In *Structure of Texts and Semiotics of Culture*, edited by Jan van der Eng and Mojmír Grygar, 225–302. The Hague: Mouton, 1973.

– "Prostranstvo i tekst." In *Tekst: semantika i struktura*, edited by T.V. Tsiv'ian, 227–84. Moscow: Nauka, 1983.

Torrance, Thomas F. *Space, Time, and Incarnation*. Oxford: Oxford University Press, 1969.

Tucker, Robert C., and Stephen F. Cohen, eds. *The Great Purge Trial*. Translation of *Sudebnyi otchet po delu anti-sovetskogo "Pravo-Trotskistkogo bloka*. New York: Grosset and Dunlap, 1965.

Tumarkin, Nina. *Lenin Lives!: The Lenin Cult in Soviet Russia.* Cambridge, MA: Harvard University Press, 1983.

Turner, Victor. "Are There Universals of Performance in Myth, Ritual, and Drama?" In *By Means of Performance: Intercultural Studies of Theatre and Ritual*, edited by Richard Schechner and Willa Appel, 8–18. Cambridge: Cambridge University Press, 1990.

Ulam, Adam B. *A History of Soviet Russia.* New York: Holt, Rinehart and Winston, 1976.

Vail, Petr and Aleksandr Genis. "Bulgakovskii perevorot." *Kontinent* no.47 (1986). 351–74.

Vakhtel', M. [M. Wachtel]. "Rozhdenie russkogo avangarda iz dukkha nemetskogo antikovedenia: Vil'gel'm Derpfel'd i Viacheslav Ivanov." In *Antichnost' i kul'tura serebrianogo veka. K 85-letiiu A.A. Takho-Godi*, edited by Robert Bird et al., 139–47. Moscow: Nauka, 2010.

Vaksberg, Arkady. *Stalin's Prosecutor: The Life of Andrei Vyshinsky.* Translated by Jan Butler. New York: Grove and Weidenfeld, 1990.

van Baak, J.J. *The Place of Space in Narration: A Semiotic Approach to the Problem of Literary Space: With an Analysis of the Role of Space in I.E. Babel's* Konarmija. Studies in Slavic Literature and Poetics, vol. 3. Amsterdam: Rodopi, 1983.

Varlamov, Aleksei. *Mikhail Bulgakov.* Moscow: Molodaia gvardiia, 2008.

Volkov, Solomon. *St. Petersburg: A Cultural History.* Translated by Antonina W. Bouis. New York: The Free Press, 1995.

von Geldern, James. *Bolshevik Festivals, 1917–1920.* Berkeley: University of California Press, 1993.

Wachtel, Andrew, ed. *Petrushka: Sources and Contexts.* Evanston: Northwestern University Press, 1998.

Wagner, David. "Peirce, Panofsky, and the Gothic." *Transactions of the Charles S. Peirce Society* 48, no. 4 (Fall 2012). 436–55.

Wagner, Richard. "Art and Revolution." In his *The Art-Work of the Future and Other Works.* Translated by W. Ashton Ellis, 21–65. Lincoln: University of Nebraska Press, 1993.

– "The Art-Work of the Future." In his *The Art-Work of the Future and Other Works.* Translated by W. Ashton Ellis, 67–213. Lincoln: University of Nebraska Press, 1993.

– *The Art-Work of the Future and Other Works.* Translated by W. Ashton Ellis. Lincoln: University of Nebraska Press, 1993.

Warner, Elizabeth A. *The Russian Folk Theatre.* Slavistic Printings and Reprintings no. 104, edited by C.H. Van Schooneveld. The Hague: Mouton, 1977.

Weiner, Adam. *By Authors Possessed: The Demonic Novel in Russia.* Evanston: Northwestern University Press, 1998.

Wood, Elizabeth A. *Performing Justice: Agitation Trials in Early Soviet Russia.* Ithaca: Cornell University Press, 2005.

Wortman, Richard. *Scenarios of Power: Myth and Ceremony in Russian Monarchy.* Princeton: Princeton University Press, 1995.

Zamiatin, Evgenii. *My.* In his *Socheneniia*, vol. 3, 113–263. München: A. Neimanis Buchvertrieb und Verlag, 1986.

Zholkovskii, Aleksandr. „Dialog Bulgakova i Oleshi o kolbase, parade chuvstv i Golgofe." *Sintaksis* 20 (1987): 90–117.

Index

Adorno, Theodor, 10
"Advent" (Esenin), 134, 135, 210n1
"agitational trials" *(agitsud)*, 168–9
agitational vehicles and trains, 15,
    17, 74, 139–41
agitprop (political propaganda), 142
Akhmatova, Anna, *Poem without a*
    Hero. A Triptych. 1940–1962, 179
Alekseev-Iakovlev, Aleksei, 121
allegory, genre of, 68, 70
All-Union Agricultural Exhibit, 160
Al'tman, Natan, 122
Amalarius, Bishop of Metz, 59
Andreevskii, I.E., 59, 188n19
Anna Ioannovna, Empress of Russia, 93
Anna Karenina (Tolstoy), 12, 23, 184n2
Antichrist, The (Bely), 94–5, 134
anti-religious campaigns, 134, 135,
    136, 154
Anti-Soviet Trotskyite trial, 173
Antov-Ovseenko, A., 173
"Appearance of Christ before the
    People, The" (painting), 23
architecture: avant-garde, 31; Gothic,
    90; music and, 87–8; Stalinist, 31,
    164, 166
Argenbright, Robert, 140
Aristotle: *Poetics*, 52
art of the future, 87

Artsybashev, Mikhail, 168
automatic devices, 103
avant-garde, 13, 31, 45, 111, 120,
    122–3, 160, 163, 180, 211n7
Avignon carnival, 157

Baba Yaga (folkloric character), 31
Babel, Isaak: *Konarmiia*, 147
Bachelard, Gaston, 44–5
Bakhtin, Mikhail: book on Rabelais,
    157; on carnival, 18, 59, 143, 145,
    156, 157–8, 161, 199n11, 199n14,
    212n19; on city, 107; concept of
    polyphonic novel, 35, 157, 194n49;
    on Gospel account of the Passion,
    199n16; interpretation of the Stalin
    era, 158; on marionettes, 205n17;
    political views of, 214nn11–12;
    Rabelais and His World, 18
Bakunin, Mikhail, 82, 84
balagan (fairground booth): demonic
    connotations of, 97, 207n24;
    modernist fascination with, 74,
    106, 107, 207n28; in Russian and
    Soviet tradition, 17, 106–7, 108,
    142; as site for disruption of the
    established order, 107, 109
Balandier, Georges, 156
ballet, 89–90, 203n4